1991

Tournament of Lawyers

TOURNAMENT OF LAWYERS

The Transformation of the Big Law Firm

Marc Galanter and Thomas Palay

The University of Chicago Press
Chicago and London

MARC GALANTER is the Evjue-Bascom Professor of Law and South Asian Studies, and is director of the Institute for Legal Studies, and of the Disputes Processing Research program, at the University of Wisconsin, Madison. THOMAS PALAY is Professor of Law at the University of Wisconsin, Madison.

The University of Chicago Press, Chicago 60637
The University of Chicago Press, Ltd., London
© 1991 by The University of Chicago
All rights reserved. Published 1991
Printed in the United States of America
00 99 98 97 96 95 94 93 92 91   5 4 3 2 1

⊗The paper used in this publication meets the minimum requirements of the American National Standard for Information Sciences—Permanence of Paper for Printed Library Materials, ANSI Z39.48–1984.

Library of Congress Cataloging-in-Publication Data

Galanter, Marc, 1931–
    Tournament of lawyers : the transformation of the big
law firm / Marc Galanter and Thomas Palay.
      p. cm.
    Includes bibliographical references (p.) and index.
    ISBN 0–226–27877–8
    1. Law firms—United States.   I. Palay, Thomas
        II. Title.
KF300.G35   1991
340'.06'073—dc20
                                 90–45088
                                    CIP

For Eve, Seth, Rachel and Sarah
and
Diane, Daniel and David

Contents

Preface

Not very long ago large law firms were relatively rare. They eschewed the public stage and flourished remote from popular attention. Information about such firms was closely restricted and did not circulate widely. Few people were curious about them. Today there are many large firms, there is much accessible information about them, and curiosity about them has broken beyond the circle of those directly involved with them. The change is symbolized by the popularity of the television series "L.A. Law," which since 1986 has retailed the fortunes of the lawyers in MacKenzie, Brackman, Chaney, Kuzak & Becker. "L.A. Law" differs strikingly from earlier portrayals of lawyers on television (and in the movies) like "Perry Mason" or "The Defenders." There are more lawyers in the office—more than would be involved on any single case. We are made aware of the firm as a presence that enlarges and limits its lawyers and binds them (at least temporarily) to a common fate. Their practice is primarily civil rather than criminal. They are connected to the world of corporate affairs as well as to the realm of individual predicaments. Their engagements, typically, are not to vindicate the one right side but to champion one side of a tangled, ambivalent issue in which there are contending equities and no clear right answer.

A simple count might suggest that Mackenzie Brackman is a small firm since it has less than a dozen lawyers. But this would be misleading, for it is really a homunculus, a miniaturized large firm. It has grown to its present size over a period of decades. Its lawyers are divided into partners of varying seniority and associates worried about the prospects for promotion. They are specialists who work in shifting work groups and often dispute about the staffing of cases. The firm serves many clients and is particularly concerned to retain its repeat corporate clients and to obtain new ones. It exists in a volatile, unstable environment with competitive pressures. During the past season Mackenzie Brackman shuffled top slots in response to the threatened departure of a partner with his clients and struggled to absorb a laterally recruited rainmaker, who was elevated to managing partner and then deposed by her predecessor.

Mackenzie Brackman is atypical of large firms in several ways: it has a low ratio of associates to partners; a large portion of its work is representing individuals (product liability plaintiffs, criminal defendants, divorcing spouses); and its lawyers conduct an extraordinary number of trials. These departures, like downsizing, respond to the exigencies of condensation and packaging for popular consumption and dramatic effect. What we see is the world of the large firm scaled down to faces that we can remember and causes that we can understand and identify with.

Some observers credit "L.A. Law" with responsibility for the late 1980s surge of applications to law schools and see it shaping perceptions of the legal system for both the general public and for lawyers themselves. Whether it has these wider effects we don't know. Even if it doesn't, it is important for us because it marks the arrival of the law *firm* (as opposed to the lawyer) as part of the familiar and observed moral landscape of American life.

What is the message of "L.A. Law" for large-firm practice? First, that it offers not only affluence, glamour, and fun, but above all an appropriate site for fulfillment of oneself as a person. Like other "work operas" such as "Hill Street Blues" and "St. Elsewhere," it depicts the job as the principle locus for emotional life. Home is "R and R"; on and at the job is where one experiences the agonies and ecstasies of personal fulfillment. Second, it tells us that as a professional one recurrently encounters complex questions with no clear blacks and whites but lots of grays, and ethical dilemmas that often have no satisfying resolution. Third, it teaches us that the inevitable tensions between self-interest and idealism can be reconciled through devotion to craft.

That lawyers like to watch the show suggests that they tolerate its distortions for the thrill of the public depiction of one's familiar world. Lawyers are searching for an understanding of the rapidly changing world of law practice. We offer this book as another path to understanding that world. It takes one prominent characteristic of that world, the relentless increase in the size of firms, and tries to demonstrate that this growth is neither an incidental feature nor merely the result of the play of external forces. Instead, we argue, it gives expression to the fundamental structure of the law firm that crystallizes around the exchange between senior and junior lawyers. Although our analysis addresses directly the large law firm that serves corporate clients, we believe that it can also illuminate the organization of other practice formats.

Just as "L.A. Law" refracts the world of law practice through the distorting mirror of story, making it more compact, more orderly, more dramatic, and richer in meanings, so our account simplifies and distorts in a different way. We strip away the passion and politics of particular firms, clients, and controversies in favor of less dramatic but fundamental patterns of organization and growth. We aim to give the reader a sense of the larger structures that underlie and frame the sequence of stories that make up the career of the firm. We hope that we can also convey a sense of the uneven and changing mix of constraints and opportunities that surround those who inhabit these complex organizations. We believe that we have identified within the firm some structural forces that have been enormously influential. But we make no claim that the future of law practice is fated and known to us. We think it is unknowable precisely because it is shaped by a mix of determinants and incentives. The organization of legal services in the future depends on how lawyers grasp the opportunities for choice offered by a setting in which many veins of determinacy intersect. Lawyers (and policy makers) enjoy a degree of freedom to reshape the world of law firms. Effective use of this freedom depends on an appreciation of the various strands of determinism that surround and entwine us.

Like the firms it describes, this book has grown exponentially, and we have accumulated a corresponding debt to those who have helped us in various ways. Richard Abel, Jim Atleson, Ian Ayres, Steven Beyer, Bill Broder, Peter Carstenson, John Coffee, Rajeev Dhavan, Gerald Faulhaber, William L. F. Felstiner, Marvin Frankel, Seth Galanter, Bryant Garth, Victor Goldberg, Henry Hansmann, Willard Hurst, Neil Komesar, John Leubsdorf, David Luban, Scott Masten, Frank Munger, Robert Nelson, Michael Powell, Deborah Rhode, Theodore Schneyer, Justin A. Stanley, Arthur Stinchcombe, David Trubek and Oliver Williamson supplied helpful commentary, suggestions, and bibliographic help. Dr. Wayne Hobson of California State University, Fullerton, kindly granted permission to reproduce Table 2. Our partners in the Business Disputing Project, Stewart Macaulay and Joel Rogers, provided continuing stimulation and unfailing support. We received valuable guidance from participants in the symposium on "Rehnquist Revisited: The Growth of Large Law Firms and Its Effect on the Legal Profession and Legal Education," held at the Indiana University School of Law, Bloomington, March 9–10, 1988; the American Bar Foundation Conference on Professionalism, Ethics, and Economic Change, held in Evanston, Illinois, September 22–24, 1988; the University of Wisconsin-American Bar Foundation Workshop on the Large Law Firm, held in Madison, July 13–16, 1989; and workshops at Columbia University, Marquette University, Northwestern University, Stanford University, Yale University, and the University of California at Berkeley.

A small legion of Wisconsin law students sacrificed their eyesight to assemble our main data set. We want to thank Jeff Baxendale, Laurie Baxter, Mary Casper, Chris Halverson, Jacob London, Deb Nudelman, Howard Smith, Cari Sullivan, Kevin Sweeney, John Talis, Mark Tyczkowski, Jeff Vail, Pamela Walgren, and Joseph Welsh for their help. John Esser, Linda Jurgella, Jacob London, Jesse Wing, and Shari Wolinsky provided able and dedicated research assistance, as did Kevin Sweeney and Pamela Walgren, who deserve special mention as supervisors of the data set assembly.

We are indebted to Michael Morgalla for unflagging library support and Brenda Storandt for painstaking and efficient preparation of the manuscript.

We are grateful to the American Bar Foundation, the Graduate School of the

University of Wisconsin-Madison, the University of Wisconsin Law School, and the Disputes Processing Research Program of the University of Wisconsin Law School under a grant from the William and Flora Hewlett Foundation, for support of various phases of this research.

Portions of Chapter 5 appeared in the *Virginia Law Review* 76, no. 4 (May 1990): 747–811, and are used here with permission.

1 Introduction

The characteristic features of the American legal profession are not new—large numbers, relatively easy entry, intensive specialization, a high degree of stratification, organization into large firms, strong ties to clients, weak controls by the state and by professional bodies, extraordinary prominence in public life, a protean entrepreneurial quality, and an unparalleled scope of professional activity. American lawyers do more things for more clients and in more settings (not only in courts), than do their counterparts elsewhere. These features are less prominent in the legal professions of other industrial societies. There is nothing to suggest that they are being effaced in the American setting; instead they seem to have become more general and more accentuated.

At the center of the picture is the great innovation in lawyering in the past century, the development of the large law firm and the distinctive style of lawyering associated with it. Lawyers in the United States nominally form a single profession. But the profession is intensely stratified. The upper strata of the private bar consist mostly of large firms whose members are recruited mainly from elite schools and who serve corporate clients; the lower strata practice as individuals or small firms, are drawn from less prestigious schools, and serve individual clients.[1] Law practice is a bifurcated structure, organized around different kinds of clients. Much of the variation within the profession, Jack Heinz and Edward Laumann conclude, is accounted for by "one fundamental distinction—the distinction between lawyers who represent large organizations (corporations, labor unions, or government) and those who represent individuals. The two kinds of law practice are the two hemispheres of the profession. Most lawyers reside exclusively in one hemisphere or the other and seldom, if ever, cross the equator."[2]

The profession's organizational hemisphere is populated almost entirely by large law firms that represent, for the most part, large organizations. We ignore for the moment how the big firm has changed over time, and the variation among big firms, in order to provide a brief composite, and therefore blurry,

---

1. In their revealing study of the Chicago bar, *Chicago Lawyers: The Social Structure of the Bar*, John P. Heinz and Edward Laumann (1982) confirm the picture of stratification drawn by such historians as Auerbach (1976) and such sociologists as Ladinsky (1963a, 1963b); Lortie (1959), and Carlin (1962, 1966).

2. Heinz and Laumann 1982, p. 319.

portrait of the big firm in, say, the first two-thirds of the twentieth century. The big firm consists of a "large" number of lawyers—just how many is "large" depends on place and time. These lawyers are highly specialized. A firm is ordinarily divided into departments (corporate, banking, real estate, litigation, etc.) or working groups. Various specialists coordinate their efforts on the problems of the client. Work for clients is not confined to litigation, but includes planning, counseling, negotiation, and representation in a wide range of settings. Big firms are general chaperones of enterprise. Firms supply thorough custom-work, involving intensive investigation, elaborate research, exhaustive exploration of options. Since relations with clients are enduring, big-firm lawyers tend to take up problems early and to monitor the effects of their work.

These firms are hierarchical. The working groups that serve clients are made up of senior and junior lawyers. The latter are hired on the basis of their qualifications directly from prestigious law schools.[3] The work of junior lawyers is supervised and reviewed by seniors. Training is imparted to young lawyers in the course of a prolonged (four- to ten-year) apprenticeship, normally ended by either promotion to partnership or by departure from the firm. Lateral mobility from firm to firm was, until recently, virtually unknown. Firms tended to be socially homogeneous, cohesive, and stable; each was imbued with its own distinct culture.

The big law firm has been with us for almost a century. It is, in a Darwinian sense, a success story: big firms are flourishing; there are more of them, they are bigger, they command a bigger share of an expanding legal market. The big law firm is also a success in a deeper sense, as a social form for organizing the delivery of comprehensive, continuous, high-quality legal services. Like the hospital as a way to practice medicine, the big firm provides the standard format for delivering complex services. Many features of its style—specialization, teamwork, continuous monitoring on behalf of clients, representation in many forums—have been emulated in other vehicles for delivering legal services. The specialized boutique firm, the public-interest law firm, the corporate law department—all model themselves on a style of practice developed in the large firm. And legal professions in other countries have increasingly emulated the American big firm.

And yet, there is a palpable anxiety and dismay within the legal profession concerning commercialization and the concomitant decline of professionalism in the setting of the big law firm. Should its robust institutional success lead us to dismiss these misgivings as the tremors of the fainthearted as they experience the further development and consolidation of the big firm as an institution? Such a sanguine response is suggested by the observation that laments about

3. Or, in recent years, from some short post–law school experience like a judicial clerkship or a stint in a government law department.

commercialization and the loss of professional virtue have recurred regularly for a century.[4]

But we submit that there is something different this time around. The present "crisis" is the real thing—not in the sense of marking a decisive break from professional ideals, but because the discomfort reflects structural changes that are transforming big firms and their world in fundamental ways. In the past twenty years or so such firms have undergone a set of striking changes that is aptly described as a transformation.

Our book describes and, we hope, explains what has happened to the big law firm. We begin by examining the origins of the big firm. Next, to provide a baseline for understanding recent changes, we sketch a portrait of the big firm during its "golden age," circa 1960. Finally, we describe the transformation experienced by it since then.

In the second half of the book we examine the reasons for this rapid transformation. We argue that the changes the big firm is undergoing grow out of the seeds planted by its early pioneers. We believe that the big firm, comprising partners and associates who are incipient partners, contains an inherent dynamic of growth. This dynamic is a by-product of what we call the promotion-to-partner tournament. Historically, the big law firm has structured attorney compensation and incentives around a promotion contest, which has proven to be a simple device for fostering the efficient sharing of human capital. But along with efficient governance has come growth. If the environment permits, the firm that employs such a tournament will tend to grow exponentially. Growth changes the character of the firm.[5] Informality recedes; collegiality gives way; notions of public service and independence are marginalized; the imperative of growth collides with notions of dignified passivity in obtaining business. Eventually the firm faces the necessity of either reorganizing to support ever-larger increments of growth or reorganizing to suppress growth. Either way, collegiality, independence, and public service are likely to be jeopardized.

4. Gordon 1988, pp. 2–6, 48ff. Cf. the quotation from *The American Lawyer* (1895) below, p. 11 n. 38.

5. So does nongrowth. See below, p. 116–19. Firms do not enjoy the option of avoiding change by remaining the same size. The formation of a "promotion-to-partnership" core launches the firm on a trajectory in which change in the firm's form and character is inevitable if the firm grows or if it remains the same size.

2 The Emergence of the Big Firm

We begin by sketching some of the distinctive features of big-firm practice. Of course, any of these features can be found apart from the whole cluster, but we shall argue that the cluster hangs together in a way that gives the big firm a distinctive institutional character—a character that is changing as these features are rearranged. We shall contrast the big firm with the sorts of firms from which they emerged, with the smaller firms that exist alongside them, and with the firms that might populate an imagined future.

The big firm and its distinctive style of practice emerged around the turn of the century.[1] The break from earlier law practice can be depicted by a schematic comparison under the six headings of partners, other lawyers, relations to clients, work, support system, and new kinds of knowledge.

Partners. In the big law firm the loose affiliation of lawyers, sharing offices and occasionally sharing work for clients, is replaced by the office in which clients "belong to" the firm rather than to an individual lawyer. The entire practice of these lawyers is shared by the firm. The proceeds, after salaries and expenses are paid, are divided among the partners pursuant to some agreed upon formula.

Other Lawyers. Unpaid clerks and permanent assistants are replaced by salaried "associates" (as we have come to call them)[2] who are expected to devote

1. We use the term "firm" throughout when discussing these developments. Although "firm" was known and occasionally used, for most of the period discussed here the common term for a company of lawyers was "law office" rather than "law firm." See, e.g., the passages quoted below on pp. 8, 11, 12, and 13.

2. The use of the term "associate" goes back at least to the 1910s. It can be found in a few listings in the 1914 edition of *Hubbell's Law Directory* but not in the 1910 edition. Paul Hoffman credits the coinage to Root, Clark partner Emory Buckner. (Hoffman 1973, p. 140). Buckner used the term (or title, since he capitalizes it) in a firm newsletter he wrote in 1923, on the tenth anniversary of the founding of Root, Clark, describing the associates as part of the opening in 1913 (Mayer 1968, p. 103). But it did not become standard usage until the last twenty-five years. Many discussions omit it and use other terms. Reginald Heber Smith's 1940 report does not use the term, but refers to non-partner lawyers as "juniors" (Smith 1940a; 1940b; 1940c; 1940d). Siddall's careful 1956 discussion of firm organization does not employ it; he refers to other lawyers as "staff" (Siddall 1956, p. 48). A corporate lawyer writing in 1961 refers to " 'associates,' as lawyer-trained employees are euphemistically termed today instead of 'law clerks' " (Levy 1961, p. 38). Since

their full efforts to the firm's clients. A select group of academically qualified associates, chosen on grounds of potential qualification for partnership, are given a prospect of eventual promotion to partnership after an extended probationary period during which they work under the supervision of their seniors, receive training, and exercise increasing responsibility.

Clients. Firms represent large corporate enterprises, organizations, or entrepreneurs with a need for continuous (or recurrent) and specialized legal services that could be supplied only by a team of lawyers. The client "belongs to" the firm, not to a particular lawyer. Relations with clients tend to be enduring. Such repeat clients are able to reap benefits from the continuity and economies of scale and scope enjoyed by the firm.

Work. Firm work involves specialization in the problems of particular kinds of clients. It involves not only representation in court but services in other settings and forums. The emergence of the firm represents the ascendancy of the office lawyer and the displacement of the advocate as the paradigmatic professional figure. The preference for office work is displayed in the advice of a partner to a young lawyer aspiring to join the predecessor to the Cravath firm:

> New York is not a very good field for one who desires to make a specialty of court practice or litigated work. The business connected with corporations and general office practice is much more profitable and satisfactory and you will find that the better class of men at our Bar prefer work in that line.[3]

A new breed of lawyers took pride in the shift from inspired oratory to astute advice.[4] As one New York lawyer put it, the places of the great orators were

---

"associate" has become the universally employed term, we employ it throughout for analytic purposes even when describing situations where the participants would have used a different word.

3. Charles Steele to H. Snowden Marshall (May 4, 1896) (Swaine 1946a, pp. 554–55).

4. This new emphasis was accompanied by a change in the character of courtroom advocacy from oratorical eloquence to a crisp, businesslike efficiency. "The age of forensic eloquence has gone, with all of its attendant glories and attractions. The practical, brief, crisp, utterances of the modern lawyer have succeeded. Exordiums and perorations are abolished by rules of court, which establish the limits of legal oratory, from twenty minutes, to two hours. . . . In proportion as legal oratory has been curtailed, what are called legal 'briefs' have expanded." (Dos Passos 1907, pp. 27–28). Theron Strong observed that "courts are so crowded and judges so overwhelmed by [the amount of litigation and] . . . have . . . become so impatient with long-winded utterances, that opportunities are rarely afforded for the oratorical displays of former days and it is consequently necessary to cultivate a plain, direct and earnest style, and conciseness and brevity in the presentation of even the most important cases" (Strong 1914, p. 362), "Juries and judges have become so accustomed to business-like methods that they appreciate a simple and clear presentation of the essential facts" (Strong 1914, p. 363).

being taken by the business lawyer who "found his higher sphere and his greatest use as a special partner of the business man."[5] Such a lawyer, he continued
"is consulted at the outset and throughout the progress of every enterprise of
magnitude, that by reason of his special legal experience along business lines he
may, primarily, make the undertaking to the business man of more profit than
without his assistance, and, secondarily, may avoid the possibility of attack and
litigation."[6] This shift from courtroom advocate to business adviser was com-
memorated in 1905 in the observations of Finley Peter Dunne's Mr. Dooley:

> . . . if I had me life to live over again I'd be a lawyer. 'Tis a noble
> profissyon. It's nobler now thin it used to be in th' old days whin a
> lawyer had to go into coort an' holler till he was hoorse to arn his
> fee. . . .
>
> 'Don't ye iver go into coort,' says I. 'What wud I be doin' in a
> smelly coort room talkin' up to a man that was me chief clerk last
> year?' says he. 'No sir, th' law is a diff'rent profissyon fr'm what it
> was whin Dan'l Webster an' Rufus Choate an' thim gas bags used to
> make a mighty poor livin' be shoutin' at judges that made less. Th'
> law to-day is not only a profissyon. It's a business. I made a bigger
> honoraryum last year consolidatin' th' glue inthrests that aftherwards
> wint into th' hands iv a receiver, which is me, thin Dan'l Webster iver
> thought was in th' goold mines iv th' wurruld. I can't promise to take a
> case f'r ye an' hoot me reasons f'r thinkin' ye'er right into th' ears iv a
> larned judge. I'm a poor speaker. But if iver ye want to do somethin
> that ye think ye oughtn't to do, come around to me an' I'll show ye
> how to do it,' says he.[7]

Litigation no longer commanded the energies of the most eminent lawyers.
By 1900, Robert T. Swaine concluded, "the great corporate lawyers of the day
drew their reputations more from their abilities in the conference room and fa-
cility in drafting documents than from their persuasiveness before the courts."[8]
In 1908 Roscoe Pound remarked this shift and appraised its consequences for
reform:

> The leaders of the American bars are not primarily practitioners in the
> courts. They are chiefly client caretakers. . . . Their best work is done
> in the office, not in the forum. They devote themselves to study of the

5. Dill 1903, p. 112.

6. Dill 1903, p. 112. Another observer remarked, "The lawyer now boldly enters into the business end of his client's transactions—he sells him prudence and experience, sometimes even
usurping the client's discretion and judgment" (Dos Passos 1917, p. 4, 22).

7. Dunne 1963, pp. 35–36.

8. Swaine 1946a, p. 371. George Gawalt dates the transition even earlier: "By the mid-1880s,
the locus of the most elite practice has decisively shifted away from the courtroom to the law office
and conference room. The main work of this practice was to serve as legal brokers and intermedi-
aries between large American corporations trying to attract new capital . . . and the investment
banking communities of Wall Street and Europe" (Gawalt 1984, p. 59).

interests of particular clients, urging and defending those interests in all their varying forms, before legislatures, councils, administrative boards and commissions quite as much as in the courts. Their interest centers wholly in an individual client or set of clients, not in the general administration of justice.[9]

Theron Strong observed in 1914 that "the great leaders of the bar, such as engaged in that class of business thirty years ago, turn over the litigation of their offices to their juniors, and at the present day are more often, if not altogether occupied with those great financial interests which are transacted in the privacy of their own offices."[10] In a 1920 talk, Paul Cravath remarked the "'striking phenomenon of the New York bar' that 'advocacy had become almost a lost art.'"[11] Judge Learned Hand in 1925 observed that:

. . . in my own city the best minds of the profession are scarcely lawyers at all. They may be something much better, or much worse; but they are not that. With courts they have no dealings whatever, and would hardly know what to do in one if they came there.[12]

Support System. The emergence of the big firm is associated with the introduction of new office technologies. The displacement of copying, clerks, and messengers by the typewriter, stenography, and the telephone greatly increased the productivity of lawyers. One lawyer who lived through the transition estimated that "with the use of a competent stenographer and typewriter the busy lawyer is capable of producing in one day as much as he could formerly have produced in three."[13] The capacity of the typewriter to produce multiple copies of documents eliminated copyists and their skills. The telephone freed lawyers from extended waiting in court,[14] eliminated messengers, and "completely revolutionized" methods of transacting legal business by enabling lawyers to conduct interviews instantly and without prearrangement.[15] The communication of business information was more readily separated from the personal intercourse that accompanied frequent meetings. Strong observed that the decrease in meetings with clients led to "destruction of the personal and intimate relation, leaving only that which is purely professional."[16] Lawyers' filthy and

9. Pound 1909, pp. 231, 235. Pound remarks the consequences of this for procedural reform: "As the interest of these clients are in the vast majority of cases defensive and procedure is one of the chief weapons of defense, the best, most vigorous and most constructive talent of the profession either neglects practice in the courts entirely or is enlisted in obstructing and defeating litigation" (Pound 1909, pp. 231, 235).

10. Strong 1914, p. 505.

11. Swaine 1946b.

12. Quoted at Levy 1961, p. 13.

13. Strong 1914, p. 393.

14. Strong 1914, p. 283.

15. Strong 1914, p. 399.

16. Strong 1914, p. 385.

disheveled offices were replaced by ones that resemble "commercial or banking offices."[17] These offices were more businesslike; they were not places "for
informal and friendly visits." Strong remarks that in this new milieu "anything
but business requires an apology for the time consumed."[18] Another practitioner lamented that

> the typical old-fashioned law office is a thing of the past. . . . Close
> personal relations, mutual interest and friendliness between the law-
> yer and his younger associates are relegated to the back of the scene or
> crowded entirely off the stage. System has replaced society.[19]

With the proliferation of printed materials—reporters, digests, treatises—
law practice involved protracted research and maintenance of an extensive collection of books.[20] And with the move from episodic to continuing
representation of clients, and from oral to written performance, law offices accumulated massive files. The introduction of filing cabinets increased the
ability to store and retrieve papers and records.[21] Offices required much higher
capital investments and continuing costs for overhead than earlier forms of law
practice; these new conditions permitted new economies of scale.

New Kinds of Knowledge. Willard Hurst refers to "the revolution in the cost
of legal service after the 1870s," a revolution produced by the flood of printed
sources and the need for mastery of new areas of specialized knowledge. The
rise of the big firms rendered obsolete the style of legal research that had sus-
tained their predecessors. The progenitor of the Davis Polk firm, Francis N.
Bangs, who died in 1885, "preferred to handle his cases on the basis of fundamental legal principle rather than judicial authorities." Theron G. Strong
observed in his Diary: "In his arguments . . . [Bangs] did not often refer to
adjudged cases; he appealed to common sense and the ordinary principles of
justice." Bangs told Strong that "no man is fit to practice law who is not able to
practice it without law books."[22] Strong reflected that the proliferation of reported cases "has virtually transformed the profession from a class of lawyers
able to practice without law books to a class almost entirely dependent on the

17. Strong 1914, p. 385. Cf. the very similar observations about offices in Dos Passos (1907, p.
46).

18. Strong 1914, p. 386.

19. Chamberlayne 1906, p. 397.

20. Hobson 1986, p. 114; Hurst 1950, p. 308.

21. Strong 1914, p. 399. A Boston lawyer described the old system of "disposition of the papers
in finished matters by tossing the envelopes into a large wooden chest . . ." (Warner 1950, p. 7).
(Copy of manuscript on file with the authors.)

22. Strong (1914, pp. 258–59) reports that Columbia's Theodore W. Dwight criticized the "case
system" because it displaced lawyers educated in legal principles by "'case lawyers' . . . who
never consider a subject on principle." "The lawyers of today are case and code lawyers. The
search for *principle* is subordinate to an investigation for a *precedent*" (Dos Passos 1907, p. 16).

adjudged cases."[23] In addition there was a great multiplication of law books. Strong speaks of "the various compilations in the form of digests, encyclopedias, tables of cases, indices of citations, books of practice and forms of pleading and other legal documents."[24]

More and more lawyers were trained in law schools. Jerold Auerbach estimates that one-fourth of those admitted to the bar in 1870 were law-school graduates; by 1910 this had risen to two-thirds.[25] As we shall see, the presence of a steady supply of highly qualified but inexperienced young recruits is one of the key ingredients of the big law firm. The gap between their certified promise and their untested quality of performance underlies the promotion-to-partnership tournament.

The blending of these features into the big law firm as we know it is commonly credited to Paul D. Cravath, who in the first decade of this century established the "Cravath system" of hiring outstanding graduates straight out of law school on an understanding that they might progress to partnership after an extended probationary period; requiring them to work for the firm only, eschewing practices of their own; paying them salaries; providing training and a "graduated increase in responsibility."[26] Cravath combined a set of features that had been around for several decades into a durable and stable model of the firm. The chronicler of the Cravath firm notes that "many of Cravath's basic ideas derived from Walter S. Carter,"[27] in whose office Cravath worked, first as a clerk and then as partner, from 1886 to 1891.[28] "It was Carter who first fol-

23. Strong 1914, p. 427. But the multiplication of cases meant that individual cases commanded less deference. "This difference has become more marked as the volume of decisions of our own State has increased. Formerly great respect, and almost binding force, was given in cases in our own courts to authorities from the English courts, and to very much the same extent to cases in . . . Massachusetts. . . . The value of the decisions of other States and of England has been constantly diminishing. . . . The same is true of the different reports in our own State. The constantly changing body of the law, as it evolves, renders the early decisions of less and less value, so that at the present time, the force of authorities from the earlier reports is much diminished" (Strong 1914, pp. 225–26). Dos Passos, too, marks the paradoxical effect of the multiplication of recorded precedents: "When the law reports were few, and the precedents shone like bright stars in the legal firmament, and the lawyers knew and followed them, as astronomers to the particular planets, the application of *stare decisis* was easy and simple. But now—it flitters between the thousands of decisions as a phantom of the law—not as a vital principle" (Dos Passos 1907, p. 15). In striking contrast to these autumnal views, a Chicago practitioner of the day attributes the decline in certainty to the improvement of the law, which now "will take account of more and minuter facts; it will give them more delicate and more changeable weights; and it will apply to them more sensitive and more plastic principles" (Bowers 1904, p. 832).

24. Strong 1914, p. 401. On the multiplication of reports in this era and the appearance of digests and encyclopedias, see Warren (1911, p. 557).

25. Auerbach 1976, p. 94.

26. Swaine 1946b, pp. 2–12; Hobson 1986, pp. 195–203.

27. Swaine 1946b, p. 1.

28. Hobson reports that according to the listings in the 1892 *Hubbell's Legal Directory* this was then the largest firm in the nation. (Hobson 1986, p. 192).

lowed the practice, [later] developed by Cravath into the 'Cravath system,' of taking annually from Columbia or Harvard one or two of the men with the best scholastic records and training them for several years before encouraging their departure to practice for themselves."[29] Carter not only selected outstanding candidates but

> train[ed] them through a clerkship of several years. They then left him for their own practice or other connections. On the one hand he did not have a constantly changing group of young law students, inexperienced and usually in the office for only a few months. On the other hand, he did not have a staff of aging law clerks who had lost ambition and all hope of gaining a professional status above that of employees. He kept moving through his office a current of brilliant, ambitious young lawyers."[30]

Carter combined the selection, training, turnover, and outplacement parts of the later Cravath model, but the relationship with the younger lawyers did not hold the promise of becoming enduring and permanent. Thus one of Carter's former juniors observed that he "picked his partners as Connie Mack picked ball players, usually dropping them when they demanded or earned as much as he did."[31]

Although most fully articulated by Cravath, it seems that the elements of the big firm—highly qualified but inexperienced novices, firm clients rather than individual ones, training, promotion to partnership—were also assembled by other innovators. Cravath was not only articulate and highly visible; he was blessed with a partner who half a century later wrote the classic law-firm history and described the "Cravath system."[32] Innovative organizers elsewhere were coming up with similar combinations of these elements. "[Louis D.] Brandeis . . . was the true pioneer of modern forms of law firm organization in Boston."[33] He hired Harvard graduates of high academic achievement, paid them salaries (an innovation), and "was the first Boston lawyer to organize his office on the basis of taking bright young men quickly into partnership."[34]

The core of the big firm, we submit, is the "promotion to partner tournament" that we describe in Chapter 5. This is our shorthand for the organization of the firm around a contest in which some junior lawyers can cross the line by

29. Swaine 1946a, p. 587.
30. Swaine 1946a, p. 3.
31. Kogel 1953, p. 91.
32. This term is used by his partner, Robert T. Swaine, whose history of the firm (1946) is the classic of the genre. The term does not appear in accounts of law firms written through the 1950s: Hurst (1950); Mayer (1956a); Mayer (1956b); Klaw (1958); Smigel (1960). But the term was picked up by Levy (1961) and Smigel (1969), and has been widely used since. The hardcover edition of Smigel's book was published in 1964. Smigel added an epilogue, updating his observations, to the 1969 Indiana University Press paperback. Citations to Smigel are to that edition.
33. Hobson 1986, p. 185–86.
34. Hobson 1986, p. 186.

promotion and become partners. Partners and juniors are not equals but are arranged in a hierarchy with command and supervision in the former. The latter
are neither transient apprentices nor permanent employees. They are inchoate
peers, fellow professionals of presently immature powers some of whom, it is
anticipated, will eventually achieve full and equal stature. By adopting this
model of professional collaboration, law set out on a course different from that
of other professions such as medicine, in which young doctors became independent proprietors (and affiliates of hospitals), or engineering, where they
became salaried employees.[35]

Firms can offer this promise only when they are confident that they can expect to attract sufficient work to keep these young lawyers busy. That is, the
senior lawyers must have either clients who produce more work than the senior
lawyers can handle themselves or a reputation that will attract such clients.[36]
Typically, association with a corporation or "super capitalist" provided the
stream of work, and "the publicity from serving such clients and the expansive
contacts of these clients result[ed] in a growing network of contacts for the
emergent firm."[37]

When the big firm appeared, there was already a sense that the profession
had compromised its identity and, by too close an embrace of business, had
itself become a branch of business:

> [T]he typical law office . . . is located in the maelstrom of business
> life . . . in its appointments and methods of work it resembles a great
> business concern . . . the most successful and eminent of the bar are
> the trained advisors of business men. . . .
> . . . [The bar] has allowed itself to lose, in large measure, the lofty
> independence, the genuine learning, the fine sense of professional
> dignity and honor. . . . [F]or the past thirty years it has become in-
> creasingly contaminated with the spirit of commerce which looks
> primarily to the financial value and recompense of every
> undertaking.[38]

35. Superficially, the "promotion to partnership" law firm most resembles the academic department with its up-or-out promotion to tenured status. The analogy is limited by the different character
of the exchanges of human capital between tenured and untenured department members and the
different constraints on growth faced by the academic department. We hope to discuss these differences on another occasion.

36. For example, "When the law firm of Shearman & Sterling was established in 1873, Jay
Gould promised Shearman that he would take his legal business to the new firm. . . . Gould was
more than a rich client that assured the new firm a few large fees. At the time of the establishment of
Shearman & Sterling, there were sixty-three cases pending involving Jay Gould. One year later, the
figure had risen to ninety-seven" (Pinansky 1986–87, p. 610). On the Jay Gould litigation, see
Earle (1963, pp. 30–31, 69–87).

37. Pinansky 1986–87, pp. 593, 604. This was an era in which large amounts of capital were
controlled by single individuals who exercised vast discretion over its use.

38. *The American Lawyer* 1895, p. 84. This *American Lawyer* is not the intense monthly that has
since 1979 chronicled (and cheered on) rapid change in the world of large law firms. It is a long-

There was, of course, resistance to the new technologies—to telephones, typewriters, and dictation.[39] The frenetic pace and intense specialization of the large firm repelled many established lawyers.[40] Conventional understandings of professionalism were violated by reducing young lawyers to anonymous employees, demanding a monopoly on their energies, forbidding them independent relations with clients. This diminution of professional identity and status troubled the junior lawyers in the Boston firm of Warren & Brandeis. William H. Dunbar, in his ninth year with the firm, complained by letter:

> . . . the work I now do is not my work . . . for the most part I not only am not known, but am not in fact a principal. So far as I am successful in what I undertake, the result benefits me pecuniarily; but whatever reputation comes from the success of all our joint labors reaches me only in a dimly reflected form and only so far as my connection with you is known in a limited circle.
>
> I look upon these results as unsatisfactory both in the practical aspect that my name acquires none of the value which seems to constitute the chief capital of a professional man and in other more sentimental but perhaps to me equally important aspects. The results seem to me the necessary consequence of an organization like ours in which there is not in fact any real partnership between the different persons associated together.[41]

Brandeis responded by envisioning a practice that encompassed the elements of the new kind of firm organization—division of labor, training, specialization, shared clients, teamwork, gradual advancement, and "a connection which I hoped and still hope may continue through our professional lives . . . :"

> In such an organization . . . every man has the opportunity of trying himself at everything and anything—and by a natural law comes to do those things that on the whole he does most effectively. . . . As to that class of things which the individual makes his own, he must become in

---

extinct legal newspaper of the same name, published in New York from 1893 to 1908. A dozen years later, Dos Passos combined a similar description with a similar indictment, "From 'Attorneys and Counselors at Law' they became agents, solicitors, practical promoters, and commercial operators. . . . Entering the offices of some of the law firms in a metropolitan city, one imagines that he is in a commercial counting-room or banking department" (Dos Passos 1907, p. 46).

39. Thus Clarence Seward, senior partner of the predecessor of the Cravath firm, not only refused to answer the telephone for several years after it was installed, but refused to allow typewriters in the office on grounds that "clients would resent the lack of personal attention to their business implied in sending them machine-made letters" (Swaine 1946a, pp. 448–49). Generally, see Hobson (1986, p. 151).

40. Hobson 1986, p. 144.

41. William H. Dunbar to Brandeis (August 17, 1896), reprinted in Mason (1946).

the office in time the principal—for those dealing with the office learn that he is considered the authority there on those things and shortly follow suit. . . .

Besides the things as to which the individual becomes the principal—there must always be much as to which he is the associate, the Junior or Senior of the others in the organization and every man must stand ready to give every other man full aid. Every man must also hold himself to a stricter performance of his task—on account of his relations to the others.

Brandeis defended the emergent big firm as conjoining efficient service to clients with professional fulfillment:

The organization of large offices is becoming more and more a business—and hence also a professional necessity, if properly planned and administered—it must result in the greatest efficiency to clients and the greatest success to the individual members both pecuniarily and in reputation.

That such organizations are the most effective means of doing the law work of this country—so far as clients are concerned—is proven by the success of the great New York firms—the pecuniary success and the professional success or reputation of the individual members. This reputation has in no sense been dependent upon the individual's name appearing in the firm designation.[42]

The following year the name of the firm was changed from Warren & Brandeis to Brandeis, Dunbar & Nutter.[43]

The big firm system crystallized in a world of fluid relations among lawyers and client loyalties that ran to individual lawyers, not to firms. When Cravath, who had earlier split off from the Carter firm, joined Seward, Guthrie and Steele in 1899, he took with him "the business of the Westinghouse interests [as well as] the law office system Carter had pioneered."[44] Hobson points out that:

42. Mason 1946, pp. 83–85. Passages have been reordered. Some eighteen years later, when the large firm was more institutionalized, Theron Strong reflected on the attraction of the firm to a young lawyer who lacked the rare magnetism to develop business on his own. For him, "fidelity and usefulness bring about the desired result, for the death and retirement of the senior will leave him in full possession; but this means a series of long years—years as a junior—occupied with details, and as a subordinate, subject to direction and dictation, having no individuality, being a part of a large machine, where one's name signifies little or nothing in point of reputation in the public mind—the office is everything and he is nothing. But in the course of time, when his seniors are dead, and his hair has turned grey or departed, he will have his reward in being at the head of a flourishing business, but without the tremendous satisfaction which a lawyer is entitled to feel, who, either by his unaided efforts or with some congenial partner, has built up a business, and in doing so has acquired standing and reputation and made a name for himself" (Strong 1914, pp. 441–42).

43. Mason 1946, p. 85.

44. Hobson 1986, p. 197.

Cravath was creating a system of law office organization which would, when it became the general rule in the 1920s make nearly impossible the kind of career he and his young colleagues on the Carter firm had known. They had established major reputations as young men. For example, [Charles Evans] Hughes was only twenty-six and Cravath twenty-five when they were made partners in Carter's firm in 1888. These men had been able to move easily from firm to firm, often creating new firms themselves and carrying their clients with them. In addition, they often became known by the public . . . because they were active in court practice . . . [or] because they became involved in . . . politics. But the Cravath system, once institutionalized, churned out anonymous organization men, steadfastly loyal to the firm that had hired them fresh out of law school, moving only if the firm informed them it could not advance them to partnership.[45]

Law firms grew in size. First in New York, then in other large cities, then in smaller cities, there were more, bigger law firms. This progression can be seen in Wayne Hobson's compilation of the number of firms with four or more lawyers, which grew from 17 in 1872, to 39 in 1882, to 87 in 1892, to 210 in 1903, to 445 in 1914, to "well over 1000" in 1924.[46] As table 1 shows, this growth started first in New York and a few other cities, but then spread to many localities.[47] Table 2, taken from Hobson, shows that, as time went on, the population of firms included ever more firms of larger and larger size.[48]

The large law firm—and with it, the organization of law practice around the "promotion to partnership" pattern—became the industry standard.[49] Gradually, the older patterns of fluid partnerships,[50] casual apprenticeship, and nepotism were displaced. At Sullivan & Cromwell, before Royal Victor became the managing partner in 1915, the firm "had not yet instituted its policy of taking young lawyers just out of law school to train them in the Sullivan & Cromwell way. Instead, associates came and went haphazardly, reflecting no policy except that they could not expect to become partners."[51] Victor "started recruiting lawyers from law schools to establish a pool from which future part-

45. Hobson 1986, pp. 199–200.

46. Hobson 1986, p. 161.

47. Hobson's data are based on his examination of *Hubbell's Legal Directory* and may reflect the expansion of the directory's coverage as well as the diffusion of the big law firm. Hobson (1986, pp. 160–61) discusses the limitations of the data source.

48. Of course not all firms grew steadily; some got smaller or broke up instead of growing. Hobson discusses fluctuations in firm size (Hobson 1986, p. 172).

49. See Hobson (1986, pp. 201ff.).

50. Looking back from 1914, Theron Strong observed that "life-long partnerships . . . after all . . . are exceptional and the partnership changes which occur in the course of years are almost as great as the changes of the figures in the constantly turning kaleidoscope" (Strong 1914, p. 360).

51. Lisagor and Lipsius 1988, p. 57.

Table 1   Growth in the Number of Firms with Four or More Lawyers, 1872–1914

Location	Years				
	1872	1882	1892	1903	1914
New York	10	23	39	64	85
Next nine "Top Cities"*	4	8	19	77	131
Other cities	1	8	29	69	229
Total	15	39	87	210	445

Source: Compiled from data in Hobson 1986, pp. 161, 168, 171.

*These were Chicago, Boston, Cleveland, Detroit, Philadelphia, Buffalo, Kansas City, Milwaukee, and Cincinnati. They were selected because they had "an especially high density of large or major firms during the period" (Hobson 1986, 163n.)

Table 2   Development of Large Firms Outside Top Ten Cities, 1882–1914

Size of Firm	Years			
	1882	1892	1903	1914
4-member firms	5	23	50	121
5-member firms	3	3	14	53
6-member firms	0	3	3	26
7–9-member firms	0	0	2	23
10–14-member firms	0	0	0	6
Total firms	8	29	69	229
Total cities	8	22	52	106

Source: From Hobson 1986, table 10, p. 171n.

ners would be chosen."[52] He began out-placing rejected associates. To induce the partners to enlarge their ranks, Victor arranged for promotions in pairs: "for every one who worked his way up in the firm, he made a partner of an existing partner's relative."[53]

As firms grew, the lawyers in them became more specialized. Strong reported that there were "separate departments in the great offices, each identified with some special line of practice: corporations, real estate, litigations, surrogate proceedings, including wills and trusts, as well as others, sometimes making the modern law office resemble one of the large department stores, where many distinct lines of business are conducted under the same manage-

52. Lisagor and Lipsius 1988, p. 58.
53. Lisagor and Lipsius 1988, p. 58.

ment."[54] Though ascendant in the profession, these successful lawyers were subservient to their business clients. Strong remarks on the decline of the respect and deference earlier shown by clients to "old time lawyers." Relations with clients had

> undergone a complete and marvelous change. The advent of the captains of industry, the multi-millionaires, the mighty corporations and the tremendous business enterprises, with all the pride of wealth and luxury which have followed in their train, have reversed their relative positions, and the lawyer, with a more cultivated intellect than ever and as worthy of deference and respect as formerly, is not treated with the deference and respect of early days. This is accounted for to some extent by the keen competition which exists in the profession, placing the lawyer in the attitude of reaching out for retainers, instead of being regarded as conferring a favour by accepting them. The lawyer no longer receives the obsequious client hat in hand, but is subject to the beck and nod of the great financial magnate, who, whenever he desires to see his lawyer, "sends for him." It would never do for the lawyer who values his practice to insist that his client should call upon him, instead of he calling upon the client.[55]

While firms grew and flourished, they were dependent on their business clients. Lawyers on annual retainers to corporations, Strong thought, "become little more than . . . paid employee[s] bound hand and foot to the service of [the corporation] . . . . [the lawyer] is almost completely deprived of free moral agency and is open to at least the inference that he is virtually owned and controlled by the client he serves."[56]

By the 1930s, the scale and stability of these firms was recognized in the pejorative phrase "law factory."[57] In a 1932 *New Yorker* profile of Paul Cravath, the author notes that "[t]he blasphemous youngsters just out of law school

54. Strong 1914, p. 360.

55. Strong 1914, p. 378. Cf. Dos Passos' earlier observations on the disappearance of lawyers' "aristocratic and social prestige": "Wealth has stolen his social position . . . the cultivation of eloquence has fallen into desuetude . . . the lawyer stands before the community shorn of his prestige, clothed in the unattractive garb of a mere commercial agent—a flexible and convenient go-between, often cultivating every kind of equivocal quality as the means of success" (Dos Passos 1907, p. 33).

56. Strong 1914, pp. 353–54.

57. This term is used by Karl Llewellyn in a 1931 book review (1931, p. 1218). That this was a then recent coinage is suggested by its absence from several earlier accounts that would surely have welcomed it: Lee (1923); Harrington (1927). Earlier, critics used the metaphor of the machine to describe the large firm: it was "a money making mechanism . . . into which the young man . . . fits . . . like a fresh, adjusted cog into a well-oiled machine" and a "mill" that "grind[s] out dollars" (Chamberlayne 1906, p. 397). See also Strong (1914, pp. 353–54).

refer to [the Cravath firm] . . . as 'the factory' and it does have, indeed, the efficiency and production of a first-rate industrial plant."[58] Describing the bar in 1933, Karl Llewellyn focused on the emergence of "a key phenomenon—the 'law factory' . . . [in which] the mass of the work is done by the ablest young men from the best law schools, while the product goes out under the name and over the name of three senior partners."[59] They worked in offices and conference rooms and had little connection with the courts.[60] Corporate practice had become "itself a business. . . . [with] a large staff, a highly organized office, a high overhead, intense specialization." These firms attracted the "ablest of legal technicians" and fostered a "lopsided" business perspective that ignored the wider public functions of the bar.[61]

In the *Encyclopedia of the Social Sciences,* published that same year, we find another of the earliest academic characterizations of the large firm. Professor A. A. Berle reports that "at the top [of the profession's hierarchy] is the 'legal factory'—the great corporation offices of New York and Chicago, having 30 or 40 partners and perhaps two hundred [sic!] or more associated attorneys."[62] In the development of the large firm, Berle saw the abandonment of the notion that the lawyer "was an officer of the court and therefore an integral part of the scheme of justice" and its replacement by a notion of the lawyer as "paid servant of his client. . . . [T]he complete commercialization of the American bar has stripped it of any social functions it might have performed for individuals without wealth."[63]

This grim assessment was shared by Chief Justice Harlan Fiske Stone, who described "[t]he successful lawyer of our day . . . [as] the proprietor or general manager of a new type of factory, whose legal product is increasingly the result

58. Mackaye 1932, pp. 21, 23. Extending the industrial imagery, he describes Cravath himself as having been formerly "in a large sense, a mental machine" (Mackaye 1932, p. 23).

59. Llewellyn 1933, p. 177. Llewellyn is careful to note that the "ablest" are only "of those who are deemed personable and socially unobjectable. There is a caste tradition to be maintained, or at least not to be 'unduly' diluted" (Llewellyn 1933, p. 177 n. 3).

60. Llewellyn endorses (1933, p. 177) the observations of a distinguished practitioner, who reported in the same symposium that among the great law firms of the largest cities "the volume and business and the returns from practice in the courts are less than 20 per cent of the gross receipts from the work of all the members of the firm" (Untermeyer 1933, p. 175). Some firms distanced themselves from the courts even more: before 1935 Sullivan and Cromwell preferred to regard itself as a firm of "solicitors" and would hire "well-known 'barristers' . . . to appear for it in court" (Lisagor and Lipsius 1988, p. 115). In 1934, when the firm had sixty-eight lawyers, including sixteen partners, the litigation group consisted of two partners and three senior associates (Lisagor and Lipsius 1988, p. 108).

61. Llewellyn 1933, pp. 177, 179.

62. Berle 1933, p. 342. As far as we are able to tell, the largest firms in 1933 had a roster of about seventy lawyers.

63. Berle 1933, p. 343.

of mass production methods."[64] Stone deplored the commercialization and de-professionalization of the big-firm lawyer:

> More and more the amount of his income is the measure of success. More and more he must look for his rewards to the material satisfactions derived from profits as from a successfully conducted business, rather than to the intangible and indubitably more durable satisfactions which are to be found in a professional service more consciously directed toward the advancement of the public interest. . . . it has made the learned profession of an earlier day the obsequious servant of business and tainted it with the morals and manners of the marketplace in its most anti-social manifestations.[65]

The factory metaphor was felt to be telling, in labeling something about these offices that was profoundly at odds with professional traditions of autonomy and public service. It accurately catches not only the instrumentalism, but the systematization, division of labor, and coordination of effort introduced by the large firm.[66]

Elements of the style of practice found in the big firm have been emulated in other practice settings. Corporate law departments have borrowed many features of large-firm practice, as have government law offices, specialized "boutique" firms, and public-interest law firms. The scope, specialization, teamwork, and continuity that the big firm affords its client is the model for what legal representation should be like. As a fund-raising letter from the Council of Public Interest Law succinctly put it, "The idea . . . [is] to give . . . ordinary citizens . . . the same kind of legal representation which historically has been enjoyed only by the very rich, the giant corporations and the government."[67] The attraction of this style of lawyering is not confined to

64. Stone 1934, p. 6.

65. Stone 1934, pp. 6–7. The "earlier day" of the virtuous profession lies just over the horizon of personal experience. Just after the turn of the century, John Dos Passos, deploring the commercialization of the profession, reported: "It may . . . safely be said that the prevailing popular idea of the lawyer, too often justified by facts is, that his profession consists in *thwarting* the law instead of *enforcing* it. . . . The public no longer calls them "great" but "successful" lawyers. . . . It is the common belief, inside and outside of the profession, that the most brilliant and learned of the lawyers are employed to defeat or strangle justice" (Dos Passos 1907, pp. 130–31).

66. Some sought to wring further parallels, attributing to large firms the standardization, "robotization," and monotony of thought characteristic of factories. In 1939, muckraking journalist Ferdinand Lundberg entitled the last of his series of *Harper's* articles on lawyers, "The Law Factories: Brains of the Status Quo" (Lundberg 1939). Lundberg explains that "The term 'law factories,' widely used in the legal profession, may be derisive, but it is accurate. The great law firms are organized on factory principles and grind out standardized legal advice, documents and services as systematically as General Motors turns out automobiles" (Lundberg 1939, p. 182).

67. Emulation of the large-firm style by public interest and other groups is discussed in Galanter 1983, 167 ff.

68. Arthurs, Weisman, and Zemans 1988.

the United States. In recent years, the American big firm became a model for firms in Canada,[68] Australia,[69] England,[70] Holland,[71] Venezuela,[72] and elsewhere.

But ironically the triumph of the big firm as an organizational form and a style of practice has been accompanied by changes that jeopardize its identity. But before we detail these recent changes, we want to portray the big firm in its "golden age."

69. Mendelsohn and Lippman 1979; Tomasic and Pentony 1989.
70. Flood 1989.
71. Schuyt 1988, p. 208.
72. Perez Perdomo 1988, p. 389.

3 Circa 1960: The Golden Age of the Big Law Firm

Before the Second World War the big firm had become the dominant kind of law practice. It was the kind of lawyering consumed by the dominant economic actors. It commanded the highest prestige. It attracted some of the most highly talented entrants to the profession. It was regarded as the "state of the art," embodying the highest technical standards. In the postwar years this position of dominance was solidified.

To get a reading on the changes over the past generation, we will develop as a baseline a portrait of the big firm in its golden age, before the transformation that it is now undergoing. We locate this golden age in the period of the late 1950s and the early 1960s—let us call it "circa 1960"—when big firms were prosperous, stable, and untroubled. The form had been tested; it was well established; it exercised an unchallenged dominance. It was a time of stable relations with clients, of steady but manageable growth, of comfortable assurance that an equally bright future lay ahead—which is not to say that its inhabitants did not look back fondly to an earlier time when professionalism was unalloyed.

One of the salient features of that world was that information about law firms was not abundant.[1] Information about firms—especially about firm organization, finances, billing, income, relations with clients, even their identity—was not shared with outsiders—or with very many insiders.[2] Systematic collection of information about big-firm practice was, to say the least, discouraged. The first scholar to venture into this area recounted his difficulty in obtaining inter-

---

1. Perhaps coincidentally, the period of the late fifties and early sixties was one in which the portrayal of lawyers in the popular media was unprecedentedly favorable. On the first "golden age" of the law film, see Nevins (1984, p. 11) (lawyers depicted as virtuous, independent, defenders of the victimized); Chase (1986); Stark (1987, p. 255) ("These mid-1960s dramas, which began with 'The Defenders,' were truly the tales of 'public servants,' and the show's visions harkened back to an earlier era of small-town America, where a true community of values existed that transcended the generational and ideological differences that came to dominate the news of the decade. . . . the shows presented a very positive view of the legal profession").

2. Restraints on information flow and their subsequent removal are discussed below, pages 68–76.

views and securing information about "taboo topics." Many lawyers felt, he reported, that "an outsider had no right to probe into their affairs."[3]

Since information flows were restricted, even participants in the big-firm world were not necessarily well equipped to generalize about it. To get a sense of how it was organized, it is necessary to piece together fragmentary accounts from various sources. Fortunately, we have a series of descriptions of big-firm practice in this period from different perspectives. These include accounts by practitioners,[4] journalists,[5] and a pioneering sociologist, Erwin O. Smigel, who between 1957 and 1963 interviewed 188 out of 1,700 lawyers in eighteen large Wall Street firms, 44 lawyers in four large firms outside New York, and 43 lawyers in twenty smaller Wall Street firms.[6] Supplementing these observations of big-firm organization are studies of lawyers' recruitment and career patterns[7] and of legal ethics.[8] In addition to these contemporary observers, we have a retrospective portrait of the Chicago big firms in Robert Nelson's recent study.[9] From these varied sources we can assemble a composite profile of the large law firms in this period. Useful contrast is supplied by Smigel's 1969 Epilogue and Paul Hoffman's 1973 book[10] that look back to this period as a baseline and provide a reading of changes immediately after our period.

New York firms loom disproportionately large in our sources on the golden age, since almost all of our witnesses focused on New York. The major exceptions are Nelson and Roger Siddall, who report the results of an unsystematic national survey conducted in 1954.[11] The Siddall data cannot be taken as representative, but they provide useful information about prevailing practices and about variation, information that is filtered through the mind of a knowledgeable and thoughtful practitioner. In addition, Smigel has some "control" firms outside New York; Edwin Austin contrasts big firms in other cities with those in New York; Dan Lortie and Jack Ladinsky shed some light on recruitment in Chicago and Detroit. It should be recalled, too, that New York City was the home of a much larger share of big-firm practice then than it is now.

3. Smigel 1969, p. 20. (Originally published in 1964. See above, p. 10 n. 32.)

4. Siddall 1956; Austin 1957; Levy 1961. A 1965 Practicing Law Institute Forum preserves practitioner observations on many aspects of firm organization (Practicing Law Institute 1965).

5. Mayer 1956a, 1956b, 1966; Klaw 1958.

6. Smigel 1969, pp. 30–32.

7. Lortie 1959; Ladinsky 1963a, 1963b.

8. Carlin 1966 (includes a survey of New York lawyers conducted in 1960).

9. Nelson 1988.

10. Hoffman 1973. This book was in turn updated (Hoffman 1982). Hoffman tells us that the latter started as a revised version of the earlier book but because there was so much change in the interval "[i]t became, perforce, an almost wholly new book" (Hoffman 1982, p. xi).

11. Siddall sent questionnaires to two hundred law firms that were the largest in their forty-seven localities. (They averaged fifteen partners and ranged from seven to forty partners.) He received forty-two completed questionnaires.

In the early 1960s, there were twenty-one firms in New York with 50 lawyers or more and only seventeen firms of that size in the rest of the country outside New York.[12] A few years earlier, the largest firm in New York (and the country) was Shearman & Sterling & Wright with 35 partners and 90 associates, a total of 125 lawyers. Three other Wall Street firms had over a hundred lawyers. The twentieth largest firm in New York had 50 lawyers.[13]

We supplemented this contemporary survey with a retrospective look from the late 1980s. We use data that we compiled from the *Martindale Hubbell Law Directory* on two sets of firms: Group I consists of fifty firms that were among the largest in 1986; Group II consists of fifty smaller but still large firms ranked roughly between two-hundreth and two-hundred-fiftieth in the United States in 1988. The two data sets are described in Appendix A. For reasons noted there, *Martindale-Hubbell* is a far from perfect source for size data on law firms. Unfortunately, there is no systematic compilation of law-firm growth statistics. Published data tend to be grossly incomplete and often constructed from two or more incompatible sources.[14] To fill in the gap in the available data our research assistants have literally counted the names associated with select firms listed in *Martindale-Hubbell*. Despite the problems,[15] we believe that these data sets surpass anything previously available.

Using these data sets we were able to examine the sizes of thirty-five Group I firms and thirty-seven Group II firms[16] in 1955 and 1965. In 1955, our thirty-five Group I firms ranged in size from 7 to 84 lawyers, with an average size of 40 lawyers. By 1965, their size ranged from 13 to 112 lawyers, with an average of 62.6. The thirty-seven firms in Group II ranged from 6 to 35 lawyers in 1955, with an average of 15.6; in 1965, they ranged from 8 to 46 with an average of 25.1 lawyers.

This was a period of prosperity and manageable growth for big firms. Over the decade ending in 1965, the Group I firms that twenty years later figured among the fifty largest grew at an annual rate of 5.3 percent. The Group II firms grew at an annual rate of 5.6 percent.[17]

12. Smigel 1969, p. 43. The roster of New York firms, based on Klaw's count in December 1957, can be found in Smigel (1969, pp. 34–35).

13. Figures from Klaw (1958, p. 194); Smigel (1969, pp. 34–35).

14. Because *Martindale-Hubbell* and other sources, such as the *National Law Journal*, use different methods to count attorneys, the data provided by these sources should not be combined. See Appendix A.

15. The principal problem is that *Martindale-Hubbell* systematically undercounts associates; therefore, these data sets generally underestimate the total number of attorneys working for a given firm in a given year. As we discuss in Appendix A, a significant portion of the undercount is attributable to *Martindale-Hubbell*'s practice of counting only those attorneys admitted to the bar.

16. All calculations are based on the firms for which data were available in both years in question.

17. Our figures on growth are a little higher than those reported by Smigel. He reports that, from

Firms were located in and identified with a single city. An earlier wave of European and Washington offices had been largely abandoned.[18] "Formation [in 1957] of a nationwide [sic] law firm with offices interlocking in Illinois, Washington, D.C. and New York" was startling, "so unusual that it had to be approved in advance by the Bar Association."[19]

Hiring. Firms were built by "promotion to partnership." Siddall observes that internal development rather than lateral hiring is

> pretty much a settled characteristic of our large law offices. Generally they add to their staffs only young men who are just starting to practice and advancement takes place by meritorious development within the organization rather than by competition from the outside. Normally the successful lawyers in the large offices located themselves where they are in their youth and then just stayed put.[20]

There were a few exceptions: unsuccessful presidential candidates were the most visible lateral recruits,[21] but more common were those leaving less exalted government posts and the occasional specialist.[22]

Big firms did not hire from one another. Smigel reported that "[c]ompetition for lawyers among the large firms in New York City is limited in two major ways: the firms will not pirate an employee from another law office, and they maintain a gentlemen's agreement to pay the same beginning salary."[23] Lateral movement was still conspicuously absent in the early 1970s when Hoffman observed that "the Brahmins of the Bar don't shop around for better-paying positions. . . . as if by an unwritten agreement, there is almost no 'raiding' by one firm of another's talent."[24]

Partners might leave and firms might split up, but it didn't happen very

---

1957 to 1962, the number of partners in twenty large New York firms increased by 16 percent and that the total number of lawyers in the seventeen large firms outside New York had grown by 37 percent from 1951 to 1961 (Smigel 1969, p. 351). Since we were looking at firms that succeeded in becoming very large two decades later, it is not unlikely that our sample is biased toward greater growth.

18. Smigel 1969, p. 207.

19. Levy 1961, p. 20. The arrangement in question was the association of Adlai Stevenson and his three partners with Paul Weiss, which then had twenty-one lawyers (Johnston 1957, p. 1). The bar association approval (by a divided vote) is reported in the *New York Times* (1957, p. 38). The arrangement lasted until 1961 (Brooks 1983, pp. 46, 74).

20. Siddall 1956, p. 34.

21. After his unsuccessful 1960 campaign for president, Richard Nixon followed the precedent of Thomas E. Dewey and Adlai Stevenson in joining a big firm.

22. Smigel 1969, pp. 42, 90.

23. Smigel 1969, p. 57.

24. Hoffman 1973, pp. 60–61.

often.[25] Looking back across our period, Hoffman reports that: "[t]here has not been a significant split in a major Wall Street or Park Avenue firm for more than twenty-five years. Except for departures to government service, none has lost more than one partner at a time."[26] Lawyers were locked in by client loyalties to firms, by the hard-to-reproduce advantages of the institutional setting, and by the value of the firm connection. "[T]he partnership name is worth money."[27]

Hiring of top law graduates soon after their graduation was one of the building blocks of the big firm. Most hiring was from a handful of law schools. By our circa 1960 period most firms had a "hiring partner" in charge of recruitment, and firm members made recruiting visits to law schools.[28] The practice of having "summer boarders" as they were called then was just taking off.[29] But links between firms and law schools were loose and informal. Walk-in interviews during the Christmas holidays were at the heart of the hiring process.

Starting salaries at the largest New York firms were uniform; the "going rate" was fixed at a luncheon, attended by managing partners of prominent firms, held annually for this purpose.[30] Salaries rose from $4,000 in 1953 to $7,500 in 1963.[31] The era of an arranged "going rate" and incremental raises ended abruptly in 1968 when the Cravath firm unilaterally raised salaries to $15,000 from the scheduled going rate of $10,500.[32]

Big firms aspired to hire "the best men." Academic qualifications were necessary but not sufficient.[33] In addition to academic qualifications, Smigel

25. The 42 firms that responded to Siddall had been in existence an average of 58 years. He asked them to detail the "number of splits in the line of succession": 29 of the 42 had none; the other 13 had undergone a total of 56 splits (Siddall 1956, p. 33).

26. Hoffman 1973, p. 60.

27. Smigel 1969, p. 258.

28. Smigel 1969, pp. 55, 59.

29. Smigel 1969, pp. 56, 62. A Columbia survey found that students taking summer jobs increased from 22 in 1957 to 222 in 1967 (Smigel 1969, p. 368).

30. Smigel 1969, p. 58; Mayer 1966, p. 332. This practice originated in 1927 when Emory Buckner, a partner at Root Clark, disturbed by the thought that young law graduates were exercising poor judgment by responding to small differences in salary, established "the big employers' trust. . . . I called twenty firms to lunch—knowing someone in each—and we made an effort to stabilize the situation" (Letter of Buckner to Felix Frankfurter [November 25, 1928], quoted in Mayer (1968, pp. 147–48). Cf. Swaine's account that after objections from law school faculties, competitive bidding "was abandoned after World War I, following a conference among the managing partners of the larger offices" (Swaine 1946b, p. 6).

31. Smigel 1960, p. 58.

32. Smigel 1969, p. 366. The impact of this is discussed below, pp. 55–57.

33. In a much-cited 1920 talk at Harvard Law School, Paul Cravath had spelled out his image of the desirable recruit: "Brilliant intellectual powers are not essential. Too much imagination, too much wit, too great cleverness, too facile fluency, if not leavened by a sound sense of proportion, are quite as likely to impede success as to promote it. The best clients are apt to be afraid of those qualities. They want as their counsel a man who is primarily honest, safe, sound, and steady" (Swaine 1946b, p. 266).

concluded, "they . . . want lawyers who are Nordic, have pleasing person-
alities and 'clean-cut' appearances, are graduates of the 'right' schools, have
the 'right' social background and experience in the affairs of the world, and are
endowed with tremendous stamina."[34]

Historically, the big firms had confined hiring to white Christian males.[35]
Few blacks or women had the educational admission tickets to contend for these
jobs. But there were numerous Jews who did and, with a few exceptions,[36] they
were excluded.[37] Exclusion of Jews had led to the organization of separate
"Jewish firms," some of which had grown into big firms much like their Wall
Street counterparts—but typically with smaller clients.[38] There were also a
small number of large firms that were conspicuously "mixed," including both
Jewish and non-Jewish partners.

This exclusion began to break down after the Second World War. Jewish associates were hired and some moved up the ladder to partner.[39] Cravath
appointed its first Jewish partner in 1959;[40] the first Jewish partner at Davis
Polk was appointed in 1961.[41] By the early 1960s, Jews were being hired and
exclusion had been tempered into concern about having "too many" Jews. By
the late 1960s, when he wrote his Epilogue, Smigel reports the "tremendous
lessening of discrimination—especially toward Jews" since he gathered data a
decade earlier. He concludes that discrimination against Jews in hiring was "essentially gone" in Wall Street firms.[42]

Circa 1960, blacks and other minorities of color were hardly visible in the
world of large law firms. Smigel reports that "[i]n the year and a half that was

34. Smigel 1969, p. 37.

35. Some women and Jews were hired during World War II, when the normal supply of desirable
candidates had dried up.

36. Among the notable exceptions was the Jewish participation in the early development of Sullivan & Cromwell. Alfred Jaretski, who had gone to Harvard with Sullivan's son, joined the firm in
1881 and became a partner in 1894 (Lisagor and Lipsius 1988, pp. 21, 31; Sullivan & Cromwell
1981, p. 43). As part of the enlargement of the partner's roster (see above, p. 15 n. 53) both his son
and his son-in-law became partners and "played an important part in the firm over the next four
decades" (Lisagor and Lipsius 1988, p. 59). Another notable exception was the Root Clark firm.

37. A *Yale Law Journal* survey found that Jewish students from the Yale classes of 1951–62,
especially those below the top third of their class, were less successful in obtaining work in the
larger, higher-paying firms. During the 1950s and early 1960s, Jews graduating from Yale went to
firms roughly half the size of those joined by their Gentile classmates and earned the equivalent of
classmates ranking an average of one-third of a class lower in law school ranking (*Yale Law Journal*
1964). This study was based on interviews with Yale students, with hiring partners, and a survey of
Yale graduates of 1951–62 who worked in New York. The exclusion of Jews and others from the big
firms (and from the bar) is chronicled by Auerbach (1976, Chapter 4 and passim).

38. Smigel 1969, pp. 174–75; *Yale Law Journal* 1964, pp. 651–52.

39. O'Melveny & Meyers, then the largest firm in Los Angeles, hired its first Jewish associate in
1955 (Zweigenhaft and Domhoff 1982, p. 39).

40. Cf. Hoffman (1973, p. 12).

41. Auerbach 1976, p. 232.

42. Smigel 1969, p. 370. Cf. Nelson (1988, p. 130) on hiring of Jews by Chicago big firms.

spent interviewing, I heard of only three Negroes who had been hired by large law firms. Two of these were women who did not meet the client." Because few blacks went to the "right" colleges or law schools, "[s]o few Negroes are 'eligible' for positions in these firms that the issue of employment is rarely raised."[43] There were few Catholics, particularly "ethnics."[44]

Women were excluded from the world of big law firms. In 1956 there were something like eighteen women working in large New York firms—something less than 1 percent of their total complement of lawyers. Smigel encountered only one woman partner.[45] As late as 1968, Cynthia Fuchs Epstein estimated, "only forty women were working in Wall Street firms or had some Wall Street experience."[46]

The lowering of barriers to Jews was part of a general lessening of social exclusiveness. In 1957, 28 percent of the partners in the eighteen firms studied by Smigel were listed in the Social Register. By 1968, the percentage had dropped to 20. Of those who had become partner after 1957, only 13 percent were listed.[47] A study of two large Pittsburgh firms in the late 1960s depicts a similar shift from particularistic to meritocratic hiring criteria. Informal hiring practices that recruited "only qualified sons of friends or relatives of partners" were replaced by appointment of a hiring partner and systematic recruitment of new associates, including Jews and Catholics.[48]

Promotion and Partnership. Only a small minority of those hired as associates achieved partnership. Of 462 lawyers hired by the Cravath firm between 1906 and 1948, only 44 (9.5 percent) were made partners.[49] Six of these were hired as partners and two more became partners after very brief periods as associates.[50] Thus, of those hired as beginning associates, only 36 of 454 (just under 8 percent) became partners. Sixteen of the 418 who did not become partners remained as permanent associates and 402 left.[51]

Cravath may have been among the most selective but it was not out of line with other firms. In 1956 Martin Mayer reported that the "chance of becoming

43. Smigel 1969, p. 45.

44. Smigel reports that discrimination against Catholics was not on grounds of religion per se, but "is based more on their 'lower class' origins, their foreign-born parents, and their lack of 'proper' education. Their religion does not seem to be a significant bar to employment although some firms will not make them partners" (Smigel 1969, p. 45).

45. Smigel 1969, p. 46.

46. Epstein 1981, p. 176. Epstein reports that "[o]f the thirty-four women partners on Wall Street in 1979, only three achieved partnership before 1970" (Epstein 1981, p. 180).

47. Smigel 1969, p. 372.

48. Delany and Feingold 1970, p. 192.

49. Smigel 1969, p. 116.

50. Smigel 1969, p. 137.

51. Smigel 1969, p. 116.

a partner . . . varies from one in seven to one in fifteen, depending on the firm and the year in which he joins it."[52] The "average chance at a partnership . . . is only one in twelve."[53] Spencer Klaw, writing two years later, provides a more optimistic assessment that partnership is achieved by "perhaps one out of every six or seven."[54]

The amount of time that it took to become a partner varied from firm to firm and associate to associate. But for the lawyers becoming partners around 1960 the average time seems to have been just under ten years. Smigel found that average time to partnership for his entire sample of Wall Street partners was 8.5 years,[55] but he portrays some firms with higher averages.[56] At Cravath, the average wait for partners who "worked their way up through the firm" after 1906 was 6.8 years.[57] Circa 1960, some thought that time to partnership was shorter than it had been earlier. One mid-level partner told Smigel that "In the pre-war days, there used to be a standard theory that a man should stay for ten years. Then the firm would decide to keep him or place him somewhere. Things have speeded up a great deal now. Our feeling is that finding a permanent place should start after six or seven years."[58]

Something very close to the seven-year figure emerges from Nelson's analysis of data on nineteen large Chicago firms. For the period 1950–59, it took an average of 7.5 years to attain partnership; in the following decade this dropped to 7.21 years.[59] Apparently the time to partnership dropped during the 1960s in New York as well. At a 1965 Practicing Law Institute forum on managing law offices, a Davis Polk partner observed:

> In our firm . . . [time to partnership] used to be a little more than ten years, except in the rarest cases. More recently, it has been five, six, or seven years though in some cases it may still take ten years or more. The time varies with the individual, his department and the need of the firm for another partner from a particular department.[60]

52. Mayer 1956a, p. 52.

53. Mayer 1956a, p. 54.

54. Klaw 1958, p. 142.

55. Smigel 1969, p. 93.

56. In a hundred-lawyer firm with twenty-six partners studied in 1956, partners had taken an average of 9.1 years to partnership (Smigel 1969, p. 137). In Simpson Thacher those who became partners between 1945 and the late 1950s had spent an average of 10.6 years with the firm (Smigel 1969, p. 79). In a firm that Smigel identifies as a "social" firm the average time to partnership was 11.7 years (Smigel 1969, p. 92). A respondent at Sullivan & Cromwell reported that "it now takes longer than ten years to become a partner" (Smigel 1969, p. 84). Cf. Mayer's report that most partners felt that "ten is about right" (Mayer 1956a, p. 53).

57. Smigel 1969, p. 137.

58. Smigel 1969, p. 79.

59. Nelson 1988, p. 141.

60. Practicing Law Institute (PLI) 1965, p. 156. Other participants presented a more mixed pic-

In his 1969 Epilogue, Smigel observes:

> A young lawyer no longer must serve as an associate for ten years before he can become a partner. While the apprenticeship period varies with each firm, the average length of time seems to be seven years, with a range between five and ten. There is no question, however, that it now takes less time to become a partner.[61]

One of the basic elements of the structure of the big firm is the "up-or-out" rule, which prescribes that after a probationary period the young lawyer will either be admitted to the partnership or will leave the firm. In this model, there can be no permanent connection other than as a partner. It is easy to overestimate the rigor with which the up-or-out rule was in fact applied.[62]

In his 1958 study, Klaw observed that "[f]ew Wall Street firms have an absolutely rigid up-or-out policy, but most of them discourage men from staying on indefinitely as associates."[63] Many firms had an explicit up-or-out rule—in some cases quite recently minted[64]—but there was at work a competing and powerful norm, that it was not nice to fire a lawyer. In 1956, Mayer reported that "nobody is ever fired except for immediate and specific cause."[65] Smigel reports a "widespread feeling that it is not professional to fire a lawyer."[66] Termination tended to be long-drawn-out and disguised. "Failure . . . is carefully disguised by the firms with the knowing help of their members and associates."[67] Addressing a PLI forum in 1965, a Shearman & Sterling partner says of those passed over: "Naturally, we don't desert these fellows. Anybody who has

---

ture: a Milbank Tweed partner said "generally eight to ten years is the range within which a man can expect to become a partner, but there are a good many instances of it taking longer. One man recently did it in six years" (PLI 1965, p. 157). A Proskauer Rose partner said "We do not make even a deserving man a partner ahead of his contemporaries. He must wait his turn. . . . [A man became a partner] in his ninth or tenth year. We have never made a man a partner early" (PLI 1965, p. 157). In a prepared talk on "Retention and Weeding Out" at the PLI forum, William Rockefeller of Shearman & Sterling observed, "In recent years the men that have been selected [as partners] are at least eight years out of law school. Although the figure has been coming down almost every time we take in partners, the average is more nearly ten years" (PLI 1965, p. 198).

61. Smigel 1969, p. 373. Writing a few years later, Paul Hoffman observed that "The period of apprenticeship has shrunk from ten to about seven years" (Hoffman 1973, p. 114).

62. Thus in a recent paper Gilson and Mnookin attempt to explain the economic logic of the up-or-out system which they define as meaning that "as a general rule, a firm *never* retains an associate who is not promoted" (Gilson and Mnookin 1989, p. 575 n. 28) a system that "appears to have dominated employment practices over the entire period in which the institution of the modern corporate law firm has existed" (Gilson and Mnookin 1989, p. 571).

63. Klaw 1958, p. 197.

64. Smigel 1969, p. 44.

65. Mayer 1956a, p. 54.

66. Smigel 1969, p. 77.

67. Smigel 1969, p. 78.

been with us that long is entirely welcome to stay, and they are so few that we can accommodate them as valued 'permanent' associates because they have demonstrated their ability."[68]

For associates who did not make partner, firms undertook outplacement, recommending them for jobs with client corporations and with smaller firms.[69] Ties might be maintained as the firm referred legal work to them or served as outside counsel to the corporation.

Although departure from the firm was decreed by the up-or-out norm, there were some lawyers who were permanent but not partners. These included managing clerks and a few specialists who because of a low-status specialty (such as immigration or labor law) or low-status origins had no expectation of being considered for partnership, although they were professionally respected and well paid.[70] But most permanent associates were "failures," "second-class citizens" who had not been promoted but stayed on and were assigned routine work—especially "back office" work which did not involve dealing with clients.[71] Permanent associates were not as rare as the up-or-out norm might suggest. Smigel gives figures on two firms in 1856: one 100–lawyer firm had 9 permanent associates; an 89-lawyer firm had 22 permanent associates (24.7 percent). Of all those who had started out at the Cravath firm from 1906 to 1948, 16 remained as permanent associates—almost half as many as became partners.[72]

In the course of the 1960s, there was a decline in the number of permanent associates; or, to put it another way, the up-or-out norm was enforced more vigorously. In his Epilogue, Smigel notes the "reduction in the number of permanent associates. The firms . . . no longer consider the permanent associate desirable."[73] He suggests a number of possible reasons for this: that the firms' work may have become more complex; that the work formerly done by permanent associates was now being done by in-house corporate counsel; that the permanent associate was viewed as an undesirable model of failure for associates.[74] In the early 1970s, Hoffman reported that "[p]ermanent associates are a dying breed . . . being phased out by attrition at most firms."[75] As we shall see, it was not to be long before they were phased back in.

68. PLI 1965, p. 199.

69. Smigel 1969, p. 64. In our "circa 1960" period, corporate legal work in many cases paid better than law firm work (Siddall 1956, p. 107).

70. Smigel 1969, pp. 119, 231.

71. Smigel 1969, pp. 164, 231.

72. Smigel 1969, p. 116. In 1934, when Sullivan & Cromwell had sixteen partners, "the firm had eight senior associates who had been there more than fifteen years and never expected to make partner" (Lisagor and Lipsius 1988, p. 108).

73. Smigel 1969, p. 375, n. 11.

74. Smigel 1969, p. 375, n. 11.

75. Hoffman 1973, p. 44.

Partners were chosen for proficiency, hard work, and ability to relate to clients.[76] But in many cases there was some consideration of the candidate's ability to attract business:

> Business-getting ability has not been important to the man as an associate (some firms will split the fees with an associate who brings in business, some will not . . .). Now a judgment on whether he can pull his weight in the acquisition of clients—either because of his connections or salesmanship or because his quality in his specialty forecasts referral business from other lawyers—will become a matter of considerable importance.[77]

And selection depended on the perceived ability of a firm to support additional partners. Sullivan & Cromwell partner Arthur Dean identified "the need of the firm for a partner" to fill a particular "slot" as the most important reason for promotion.[78] One managing partner confessed to Mayer:

> Often we'll have a sudden expansion of work, and we'll simply need three or four more men with status. We'll look around the office and sigh about associates who left us last year or the year before because we couldn't see any real chance of a partnership for them. And the men who get the partnerships may not be as good as the men we lost.[79]

What were perceived as merely temporary fluctuations in demand could be addressed in other ways than by enlarging the firm: by use of temporary lawyers, by contracting work to outside lawyers, and by cultivating satellite firms.[80]

Achieving partnership, the "strongest reward," meant not only status but security and assurance of further advancement: "they . . . know that they have tenure and feel certain that they will advance up the partnership ladder."[81] There was certainly pressure to keep up with one's peers, but competition between partners was restrained. In this environment "[a]dmission to the partnership of a leading firm was a virtual guarantee not only of tenured employment but of a lifetime of steadily increasing earnings unmatched by a lawyer's counterparts in the other learned professions."[82]

Even today the compensation of partners is a topic that is deeply confidential. Not surprisingly, in 1960 it was made clear to Smigel that this was a "taboo topic."[83] "The subject of percentages and salary is particularly 'hush,

76. Smigel 1969, p. 97.
77. Mayer 1966, p. 334.
78. Lisagor and Lipsius 1988, p. 190.
79. Mayer 1956a, p. 52.
80. Smigel 1969, pp. 88, 89, 193, 228.
81. Smigel 1969, pp. 259, 302. Cf. Smigel (1969, p. 257).
82. Stevens 1987, p. 8.
83. Smigel 1969, p. 18.

hush' "[84] Even senior associates were in the dark on partners' income. "Nobody knows for sure the income of his opposite numbers in rival firms."[85]

There seems to be an impression that the classic pattern of dividing the proceeds of the big-firm partnership was some approximation of giving each partner an equal share—or a share by seniority (the so-called "lockstep" system).[86] If this was ever true, by circa 1960 the prevailing practice was to divide profits according to individualized shares rather than by a norm of equal participation.[87] The prevalence of unequal shares is confirmed by Mayer, who reports that:

> Though some of the old firms worked on the principle that all men admitted to the firm at the same time should receive the same percentage, everybody growing at the same rate as the group got older, the business-getters eventually refused to put up with this equality. Over the long run, a man's share of the firm (and his importance in its management, if he cares) will reflect the significance of the clients he controls. Shifts in partnership shares as new business arrives will normally give two-thirds of the added profit to the man who found the business (and who is, also, of course, the lawyer actually advising the client), one-third to the man who works on it.[88]

It is not clear whether Mayer is proposing that marginal-product-based compensation was already "there" throughout our circa 1960 period or is a departure from an equal-shares scheme that once generally prevailed.[89] Any sense of trends is elusive. Hoffman suggests that shares may have become *more* equal as firms became larger and less dominated by founders or renowned stars "who took whopping percentages of the firms' income."[90] Yet since there was little

84. Smigel 1969, p. 92. "On no subject is the blue chip bar more secretive" (Hoffman 1973, p. 58).

85. Mayer 1956a, p. 51.

86. Cf. Gilson and Mnookin (1985) who refer to "traditional methods" of apportionment. The persistent reports about the secrecy of these matters (see above, nn. 83–85) suggest that there was more to keep secret than an "equal shares" formula.

87. Siddall reports a great variety of compensation schemes among his forty-two firms (Siddall 1956, p. 43). The data here do not tell us how much of the variation may be accounted for by seniority. But they cast some doubt on the notion that many or most law firms were equal-shares partnerships. At least some of these firms attempted to apportion rewards according to the contribution of each partner to income (Siddall 1956, p. 48).

88. Mayer 1966, p. 336. This is presumably based on research conducted in the years before Mayer's book was published in 1967. Mayer had an earlier round of researching Wall Street firms for his 1956 *Harper's* articles.

89. In 1958 Klaw reported on one "equal shares" firm but suggested that generally a Wall Street partner makes "a good deal more" if he "consistently attracts important new clients" (Klaw 1958, p. 198).

90. Hoffman 1973, p. 58.

opportunity for partners to leave, there was no assurance that disparities between productivity and compensation would be remedied.[91]

In the mid-fifties few firms had standing arrangements for retirement.[92] The passage of the Keogh Act in 1962 made it possible for firms to set up tax-free pension funds. Compulsory retirement and pension plans were introduced for the most part after our circa 1960 period.[93]

Work and Clients. The work of the big firm was primarily office work in corporations, securities, banking, and tax with some estate work for wealthy clients. Divorces, automobile accidents, and minor real-estate matters would be farmed out or referred to other lawyers.[94] Mayer estimated that "litigation occupies less than one-tenth the time of a large law firm" and reported that "[s]ome firms avoid it entirely."[95] Elite lawyers took pride in the minor role of litigation in their practices. A practitioner's account of "The New Role of the Lawyer in Modern Society" emphasized that "[p]reventive law, as against crisis law, is the kind of law which lawyers practice today."[96] Litigation was not prestigious work and it was not seen as a money-maker. It was necessary to have a litigation department "even though it may be the least lucrative branch of the firm." Alternatively, the firm could "have a firm of trial lawyer specialists with which it will work in close association."[97] It was explained to Klaw in 1958 that although litigation is not always profitable, "it's a service we have to provide, and at worst it can be looked on as a sort of loss leader."[98] As late as the early

91. In 1973, after our circa 1960 period, a story of a Sullivan & Cromwell partner who twice threatened to quit unless given a bigger slice of the pie was deemed sufficiently unusual to be worth recounting (Hoffman 1973, p. 59).

92. Siddall suggests that retirement arrangements are rarely matters of pre-formed policy (Siddall 1956, p. 80). Mayer (1956a, p. 54) says firms with pensions for secretarial staff never extend them to the legal staff. Mayer (1966, p. 335) says some large New York firms in recent years have addressed the retirement problem by requiring new partners in effect to buy out the older men. "The actual procedure is a compulsory deduction from the new man's partnership share to make up a 'retirement fund' to which not all the established partners contribute."

93. Hoffman 1973, p. 59. E.g., Cravath adopted a retirement plan in 1967, under which partners were phased out from age sixty-five and compelled to retire at seventy-two (Hoffman 1973, p. 12).

94. Levy 1961, p. 35.

95. Mayer 1956b, p. 36.

96. Levy 1961, p. 165. The quoted phrase is the subtitle of Levy's book.

97. Levy 1961, p. 64. A study of judicial selection in Kansas City in the early 1960s noted that members of large corporate law firms "rarely become involved in actual courtroom litigation but, instead, devote most of their time to out-of-court legal matters." Echoing the observations of Llewellyn thirty years earlier (see Llewellyn 1933), the authors note that lawyers in large corporate firms "do not have a very wide acquaintance with the Bar, are never significantly involved in trial practice, have few contacts within the political community, and are not very interested or knowledgeable about the judiciary, particularly at the trial court level" (Watson and Downing 1969, p. 76).

98. Klaw 1958, p. 144.

1970s, Hoffman reports that "[f]ew firms make money from litigation. They look upon the litigation department as a loss-leader, something to lure clients into the office."[99]

Mayer describes big-firm litigation in the early 1960s as involving taxes, contracts, personal-injury defense, and defense of corporations and directors from shareholders' suits. "But to most large law firms, the word 'litigation' connotes an antitrust suit, not because the number of such cases is large but because each of them represents so enormous a quantity of work."[100] The surge of antitrust litigation tended to elevate the standing of litigators, who had been "overshadowed by office-lawyer partners . . . who seldom, if ever, went near a courtroom."[101] Where big firms were involved in litigation, it was typically on the defendants' side.[102] Big firms usually represented dominant actors who could structure transactions so that they got what they wanted; it was the other side that had to seek the help of courts to disturb the status quo. Disdain of litigation reflected the prevailing attitude among the corporate establishment that it was not quite nice to sue.[103]

Relations with clients tended to be enduring. "A partner in one Wall Street firm estimate[d] its turnover in dollar volume at 5 per cent a year, mostly in one-shot litigation."[104] Many big-firm partners sat on the boards of their clients[105] (a practice that had been viewed as unprofessional earlier in the century and would lose favor later).[106]

99. Hoffman 1973, p. 42.

100. Mayer 1966, p. 321.

101. Klaw 1958, p. 144.

102. This tilt to big-firm participation in litigation was noted by an earlier writer about Wall Street law practice: "[M]ost of the legal cases handled by the big law firms . . . place them on the side of the defense. . . . So imbued do the corporation lawyers become with a defensive psychology that they have unconsciously evolved a folklore—familiar to all newspaper men who report Wall Street—in which plaintiffs figure as racketeers or Bolshevists, in spirit if not in fact. To the average Wall Street corporation lawyer, in whose very fibre is burned the conviction that the management is always right, stockholders who bring suit against the management are simply racketeers and their lawyers are little better; anyone who is injured in a train wreck and who sues the great and good railroad company is little more than a scoundrel. . . . Again, the bondholder who finds that he has been sold securities by means of a misleading prospectus, and who brings suit, is a knave, and his lawyer is probably more of a knave, meriting disbarment. . . . Similarly, lawyers who chase ambulances in search of clients are little better than pickpockets and their clients hardly more than criminals" (Lundberg 1939, p. 187–88).

103. Macaulay 1963.

104. Hoffman 1973, p. 72.

105. Mayer noted that "lawyers want to sit on boards because . . . it sews up the client's legal business" (Mayer 1956a, p. 56).

106. Gartner (1973, p. 4) reported that liability and conflict of interest concerns were leading law firms to reappraise the desirability of directorships.

As they had grown, many firms had broadened their client base, becoming less dependent on a single main client. Smigel reported that

> Today, a firm's ability to retain its independence is further strength-
> ened because it has a number of clients, with no one client providing
> enough income to materially or consciously influence the law office's
> legal opinion. This was not always true, for at their inception many of
> these firms depended upon one major client or at best upon a very few
> important ones; they resembled the legal departments of large corpo-
> rations and were much more subject to a major client's demands.[107]

Corporations had strong ties to "their" law firms. Relations tended to be enduring and unproblematic. A 1959 Conference Board survey on the legal work
of 286 manufacturing corporations found that "three fourths of them retain outside counsel on a continuing basis. . . . Companies most frequently report that
'present outside counsel has been with us for many, many years,' or that 'we are
satisfied with the performance of our outside counsel and have never given any
thought to hiring another.' "[108] In-house corporate counsel were conduits to
and handmaidens of their outside law firms, not managers and rivals as they
would become later. A prosperous corporate America, enjoying . igh margins
of profit and untroubled by international competition,[109] was disinclined to
question the charges of the big firms. As one corporate counsel said, legal advice "is probably the only service we buy without some kind of survey of
alternate cost. I don't know how much longer lawyers can operate in this
way."[110]

Bills to clients, Klaw reported at the beginning of our period, "are almost
never itemized."[111] Each lawyer in a firm kept a diary or time sheet to keep
track of time spent on the work of various clients. In some firms timekeeping
was fairly recent.[112] Each lawyer was assigned an hourly billing rate for com-
putational purposes, although it was not always the case that clients were
charged that amount.[113] Some firms began billing by the hour, a practice that
proved popular with clients, so that by the middle 1960s billing for lawyer
hours became the standard method of calculating fees.[114]

107. Smigel 1969, p. 344.
108. National Industrial Conference Board 1959, p. 464.
109. On the comfortable position of American corporations in this period, see Business Disputing Group (1989).
110. PLI 1965 forum on managing law offices, cited in Mayer (1966, p. 337).
111. Klaw 1958, p. 202.
112. Thus, the Shearman & Sterling firm history reports that "prior to 1945 the Firm kept no time
records" (Earle and Parlin 1973, p. 354).
113. Klaw 1958, p. 202.
114. Telephone interview with Mary Ann Altman of Altman & Weil, Inc., August 7, 1989.

We have no evidence about how many hours people actually worked or billed. Smigel reported that "[s]ome firms believe an associate should put in 1800 chargeable hours a year and a partner 1500, with the hours decreasing as the partner gets older."[115] It was widely believed, perhaps with some basis, that lawyers (especially associates) were not working as hard as they had in earlier times.[116]

Circa 1960, New York still dominated the world of big-time law practice. Big firms elsewhere were constructed along the same promotion-to-partnership lines, but tended to operate a bit differently. They had a smaller turnover of associates and less up-or-out pressure. Partnership was easier to attain and came earlier.[117] Outside New York, firms were less highly leveraged. The ratio of associates to partners in Smigel's nineteen New York firms was 2 to 1; in his non–New York firms it was between 1 to 1 and 1.5 to 1.[118] A Chicago big-firm lawyer observed that New York firms "frequently employ two or three or even more associates per partner. In Chicago these ratios are lower; and there has been a well-defined trend in recent years, toward increasing the number of partners in the larger firms as compared with the number of associates."[119] Outside New York there was more use of such intermediate classifications as junior or limited partners.[120] There was more lateral hiring.[121]

Firms outside New York tended to be more recently founded.[122] There was less departmentalization; lawyers were less specialized, and less supervised.[123] Firm organization was less formal: there was less elaboration of rules about meetings, training, conflicts of interest, and so on.[124]

115. Smigel 1969, p. 220. In a detailed explication of law-office organization in 1941, Reginald Heber Smith suggested as approximations of "the number of hours experience indicates [lawyers] will actually work on the average year in and year out": 1,600 from juniors, 1,520 from partners, and 1,200 from "older senior partners" who "are commonly devoting more time to public service, to charities . . ." (Smith 1940c, p. 611).

116. Smigel 1969, pp. 43, 104. Cf. Klaw (1958, p. 194). Subsequently, expectations about billable hours seem to have declined. In 1973, Hoffman reported that "[a]s late as five years ago [1968], associates were expected to produce 2,000 billable hours a year. The target is now down to 1,600 and the actual output is even less" (Hoffman 1973, pp. 130–31). It is difficult to interpret changes in these figures because "billable hours" is a product not only of actual time spent but of recording practices and billing practices, which may change independently of the former.

117. Smigel 1969, pp. 182–83. In late 1957, the twenty largest Wall Street firms (ranging in size from 125 to 46) had 2.28 associates for each partner. Calculated from data given at Klaw (1958, p. 194).

118. Smigel 1969, pp. 183, 203.

119. Austin 1957, p. 16.

120. Smigel 1969, p. 183.

121. Smigel 1969, p. 181.

122. Smigel 1969, p. 190.

123. Smigel 1969, p. 186.

124. Smigel 1969, pp. 184–85.

Summary. For big firms, circa 1960 was a time of prosperity, stable relations with clients, steady but manageable growth, and a comfortable assumption that this kind of law practice was a permanent fixture of American life and would go on forever.[125] Notwithstanding their comfortable situation, many inhabitants and observers regarded the big-firm world as sadly declined from an earlier day when lawyers were statesmen and served as the conscience of business.[126] Echoing laments that have recurred since the last century, partners complained to Smigel that law is turning into a business.[127] No longer, Mayer reflects, do young associates regard themselves as servants of the law and holders of a public trust; "they are too busy fitting themselves for existence in the 1950s, when efficiency, accuracy, and intelligence are the only values to be sought."[128]

Big law firms enjoyed an enviable autonomy. They were relatively independent vis-á-vis their clients; they exercised considerable control over how they did their work; and they were infused with a sense of being in control of their destiny. A sharp contrast with present practices and perspectives is implicit in the retrospective glance of a contemporary author:

> competition was very much a gentlemanly affair. With the banks and manufacturing corporations pacing America's industrial expansion— and with the Securities Acts and New Deal legislation complicating business transactions—the workload grew faster than the firms' ability to service it. Protected by their captive relationships, the established practices had no reason to fear competitive assaults and were not, in turn, moved to encroach on their competitors' turf. Blessed with virtual monopolies in their respective markets, they focused instead on practice standards, on establishing self-indulgent compensation systems, and on perfecting the mystique and the mannerisms of elite professionals. How cases were staffed and billed, how partners were selected and paid, and how new partners were admitted to the ranks were issues based on internal considerations rather than market factors. Free to conduct their affairs as they saw fit, the established practices could all but ignore such boorish concerns as efficiency, productivity, marketing and competition.[129]

125. For other strata of the profession, however, there was a sense of decline from a more prosperous past. The ABA's Special Committee on the Economics of Law Practice in 1959 complained that lawyers' incomes had fallen relative to those of doctors and dentists. They saw the profession "endangered by the creeping instability of its economic status" and "dwindling" as the percentage of national income spent on legal services fell to one-third of what it had been (at its all-time high in the early Depression years). The solution was minimum-fee schedules to be enforced by the profession's disciplinary bodies (American Bar Association 1959, p. 3).

126. On the "declension thesis," see Gordon (1988, p. 48).

127. Smigel 1969, pp. 303–5.

128. Mayer 1956a, p. 56.

129. Stevens 1987, pp. 8–9.

4 The Transformation

The Changing Environment of the Big Firm

In the past generation, the large-law-firm sector of the American legal profession has undergone a set of drastic changes.[1] These changes, which we will describe shortly, are not a singular eruption against a relatively unchanging background. Instead they are part of a dramatic expansion of the scale and scope of the whole world of legal institutions. In the course of this twenty-five years, there has been a great change in scale of many aspects of the legal world: the amount and complexity of legal regulation; the frequency of litigation; the amount and tenor of authoritative legal material; the number, coordination, and productivity of lawyers; the number of legal actors and the resources they devote to legal activity; the amount of information about law and the velocity with which it circulates.

Changes in the legal world reflect changes in the surrounding economy and society. Large law firms are evolving along with other institutions in the legal world. Before describing the way that large law firms have changed, we sketch some of the salient changes in their world. These changes—for example, increased expenditures on law—affect the conditions under which individual firms operate. For any given firm these changes are constituents of the environment, external and given, and not readily influenced. But as firms in the aggregate adapt to these conditions, changes in their number, size, and activities contribute to further changes in the environment. These concomitant changes can be viewed either as the causes or the effects of changes within law firms. When, as in this section, we describe the changing conditions to which firms are adapting, we emphasize these phenomena as constituents of the

1. The changes described here are in the "hemisphere" of the legal profession, made up largely of big firms, that serve corporations and other large organizations. There have been corresponding changes in the other hemisphere of the legal profession that serves individuals and small businesses (on the two hemispheres, see Heinz and Laumann [1982]). These changes include: organizational rationalization and computerization; the development of specialties like medical malpractice, product liability, toxic torts, and civil rights; development of networks for sharing information and strategic coordination, enabling far-flung congregations of unaffiliated lawyers to mount major litigation campaigns like the asbestos cases. These developments have been stimulated and paralleled by developments in legal services for the poor and public-interest law. When we come to speculate on the future in Chapter 6 below, we shall indicate how these separate, though related, lines of development might intersect.

changing environment; later, when we discuss the effects of changes in large firms, many of these phenomena will reappear as effects of changing patterns of firm activity.

This enlarged legal system serves a society that is different in many important respects from the society in which the large firm had enjoyed its golden age. Compared to 1960, the population in 1985 was larger, older, more affluent, more educated, and more diverse.[2] It enjoyed a higher level of social services, higher life-expectancy, and higher expectations of institutional performance.[3] At the same time, the period since 1960 has seen a pronounced decline of confidence in government, business, and other major institutions.[4]

The economy has grown larger. The gross national product increased by 679 percent, from $515.3 billion in 1960 to $4,014.9 billion in 1985.[5] Employment rose from 67 million in 1960 to 108 million in 1985. Participation in the workforce increased, due largely to the inclusion of women, from 38 percent of the population to over 45 percent. There has been a pronounced shift away from the making of goods to the providing of services.[6] In particular, there has been an immense multiplication of financial transactions.[7] The economy has been internationalized.[8] U.S. assets invested abroad increased from $277.0 to $853.8

2. The population grew from 179,979,000 in 1960 to 238,740,000 in 1985. The median age increased from 29.4 in 1960 to 31.5 in 1985. Per capita income grew from $9,023 in 1960 to $15,029 in 1985. The median years of school completed increased from 10.6 years in 1960 to 12.6 years in 1985 (U.S. Bureau of Census 1976, p. 224; U.S. Bureau of Census 1987, pp. 14, 121, 419, 754). All dollar amounts in 1982 dollars. Current dollar amounts were converted into 1982 constant dollars using the annual GNP implicit price deflator of the given years. See U.S. President (1987, Table B-3); U.S. Bureau of Census (1987, Table 732).

3. Public spending on social welfare increased from $169.2 billion in 1960 to $653.9 billion in 1985. Public spending on health and hospitals increased from $17.0 billion in 1960 to $56.7 billion in 1985. Average life expectancy increased from 69.7 years in 1960 to 74.7 years in 1985 (U.S. Bureau of Census 1976, pp. 1120–27; 1987, pp. 69, 251, 334). For discussion of higher expectations of institutional performance, see Friedman (1985).

4. Lipset and Schneider 1987.

5. U.S. Bureau of Census 1989, p. 421, Table 685.

6. In 1960, 51.5 percent of GNP was in goods and 37.2 percent was in services. In 1985, goods made up only 40.9 percent of GNP while services made up 49.0 percent of GNP (U.S. Bureau of Census 1976, p. 228, Series F 32–46; 1989, p. 423, Table 688).

7. The percentage of wage and salary workers employed in the financial sector increased from 4.7 percent in 1960 to 6.8 percent in 1987. From 1960 to 1986 the ratio of interest income to pre-tax profits in the United States increased fivefold, rising from 9 percent to 51 percent. The ratio of external to internal financing used by nonfinancial corporations increased from 1.5:1 to 4.6:1. (U.S. Bureau of Labor Statistics 1988, Table A-21; U.S. President 1988, Tables B-12 and B-89; Business Disputing Group 1989, pp. 28–30, Table 4).

8. Exports and imports as a percentage of gross domestic product increased from 10.5 percent in 1960 to 23.3 percent in 1985. (U.S. President 1989, Tables B-1 and B-8; Business Disputing Group 1989, Table 2).

billion, while foreign assets invested in the U.S. increased from $132.4 billion to $949.8 billion.[9]

The number of lawyers increased from 285,933 in 1960 to 655,191 in 1985—an increase of 129 percent.[10] Not only were there more lawyers, but they were younger,[11] less experienced,[12] better educated,[13] and more diverse in background and outlook than their predecessors.

In 1960, only 2.6 percent of all lawyers and 3.5 percent of law students were female.[14] By 1985, 13.1 percent of all lawyers were female,[15] a figure destined to keep increasing rapidly since women made up 40 percent of law students.[16]

Minorities made up no more than 1 percent of the profession in 1960,[17] and just over 4 percent in 1985.[18] Minorities made up only 4.3 percent of law students in ABA-approved schools in 1969–70, the first year for which figures are

9. U.S. President 1987, p. 779, Table 1389.

10. U.S. Bureau of Census 1976, p. 416; Curran 1986.

11. In 1960, 23.6 percent of all lawyers were thirty-five years old or younger. In 1980, 38.8 percent were thirty-five or younger (Curran 1985, p. 10, Table 1.3.1; p. 8, Table 1.2.3). In 1985, 30.3 percent were thirty-four or younger (Curran 1986, p. 3).

12. In 1960, 32.5 percent of all lawyers had been admitted to the bar during the preceding nine years (that is, had less than nine years of experience) (Hankin and Krohnke 1965, p. 26, Table 2, Table 9). In 1980, 42.3 percent of the lawyer population had been admitted to the bar during the preceding nine years (Curran 1985, p. 27, Figure 6).

13. E.g., the portion of lawyers listed in *Martindale-Hubbell* who received a college degree rose from 58.0 percent in 1960 to 73.3 percent in 1970, the last year for which data are available (Sikes, Carson, and Gorai 1972, p. 8, Table 4). A rise in prior educational performance can reasonably be inferred from the increasing selectivity of law schools. See Abel (1989, Table 4).

14. Curran 1985, p. 10, Table 1.3.1; Abel 1989, Table 27.

15. Curran 1986, p. 3.

16. Abel 1989, Table 27. This and the previous figure for law-school enrollments are for A.B.A.-approved law schools only.

17. There is no count of all minorities for 1960, but Schuman reports that there were 2,180 black lawyers (Schuman 1971, p. 230 n. 18). That would be about three-fourths of 1 percent of the total lawyer population.

18. Census figures showed some 3,700 Blacks and 2,500 Hispanics out of a total of 277,700 lawyers and judges by 1970. Blacks would have been about 1.3 percent of all lawyers, and Hispanics about nine-tenths of 1 percent (Holley and Kleven 1987, pp. 301–2). "As of 1980 the Census reported that the total number of lawyers and judges had almost doubled to about 529,700 while the number of Blacks and Hispanics had roughly quadrupled to about 15,300 and 9,500, respectively. If accurate, this means an increase as of that time in Black representation in the profession to about 2.9 percent, and in Hispanic representation to about 1.8 percent. As of 1984, the Census reported a total of about 678,000 lawyers and judges, of which about 2.6 percent (about 17,600) were Black and about 2 percent (about 13,600) were Hispanic" (Holley and Kleven 1987, pp. 301–2). By comparing the census figures with figures from the *Lawyer Statistical Report* and the *Review of Legal Education,* Holley and Kleven conclude that these census figures overstate both the total number of lawyers and the total number of minority lawyers. For discussion, see Holley and Kleven (1987, p. 302 n. 7).

available. By 1985–86, they made up 10.4 percent of this population.[19] The number of white males attending law school has decreased significantly since 1970.[20] Greater diversity allows—and requires—firms to be more diverse in composition.

Americans spent much more on law. The amount of Gross National Product derived from legal services more than doubled (in constant 1982 dollars) from $15.0 billion in 1960 to $35.0 billion in 1985.[21] The portion of the national income produced by legal services roughly doubled from 1960 to 1985.[22] Of these higher expenditures for legal services, an increasing portion is spent by businesses rather than by individuals. From 1967 to 1982, the portion of the receipts of the legal services industry contributed by businesses increased from 39 percent to 49 percent, while the share purchased by individuals dropped from 55 percent to 45 percent.[23] These figures underestimate the growth in total business expenditures on law, since they record only payments to "outside" lawyers; to these must be added the greatly increased spending on in-house legal services during this period.[24]

Larger firms have been receiving an expanding share of the money spent for legal services. The largest firms have been growing faster than the legal profes-

19. American Bar Association 1973, Table 1, 47; 1985, p. 65.

20. Figures are available on the number of women and minority J.D. students, but are not cross-tabulated. In order to determine the number of white male law students it is necessary to introduce assumptions about the gender composition of minority law students. If we assume a gender distribution parallel to that of whites (8.5 percent women in 1970; 42.7 percent women in 1989), there were 68,654 white male law students in 1970 and 62,346 (9.2 percent fewer) in 1989. However if we assume that the portion of women among minorities was one-and-a-half times as great as among whites (i.e., 12.8 percent in 1970 and 64 percent in 1989), then there would have been 68,780 white male J.D. students in 1970 and 65,706 in 1989 (4.5 percent fewer). Of course, if we assume that the portion of women among minorities in law school was only one-half as great as among whites (i.e., 4.3 percent in 1970 and 21.3 percent in 1989) then there would have been 68,529 white male J.D. students in 1970 and 58,992 in 1989 (13.9 percent fewer). Figures, which are for ABA-approved schools only, are derived from the 1973 *Review of Legal Education* (American Bar Association 1973, p. 48) and the 1989 *Review of Legal Education* (American Bar Association 1989, p. 68). Minority totals for 1970 may include a few graduate students.

21. U.S. Dept. of Commerce 1986, p. 254, Table 6.2; 1988, p. 78, Table 6.2.

22. Between 1960 and 1985, the share of the gross domestic product contributed by the legal-services sector increased from 0.59 percent to 1.17 percent. The share of national income contributed by the legal-services sector increased from 0.52 percent in 1960 to 0.98 percent in 1983. On the value of lawyers' work that is not counted in the legal-services sector, see Sander and Williams (1989, p. 435 n. 10).

23. The share of total legal services purchased by government decreased during this period (U.S. Dept. of Commerce, Bureau of Census 1976, Table 4; 1981, Table 9; 1985, Table 30). Figures for 1967 are from Sander and Williams (1989, p. 441). Figures for 1967 are estimates derived by combining data on the receipts distribution for a subsample of firms of varying sizes with data on the total distribution of firms by size.

24. See below, pp. 49–50.

sion as a whole.[25] Between 1972 and 1986, the market share of the fifty largest law firms doubled.[26]

The amount of law has increased exponentially. During this quarter-century the amount of regulation has multiplied. There are more federal regulatory statutes,[27] more agencies,[28] more staff,[29] more enforcement expenditures, and more rules.[30] There were comparable increases of regulation by state and local government.[31]

The corpus of authoritative legal material has grown immensely over our pe-

25. One comparison of 1967 and 1987 data suggests that the attorney population of the nation's fifty-five largest law firms increased an average of 8 percent per year between 1967 and 1987 while the total lawyer population grew an average of 5 percent to 6 percent (Sander and Williams 1989, p. 439). Sander and Williams drew the 1967 figure from the Census of Service Industries and the 1987 figure from the *National Law Journal*. They say that because these two figures are based on two different data sources, "this conclusion is only a tentative one" (Sander and Williams 1989, p. 439, n. 18).

26. Size of firm determined by using amount of receipts. The market share of the fifty largest law firms increased from 5.1 percent of total receipts in 1972 to 5.8 percent in 1977 to 7.1 percent in 1982 to 7.8 percent in 1987 (Sander and Williams 1989, Table 4).

27. There were sixty-two new consumer safety and health laws enacted from 1964 to 1979, compared with eleven during the New Deal and five during the Progressive Era. Similarly, there were thirty-two "statutes regulating energy and the environment" during 1964–79, compared to five during the New Deal and two during the Progressive Era (Vogel 1981, p. 162).

28. The number of federal regulatory agencies increased from twenty-eight in 1960 to fifty-six in 1980 (Penoyer 1981).

29. Permanent full-time staffing for fifty-five federal regulatory agencies increased from 27,661 in 1970 to 76,389 in 1984, an increase of 176 percent. The federal budget expenditures for these fifty-five agencies increased (in constant 1982 dollars) from $1,905 million in 1970 to $6,423 million in 1982, an increase of 237 percent (Weidenbaum and Penoyer 1983).

30. A rough measure of the sheer quantity of rules may be derived from the number of pages added to the *Federal Register* each year: in 1960, 14,477 pages were added; in 1985, 53,480. This is the gross addition for the year; some supplant or repeal earlier regulation and some are ephemeral. But making appropriate discounts for depreciation, it is clear that there has been a great increase in the "capital stock" of regulation. From 1961 to 1977 the number of pages in the *Federal Register* devoted to regulations increased from 14,000 to 66,000 (Meier 1985, p. 3). This extremely crude measure of the level of regulatory activity and enforcement almost surely understates its significance to business, since statutes may remain unchanged but be enforced more heavily, and governmental enforcement may be augmented by the activities of "private attorneys general" (Galanter and Rogers 1988).

31. In the absence of direct measures, we are reduced to using even rougher measures of expenditures and employment. State and local government expenditures increased from 9.7 percent of GNP in 1960 to 12.9 percent in 1985 (U.S. President 1988, p. 248, Table B-1; p. 341, Table B-79). Total civilian employees of governmental units in the United States roughly doubled in this period, from 8.8 million in 1960 to 16.7 million in 1985. More than nine-tenths of this growth was in state and local governments (U.S. Bureau of Census 1976, Series Y 272–89; U.S. President 1987, Table 479). Federal employees increased in this period from 2.398 million to 3.001 million. Granted that not all of these employees were engaged in tasks connected with lawmaking or regulation, the figures are provided here as a rough index of the increase in regulatory activity.

riod. The production of state judicial opinions added to the West Publishing Company's regional reporters increased from 63 volumes with 61,057 pages in 1960 to 127 volumes with 151,863 pages in 1985—a 149 percent increase in pages.[32] Federal material multiplied even more rapidly.[33] The year's addition of federal cases increased from 23 volumes with 21,474 pages in 1960 to 61 volumes with 93,588 pages in 1985, an increase of 336 percent.[34] The profusion of legal information has outrun these printed sources. On-line data bases, such as LEXIS (since 1973) and WESTLAW (since 1975), increase access to a vast range of legal material, including some that was previously unpublished.[35]

The amount of published commentary that glosses this authoritative material has grown apace. Michael Saks found that, between 1960 and 1985, the number of general law reviews increased from 65 to 186, while specialized reviews multiplied from 6 to 140.[36] The average annual volume in 1985 was about two-thirds bigger than its 1960 predecessor; the articles it contained were longer.[37] Parallel to the growth of these scholarly sources was a proliferation of less formal channels of legal information. In 1989 there were nearly 1,000 newsletters published in Washington, in addition to those published by the 3,200 Washington-based associations that mailed newsletters to their members.[38]

The technological infrastructure for handling this information has changed radically. At the turn of the century, legal work was reshaped by the telephone, the typewriter, expanded legal publishing, and new research devices like digests and citators. The technology of the law firm remained essentially unchanged until the 1960s. Since then, a rapid succession of new technologies—photoreproduction, computerization, on-line data services, overnight delivery services, electronic mail, and fax machines—have multiplied the amount of information that can be assembled and manipulated by legal actors and have greatly increased the velocity with which it circulates.[39]

32. Figures are for number of new volumes and pages of new cases added for year designated. Inclusion is based on copyright date of reporter volume, not date of case decision. Part of the increase is attributable to new intermediate appellate courts created in the interim.

33. The annual rate of growth in pages was 3.7 percent for the state cases and 6.1 percent for the federal cases.

34. This computation is based upon the United States Reports, Federal Reporter, and Federal Supplement.

35. Harrington 1984, pp. 552–53.

36. Saks 1989. In the Saks study, law reviews are defined as scholarly periodicals published by law schools, excluding journals by commercial publishers and scholarly and professional associations. The number of publications indexed in the *Index to Legal Periodicals* increased from 305 in 1960 to 557 in 1986. The pages taken up by a year's listings doubled. (The triennial volume covering August 1958 to August 1961 had 915 pages; the annual volume for September 1985–August 1986 contains 609 pages.)

37. Saks 1989, p. 3.

38. Weiss 1989, p. A11.

39. This is reflected in, and in turn encouraged by, the increasing length and complexity of judi-

During this period there has been more litigation. Total civil filings in the federal courts grew from 59,284 in 1960 to 273,670 in 1985.[40] Comparable figures for the state courts are not available, but a sense of the growth of state judicial activity can be gathered from the increase in lawyers employed by state courts, from 7,581 in 1960 to 18,674 in 1985, an increase of 146 percent.[41] Courts, federal and state, acquired more staff and clerks and professional administrators.[42] These larger staffs were equipped with new information technologies which increased the "production" of these institutions even faster.

An increasing portion of this litigation involves the business firms that are the primary clientele of the large law firms. With increasing frequency, these companies are targets of civil rights, wrongful discharge, and product liability claims.[43] Less visibly but more importantly, they have become more frequent and more aggressive users of the legal system in disputes arising from their dealings with one another. This is marked by the surge of contracts, intellectual property, and other business cases in the federal courts.[44] An increasing number of business disputes are not being resolved among the parties in the

---

cial opinions. Posner (1985) compares federal Court of Appeals opinions from 1960 and 1983 and finds substantial increases in length, number of footnotes, number of citations, and number of issue categories.

40. On the changing patterns of litigation in the federal courts, see Galanter (1988); Posner (1985); Clark (1981).

41. Curran 1985, p. 16, Table 1.4.8; Curran 1986, p. 3. This figure includes lawyers as judges, court officials, and support personnel.

42. Employees in the federal judiciary increased from 4,992 in 1960 to over 18,000 in 1985 to 20,244 in 1987 (U.S. Bureau of Census 1976; p. 1102, Series Y 308–17; 1989, p. 319, Table 514). The number of lawyers employed by the judicial branches, federal and states, almost tripled, from 8,180 in 1960 to 22,276 in 1985 (Weil 1968, p. 20; Curran 1986, p. 3).

43. Galanter 1988; Dungworth 1988.

44. Over the period 1960-88, contracts filings in the Federal District Courts increased from 13,268 to 44,027. (In this discussion, the contracts category does not include either recovery cases, i.e., cases by the government seeking recovery of defaulted student loans or overpaid veterans' benefits, or cases that are in the federal courts under their "local jurisdiction." Except as otherwise noted, the source of data on federal court cases is the *Annual Reports of the Administrative Office of the United States Courts.* Figures on filings are found in Table C-2.) This increase of 232 percent far outstripped the increase in tort cases, which grew by 128 percent over this period. Contracts grew at an annual rate of some 4.4 percent, almost half again as fast as the tort growth rate of 3 percent. By 1988, contracts filings made up 18.4 percent of all civil filings, having surpassed torts as the largest category of civil litigation. A more detailed comparison of contract filings with torts and other leading categories is presented in Galanter (1988). The ascendancy of contracts over torts is particularly pronounced in the diversity jurisdiction. Since the mid-1970s, there have been more contracts cases than tort cases in the diversity jurisdiction. In crude figures, diversity contracts filings have increased over eight times during this period while diversity torts increased two and one-third times. The diversity contracts filings category includes many kinds of cases among various kinds of parties, so we must be cautious in taking its growth as a measure of increasing corporate litigation. In Business Disputing Group (1989), we present evidence to justify our confidence that much of the

informal style that Stewart Macaulay described in the early 1960s.[45] It has become acceptable for corporations to be plaintiffs and to sue other corporations; there is an increased use of litigation as part of business strategy. A significant portion of this larger total of litigation is more complex and involves higher stakes, calling forth larger amounts of lawyering.[46]

At the same time that litigation has increased, the range of techniques for pursuing legal disputes has been enlarged. In 1960 what we now recognize as "alternative dispute resolution [ADR]" inhabited a few scattered enclaves— labor arbitration and mediation, commercial arbitration, divorce concilia- tion.[47] The last decade has witnessed a great proliferation of ADR institutions and programs. As late as the mid-1970s, "alternatives" were commonly viewed as diversion schemes to take up minor or marginal matters not deserving of full judicial treatment. But ADR has moved from the periphery to the center of legal work.[48] There has been a proliferation of "up-market" ADR devices (rent-a-judge, mini-trials, etc.) aimed at the kinds of business disputes that en- gage large law firms.[49] Although much of the rhetoric of the ADR "movement" militates against legal formality and adversary conflict, the growth of ADR has enlarged the repertoire of courts and lawyers.

Compared to 1960, many more groups and interests are active participants in the legal arena. The 1960s saw the appearance of legal services programs for

increase in diversity contracts cases represents an increase in cases involving businesses as parties. This report also contains documentation on the increase in other kinds of business litigation.

45. Macaulay 1963.

46. In a study of jury awards in San Francisco County courts and in Cook County (Illinois) courts, Peterson found that average jury awards in constant 1984 dollars increased from $57,000 during the 1960–64 period to $252,000 during the 1980–84 period in Cook County, and from $74,000 during the 1960–64 period to $302,000 during the 1980–84 period for San Francisco County courts. (Pe- terson 1987, pp. 28–29). Peterson's findings are confirmed by a study of contract litigation in the Federal District Court for the Southern District of New York, which found that the average settle- ment or judgment increased from $165,000 during the 1960s to $887,000 during the 1970s. Adjusting for inflation, this was a threefold increase for the decade of the 1970s compared to the decade of the 1960s (W. Nelson 1990, p. 415).

47. On the ebb and flow of interest in alternatives, see Auerbach (1983).

48. This shift is neatly epitomized by the A.B.A. committee which changed its name from the Committee on Minor Disputes to the Committee on Alternative Dispute Resolution to the Commit- tee on Dispute Resolution. Many courts, federal and state, have added ADR devices to their institutional repertoire—including court-annexed arbitration and mediation programs and a variety of settlement devices like summary jury trials. Experiments are under way to establish the "multi- door courthouse" in which various modes of dispute processing, including judicial, would be inte- grated in a single establishment. A 1986 A.B.A. Directory lists 304 ADR programs, half developed after 1980 (American Bar Association 1986a, Introduction).

49. These are chronicled in the publications of the Center for Public Resources, a nonprofit orga- nization devoted to promoting the use of ADR by corporations. See Center for Public Resources (1984) and the Center's newsletter, *Alternatives to the High Cost of Litigation*.

the poor, including specialized backup centers that generated whole new areas of organized knowledge.[50] It also saw the birth of "public interest law" firms and organizations, followed in the 1970s by "conservative" business-oriented public interest law centers.[51] More trade and voluntary associations engage in legal activity.[52] Overall, there has been a great increase in the number of organized groups with legal staffs acting as strategic players in the law game.

Increases in the number and variety of legal actors, in the number of decision-makers, in the amount of authoritative material and the span of legal theory, in the amount of available information, in expenditures for legal services and the consequent intensity of lawyer work—all of these multiply the opportunities and incentives for unforeseen juxtaposition and innovative enterprise to undermine established theories, rules, and practices. Contingency and discretion increase as rules and institutions grow in bulk.[53]

So, large law firms find themselves in an environment with more lawyers, competing with more large firms like themselves, all supplied with more technological infrastructure, involved in more contested activity in more varied arenas with more contenders, using a larger, more indeterminate and more diffusely bounded body of legal knowledge. It is in this setting that they are undergoing the "transformation" that threatens to alter the basic model of the large firm that has persisted for almost a century.

The Transformation of the Big Firm

The more numerous and more diverse lawyers of the late 1980s are arrayed in a very different structure of practice than their counterparts a generation earlier. There has been a general shift to larger units of practice. In 1948, more than six

50. Johnson 1974; Handler, Hollingsworth, and Erlanger 1978.

51. On public-interest law, see Weisbrod, Handler, and Komesar (1978); Handler (1978). On the emergence of business-oriented public-interest firms, see Weinstein (1975, p. 39); Flaherty (1983b, p. 1); Houck (1984, p. 1454).

52. In a 1979 survey by the Conference Board, 73 percent of the companies (285 of 389 companies responding) had a governmental relations unit. Of these, 164 had an office in Washington, D.C., and 29 percent of the respondents said that their company had increased its involvement and commitment in governmental relations over the preceding three years. The executive in charge of these units and the staff members of these units were more likely to have a law background than any other type of background (McGrath 1979, pp. vi, 3, 56–57, 63).

53. Katsh 1989, pp. 43–46. On the inherent entropic tendencies of legal rules within complex systems to become "increasingly vague, inapplicable, remote, ambiguous or exception-ridden," see d'Amato (1983, p. 4). Cf. the observation of Damaska that "there is a point beyond which increased complexity of law, especially in loosely ordered normative systems, objectively increases rather than decreases the decision-maker's freedom. Contradictory views can plausibly be held, and support found for almost any position" (Damaska 1975). See also Feeley 1976, p. 500. Cf. Posner's observation on the decline of the ability of judicial decisions to compel assent (Posner 1985, p. 110).

out of ten lawyers practiced alone; in 1980, only one-third of a much swollen number of lawyers was in sole practice.[54] The number of lawyers working in sizable aggregations, capable of massive and coordinated legal undertakings, has multiplied many times over.[55] One estimate was that, in 1988, there were 35,000 lawyers at 115 firms with more than 200 lawyers, and a total of 105,000 lawyers in 2,000 firms larger than 20 lawyers.[56]

Growth. In the late 1950s there were only 38 law firms in the United States with more than fifty lawyers—and more than half of these were in New York City.[57] In 1985, there were 508 firms with 51 or more lawyers.[58] Large firms were larger. Firms with more than a hundred lawyers grew from less than a dozen in 1960 to 251 in 1986.[59] In 1968 the largest firm in the United States had 169 lawyers and the twentieth largest had 106 lawyers.[60] In 1988, the largest firm had 962 lawyers and there were 149 firms larger than the largest firm in 1968.[61]

Not only were there more big firms, they were growing faster. The 35 firms from our Group I sample grew from an average size of 124 in 1975 to 252 in 1985.[62] In this period, the average size of the 37 Group II firms in our sample more than doubled, from 44 to 89 lawyers.[63] The average annual growth rate over this ten-year period was 8 percent for Group I and 8 percent for Group II.[64] These rates are considerably higher than the rates at which these same firms had been growing twenty years earlier. From 1955 to 1965, the average annual growth rate was 5.3 percent for the Group I firms and 5.5 percent for Group II firms.[65]

54. Abel 1989, p. 179; Curran 1985, p. 14.

55. In 1980, there were almost 50,000 lawyers in firms of 21 lawyers or more—they made up 9.2 percent of all lawyers, 13.4 percent of lawyers in private practice, and 26.1 percent of all lawyers practicing in firms (Curran 1985, pp. 13–14).

56. Brill 1989b.

57. Smigel 1960, p. 58.

58. Curran 1986, p. 58.

59. *National Law Journal* 1986, pp. S4ff.

60. *Business Week* 1968, pp. 78–79.

61. *National Law Journal,* 1988, p. S4. Baker & McKenzie, Hyatt Legal Services, and Jacoby & Myers were omitted from this computation.

62. The range was from 50 to 198 lawyers in 1975 and from 142 to 419 lawyers in 1985. These figures are somewhat lower than those in the last paragraph, because they are drawn from our data set, based on *Martindale-Hubbell*, rather than from the *National Law Journal* surveys. We explain the peculiarities of these data sets in Appendix A. Our data are used here because, unlike those from the *National Law Journal,* they permit comparisons with earlier periods.

63. The range was from 21 to 68 in 1975 and from 54 to 121 in 1985.

64. These ranges are confirmed by annual surveys of the 500 largest firms conducted by *Of Counsel* since 1986. The reported rate of growth for all of these firms was over 9 percent for each of the three years (Smith 1989b, p. 1).

65. For the calculations for 1955 to 1965, see above, Chapter 3, notes 16 and 17.

In 1960 big law firms were clearly identified with a specific locality, as they had been since the origin of the big firm.[66] But by 1980, of the 100 largest firms, 87 had branches. Of all firms with fifty or more lawyers, 62 percent were in more than one location and 24 percent were in three or more locations in 1980.[67] Some of this branching was by "colonization" but most of it involved mergers with firms (or with groups defecting from firms) in the new locality. Washington has been the favorite site for branches. In 1980, 178 firms from outside Washington had branches there.[68] But as branching activity has increased, Washington offices are a declining portion of all branches.

In the 1980s the home office and branch pattern was joined by the genuine multicity law firm.[69] To capture the dynamic of multicity growth, we compared twenty of the largest firms based in New York City (NY) and outside New York City (ONY) in 1980 and 1987.[70] The twenty NY firms had a total of 70 branch offices in 1980 and 99 branches in 1987. The twenty largest ONY firms had a total of 61 branches in 1980 and 124 branches in 1987. Thus there was a 41 percent increase in branches of NY firms over this seven-year period and a 103 percent increase in branches of ONY firms.

Not only did the number of branches increase, so did their size. The average size of each branch of a NY firm went from 8 lawyers in 1980 to 17 in 1987. The branches of the ONY firms grew from an average of 15 lawyers in 1980 to 30 lawyers just seven years later. The growth in branches accounted for 31 percent of the total growth of the 20 NY firms and 69 percent of the total growth of the ONY firms. The percentage of lawyers outside the largest office rose from 15 percent to 21 percent for the NY firms while doubling from 21 percent to 42 percent for the ONY firms.

We can see that branches grew much faster than main offices during this peri-

66. The occasional Washington or foreign branch office was anomalous (Smigel 1969, p. 207). Attempts at multicity firms were rare, suspect, and unstable, as displayed in the Adlai Stevenson/Paul Weiss arrangement, discussed above in Chapter 3, note 19.

67. Curran 1985, p. 53.

68. Abel 1989, p. 188.

69. Lewin 1984, p. 31. The true pioneer is Baker & McKenzie, which in the 1950s established four foreign offices, staffed largely by local lawyers, as well as a Washington office. Thirteen more foreign offices were added in the 1960s. In 1988, the firm consisted of 41 offices in 25 countries (*National Law Journal* 1988, p. S4; Lyons 1985, pp. 115–16). On the firm's organizational strategy, see also Stevens (1987, pp. 153–66). Another pioneer in the design of the multicity firm was the late Robert Kutak, whose Omaha-based Kutak Rock and Huie, founded in 1965, was established in six regional centers by 1980 (Tybor 1981, p. 8). In the late 1970s, the firm planned to open an office in one new city each year and by the end of the 1980s to have seventeen offices around the country (Kiechel 1978, pp. 112–13). The firm was unable to keep up this pace and experienced a severe contraction in late 1980 (Tybor 1981, p. 1).

70. This comparison is based on our *National Law Journal* "Two Twenties" data set, which is described in Appendix A. For convenience, we refer to "branches," but we use that term to mean an office other than the office of the firm that contains the largest number of lawyers. In 1987, only one of our forty firms (Akin Gump) had an office larger than its "home" office.

od. By 1987 there were a number of firms that had a substantial portion of their lawyers away from the largest office. Eight of the NY firms had more than 25 percent of their lawyers outside the main office (up from 4 in 1980); and 17 of the ONY firms had more than 25 percent of their lawyers outside the largest office—7 had more than 50 percent outside.

Increasingly, large firms operate on an international basis. Of the 100 largest firms in 1988, some 44 had a total of 136 overseas offices.[71] Our comparison of the 20 largest NY and 20 largest ONY firms indicates that the largest NY firms have more overseas branches, but the gap is closing. The 20 NY firms had 39 in 1980 and 43 in 1987. Their ONY counterparts had 9 in 1980 and 21 in 1987. Foreign offices tend to be a larger share of the offices of the NY firms (36 percent in 1987) than of the ONY firms (15 percent in 1987).

Over the past thirty years, there has been a marked movement away from New York City as the nation's legal center.[72] In 1957, there were 21 firms with over fifty lawyers in New York City and only 17 in the rest of the country.[73] In 1980, there were 72 firms of 51 or more in New York State[74] but in the whole country there were 287.[75] In twenty years, New York City's share of large firms had fallen from more than half to less than a quarter. New York City has retained a somewhat larger but declining share of the very largest firms. In 1987, 32 of the 100 largest firms were based in New York (down from 36 in 1975).[76] The hundred largest firms were based in 24 cities (up from 18 in 1975).[77]

Work and Clients. As firms grow larger, specialization within them has become more intense and the work of various levels more differentiated.[78] The work that big firms do has changed dramatically. We take up in turn two major causes of this change: (1) an increase in the number, size and responsibility of

71. The number of overseas offices ranges from one to thirty-two; eight firms had five or more overseas offices.

72. This reflects the dispersion of corporate headquarters and financial markets. In 1960, 128 of the Fortune 500 industrial corporations had headquarters in New York City; in 1988, only 50 were headquartered there. There were comparable shifts in other categories of corporations (*Fortune* 1960, p. 131; 1960, p. 137; 1988, p. D11; 1988, p. D7).

73. Smigel 1960, p. 58.

74. Curran 1985, p. 166.

75. Curran 1985, p. 51.

76. Abel 1989, Table 47. A 1989 survey found that 33 of the 100 firms with the largest gross revenues were based in New York City (*American Lawyer* 1989).

77. The decline in the predominance of New-York-based firms points to, but overstates, the decline of New York City as a locus of legal activity. A significant portion of the branching activity discussed in the preceding paragraphs consists of the establishment of New York branches by ONY firms. In 1980, only three of our ONY firms had offices in New York (average size seventeen). By 1987, ten of the twenty ONY firms had New York offices (average size thirty-nine).

78. Nelson 1988, pp. 147, 171; Abel 1989, p. 202.

in-house legal departments and (2) a surge of corporate litigation since the 1970s.

That corporate law departments have grown at the same time that there has been a tremendous growth of outside law firms testifies to the surge in business consumption of legal services. At the same time that outside law firms have been growing in number and size, in-house corporate law departments have also been growing in size, budget, functions, and authority.[79]

In-house law departments have been growing in size. A 1980 *National Law Journal* survey found a sharp increase in 80 percent of the responding corporations.[80] A subsequent Arthur Young survey reported further sharp increases in the size of corporate law departments between 1979 and 1984.[81] This increase was general rather than confined to a few economic sectors. A 1985 Arthur Andersen survey found that between 1980 and 1985 there was an increase in the number of corporate counsel in 14 of the 17 industry sectors they surveyed, with increases of 44 percent to 95 percent occurring in banking, brokerage, communications, utilities, leisure and publishing, and health care.[82] A 1987 American Corporate Counsel Institute (ACCI) survey of eight industrial sectors found that between 1982 and 1987 there had been an increase in the size of corporate law departments in all eight.[83]

There has been an increase in the portion of the corporation's legal work conducted in-house. A series of surveys by Altman & Weil found that, from 1976 to 1982, the percentage of firms reporting that in-house counsel do three-quarters of the corporation's legal work increased from 56.0 percent to 66.5 percent.[84]

The nature of the legal work undertaken by in-house counsel has been changing. While law departments formerly confined themselves to processing routine corporate legal matters and left major transactions and litigation work to outside counsel, they are now undertaking more work that once would have

79. There is some indication that there are more large corporations that have corporate law departments. A 1959 survey of manufacturers found that 134 of the 286 companies surveyed had legal departments. A 1987 survey found that 74 of the 126 manufacturing companies replying had in-house counsel. This is an increase from 47 percent to 59 percent. However, the degree to which these numbers are comparable is unclear (National Industrial Conference Board 1959, pp. 463–68; Arthur Andersen & Co. 1985, p. 4, Exhibit 3).

80. *National Law Journal* 1980, p. 24. See also Ayre (1982, p. 11).

81. Arthur Young survey reported in *Business Week* (1984, p. 66).

82. Arthur Andersen & Co. 1985, p. 4, Exhibit 3.

83. American Corporate Counsel Institute 1987. The ACCI sent questionnaires to a sample of 1,209 non-Fortune 1000 companies from a list of 2,418 American Corporate Counsel Association members. They had a response rate of 28.3 percent. The ACCI also sent questionnaires to 992 Fortune 1000 corporations. They had a response rate of 26.2 percent.

84. Altman & Weil, 1985, p. 76. Altman & Weil surveys corporate law departments annually. The 1982 survey received responses from 430 companies, "many in the Fortune 500." The identity of survey respondents "changes to some degree" from survey to survey.

gone to outside lawyers.[85] Some in-house counsel now conduct some or all of their own litigation.[86]

The relation of corporate law departments to outside counsel has shifted from comprehensive and enduring retainer relationships[87] toward less exclusive and more task-specific ad hoc engagements.[88] In a 1980 survey of corporate law departments by the *National Law Journal,* one-quarter of the corporations responding reported that they no longer use a general outside counsel.[89] In their relationship with outside law firms, today's enlarged corporate legal departments impose budgetary restraints,[90] exert more control over cases,[91] demand periodic reports, and engage in comparison shopping among firms.[92]

Selection of law firms by corporate counsel who are sophisticated shoppers for legal services might be expected to shift business away from large firms toward lower-cost smaller firms of high quality. But no such effect is noticeable. Corporate counsel remain drawn to large firms because (1) in a setting where quality is hard to judge and the costs of visible misjudgment are high, prestige remains a useful surrogate for quality; (2) large firms' reputation for formidability is an asset in adversary relationships; (3) their size is perceived to confer a capacity to deploy large work-teams and to respond to short deadlines; (4) "one-stop shopping" benefits the corporate buyer by reducing not only the search costs but the transaction costs of additional quality checks, dealing with different systems of billing, and so forth.

The work that is brought to large firms by their corporate clients has changed. At the same time that much routine work has been retracted into cor-

85. Berkow and Spiciarich 1985, p. 13; Strasser 1985, p. 1. The area of legal activity most frequently handled by in-house counsel tends to be commercial contracts (as compared to antitrust, compliance with governmental regulation, litigation, securities work, and labor). This pattern appears to be consistent across various industrial sectors (Arthur Andersen & Co. 1985, pp. 7–9, Exhibits 9–14).

86. "Outside counsel if he is involved at all, need only supply local support services." Temporary needs for more staff can be supplied "by the growing practice of leasing lawyers" (Salibra 1986, p. 28). See also *National Law Journal* (1980, p. 25). The 1987 ACCI survey found that 60 percent of their respondents whose organizations litigate in-house reported an increase in the size of their in-house litigation staffs during the previous five years (American Corporate Counsel Institute 1987, p. 11).

87. Cf. The 1959 Conference Board Survey, cited in Chapter 3, note 108, which found companies contentedly tied to outside counsel.

88. Chayes and Chayes 1985, p. 294.

89. *National Law Journal* 1980, p. 25; Couric (1985, p. 1) reports this is not the case with small corporations.

90. Banks 1983.

91. *Business Week* 1984, p. 66; Lavine 1981, p. 1.

92. Flaharty 1983a, p. 1; Jensen 1988a, p. 1; Couric 1988, p. 2. Sometimes inside counsel require competitive presentations, known colloquially as beauty contests, dog and pony shows, or bake-offs.

porate law departments, there has been a great surge of litigation and other risk-prone high-stakes transactions. Suddenly, the work of large outside firms shifted from its historic emphasis on office practice back toward the litigation from which the large firm turned away in its infancy.[93] The shift is marked in a 1978 report:

> at Cravath, Swaine & Moore, which has such blue-chip clients as IBM, CBS, Westinghouse and Chemical Bank, ten years ago litigation was about 20 percent of Cravath's "total effort." Now more than 40 percent of the firm's manpower is so occupied.[94]

This shift has been accentuated by a great surge of corporate litigation, which in turn reflects changing corporate attitudes toward use of law. In his classic research on business disputing in the early 1960s, Stewart Macaulay found that manufacturers avoided litigation, preferring to rely upon informal norms and sanctions to control relations with competitors, suppliers, and customers.[95] Avoidance of litigation by corporations paralleled the big firms' deemphasis on courtroom advocacy. But in the last quarter-century there has been a dramatic turnabout. A business environment that is more competitive, more insecure, and more uncertain—in which there are more large risk-prone deals, with higher stakes and more regulation to take into account, amid more volatile fluctuations of interest and exchange rates—generates new demand for intensive lawyering. Such deals spawn satellite litigation as a sideshow or a strategic ingredient. Generally, businesses are less likely to forbear from litigation when things turn out badly, and they are more inclined to use litigation as a business strategy.[96] A preliminary analysis of contract cases filed in federal courts from 1971 to 1987 suggests that the number of cases in which there are corporations on both sides has increased many times faster than the rapidly rising total of diversity contract cases.[97]

The upsurge of business litigation is marked by the rapid growth of federal court filings of diversity contract cases and other kinds of cases that might be identified as business litigation, such as intellectual property, commercial bankruptcy, and civil RICO cases.[98] The link between increased business liti-

93. Chayes and Chayes (1985) report that major corporations responding to a small survey reported half of all legal fees paid to outside lawyers were for litigation. Cf. Nelson (1988, p. 8).

94. Bernstein 1978, p. 106.

95. Macaulay 1963.

96. Business Disputing Group 1989. Recall, in contrast, the earlier equation of corporate representation with the defense posture. See Pound (1903) and Lundberg (1939).

97. Business Disputing Group (1989) based on a study being undertaken by the Business Disputing Group in collaboration with the Rand Corporation's Institute of Civil Justice.

98. Business Disputing Group 1989. A study of one key commercial district, the Southern District of New York, from 1960 to 1979, found that contract cases became an increasing portion of the caseload and registered increases in complexity, size, and presumably cost (Nelson 1989).

gation and changes in the work of big firms is suggested by William Nelson's study of contract litigation in the Southern District of New York. He estimated that during the 1960s a set of 43 major New York City law firms appeared in 17.5 percent of all contract cases in the Southern District. This increased to an estimated 24.8 percent of the much larger number of contract cases in the years 1971–79. "[L]arge firm involvement went from an estimated 73 cases per year to over 290."[99]

The large, contested, and/or risk-prone one-of-a-kind transaction—litigation, takeovers, bankruptcies, and such—makes up a larger portion of what big law firms do. Existing clients cannot provide a steady supply of such matters and those that have them increasingly shop for specialists to handle them. Hence, firms are under pressure to generate a steady (or increasing) demand for such work by retaining the favors of old clients and securing new ones, and to develop the specialty groups that can service this demand.

Competitiveness. The new aggressiveness of in-house counsel, the breakdown of retainer relationships, and the shift to discrete transactions have made conditions more competitive.[100] Firms have become more openly commercial and profit-oriented, "more like a business."[101] Firms rationalize their operations; they engage professional managers and consultants; firm leaders worry about billable hours, profit centers, and marketing strategies. "Eat what you kill" compensation formulas emphasize rewards for productivity and business-getting over "equal shares" or seniority.[102] There is more differentiation in the power and rewards of partners; standing within the firm depends increasingly on how much business a partner brings in.[103] Rising overhead costs and associate salaries put pressure on partners. In many firms, partners work more hours, but their income does not increase correspondingly.[104]

99. Nelson 1989, p. 416.

100. During this period, the profession's traditional means of suppressing intraprofessional competition, minimum fee schedules, was struck down by the Supreme Court as a violation of the Sherman Act. *Goldfarb v. Virginia State Bar,* 421 U.S. 773 (1975); and two years later the traditional ban on advertising fell. *Bates v. State Bar of Arizona,* 433 U.S. 350 (1977). The demise of minimum fee schedules did not directly affect the big firms, but the encouragement of competition and particularly the freedom from restrictions on self-promotion provided them with new means to adapt to the changing marketplace. On the indirect effects of *Bates,* see text below, at p. 71.

101. It should be recalled that similar observations have echoed periodically since the early days of big law firms. See above, at pp. 11, 17–18.

102. Heintz 1982; Gilson and Mnookin 1985, p. 313. But cf. Nelson (1988, pp. 202–4).

103. Reflecting on Smigel's contention that law firms lack the hierarchy, rules, and conflict characteristic of other organizations because they are organized around professional norms, Nelson concedes that if this was so in "the stable professional community of New York law firms in the late 1950s. . . . [i]t is clearly not accurate today. Large firms are the regimes of client-producers, and this stratum of partners dictates the policies of the firm and projects the ideology of professionalism that justifies the structure of the firm and the client-producers' role in it" (Nelson 1988, p. 276).

104. A survey by Altman & Weil of median earnings of partners in 700 large (75+ lawyers) firms

The need to find new business leads to aggressive marketing. Some firms take on marketing directors, a position unknown in 1980. In 1985, there were forty such positions.[105] By 1989 "almost 200 law firms ha[d] hired their own marketing directors."[106] The push for new business also brings about increased emphasis on "rainmaking" by more of the firm's lawyers.[107] Those lawyers who are responsible for bringing in business—"rainmakers"[108] or "finders"[109] or "business-getters"[110]—have a new ascendancy over their colleagues. The thrust for business-getting resonates throughout the structure of the firm. Thus a description of big firms in the Southeast reports that:

> Th[e] . . . shift from a traditional reliance upon a small number of rainmakers to the aggressive stance that everyone must make rain has resulted in a reduction in numbers of associates receiving a vote for partnership as well as—in many cases—a redivision of partners' profit pie. Many firms also go a step further by eliminating non-producing partners and restructuring or jettisoning non-productive departments.[111]

The search for new business has been directed not only toward coveted clients but toward existing ones. In a setting where corporations are more inclined

found 1986 earnings increased by 78 percent over ten years earlier, but inflation was up 93 percent. Average hours billed were up 8 percent to 1,685 hours annually (Jensen 1987a, p. 12). A Price Waterhouse survey of medium and large firms found that from 1978 to 1988 partner earnings rose only 1 percent after accounting for inflation. Cited by Brill (1989b).

105. Galante 1985, pp. 1, 28. The next year it was reported that "more than 60 law firms, ranging in size from 14 lawyers to nearly 600 . . . [in] about 25 cities . . . had hired a marketing administrator." A National Association of Law Firm Marketing Administrators was established in the same year (Schmidt 1986, p. 15).

106. Merrilyn Astin Tarlton, former president of the National Association of Law Firm Marketing Administrators, quoted in *New York Times* (1989, p. B6).

107. Haserot 1986, p. 15; Jensen 1987b, p. 1.

108. "Rainmaker," a term of fairly recent vintage, makes its first appearance in press accounts of lawyering in 1978. None of the material we used in describing the 1960s employed this term. For example, Mayer spoke of "the business-getters [who] eventually refused to put up with . . . [equal shares]" (Mayer 1966, p. 336). On this term, see below, note 110.

109. Nelson (1988, pp. 69–70), recounts a humorous folk categorization of big-firm lawyers into "finders, minders, and grinders"—those who acquire new clients, those who attend to existing ones, and those who grind out the work.

110. The idea of a lawyer who specializes in obtaining business has been part of the large-firm scene for a long time. The older term was the straightforward "business getter." As early as 1907, a practitioner observed that "[i]n nearly every large firm in our great cities the indispensable partner is 'the business getter' " (Andrews 1907, p. 608). An extended 1925 satirical sketch describes the business-getter as a type that "has waxed and swelled, until his work constitutes a profession in itself, and he bestrides the legal world like a colossus." Technically a lawyer, "[a]ctually he is a peripatetic electric signboard, a prospectus that walks like a man, a barker with a modulated voice, a glorified sandwich man, a solicitor in more senses than one, broadcasting the virtues of his law firm in waves more subtle than those of Marconi" (Smith 1925, pp. 199–200).

111. Bellon 1988, pp. 19–20.

to divide their custom among several law firms, firms engage in "cross-sell-ing" to induce the purchaser of services from one department to avail itself of other services from the firm.[112]

Lateral Hiring, Mergers. In the classical big firm, almost all hiring was at the entry level; partners were promoted from the ranks of associates. Those who left went to corporations or smaller firms, not to similar large firms, since these adhered to the same no-lateral-hiring norm. But starting in the 1970s, lateral movement became more frequent. At first firms made an occasional lateral hire to meet a need for litigators or to fill some other niche. But soon lateral hiring developed into a means of systematically upgrading or enlarging the specialties and the localities they could service and of acquiring rainmakers who might bring or attract new clients. As lateral movement increased, a whole industry of "headhunter" firms emerged, gaining respectability if not respect as it grew.[113] The number of legal search firms grew rapidly from 83 in 1984 to 167 in 1987 to 244 in 1989.[114]

The flow of lateral movement widened out from individual lawyers to whole departments and groups within firms and to whole firms. Mass defections and mergers became common, enabling firms at a stroke to add new departments and expand to new locations. A casual search of the legal press from 1985 to 1989 produced a list of 71 mergers involving 83 firms with more than 50 law-yers; in 58 of these mergers, at least one of the merging firms had one hundred lawyers—a sizable portion of the whole population of firms of that size.[115] Mergers were not only a way to grow; they also provided a convenient device to shake out or renegotiate terms with less productive partners.

Firms hired laterally not only by mergers but by inducing specific lawyers to change firms, "cherry picking" as it came to be called in the late 1980s. A 1988 survey of the 500 largest law firms found that over a quarter reported that more than half of their new partners were not promoted from within but came from other firms.[116] But lateral movement takes place not only at the partner level. The same survey found that one-quarter of the responding firms reported that

112. Weklar 1988, pp. 22, 26; O'Neill 1989, p. 17.

113. Legal headhunter firms emerged in New York in the late 1960s in response to the constriction in the supply of lawyers, described below, pp. 55–56. At first such activity was regarded as a discreditable departure from professional decorum. "In 1967 when Lois R. Weiner . . . decided to specialize in finding jobs for lawyers, the publishers of *Martindale-Hubbell* refused to sell her a copy" (Stevenson 1973, pp. 12–13).

114. Abel 1989, p. 188; *National Law Journal* 1989a, p. S3.

115. Compiled from data supplied by Holly Moyer of Hildebrandt & Co. According to the *National Law Journal* annual surveys, there were only 218 firms with 100 or more lawyers in 1985 and less than 300 in 1988.

116. *Of Counsel* survey, reported in Smith (1989a). Approximately 400 firms provided information on lateral hiring. The figures in this survey were close to those in a 1986 survey.

more than half their associates were hired laterally.[117] Increasingly, associates move from one big firm to another. A recent survey of promotion at 35 large firms in seven localities revealed that 33 of the 35 firms hired some associates laterally and that of 2,227 associates who entered in the late 1970s, 500 (22 percent) had not come to those firms directly from law school, but "arrived at their current firm later in their careers."[118] A recent *New York Law Journal* survey found that at 23 of the 30 largest firms in New York City, an average of 24 percent of the associates coming up for partnership were laterals.[119]

The other side of this movement is splits and dissolutions of firms.[120] As firms grow larger, the task of maintaining an adequate flow of business may become more precarious. Firms are more vulnerable to defections by valued clients or the lawyers to whom those clients are attached. Size multiplies the possibility of conflicts of interests, and the resulting tension between partners who tend old clients and those who propose acquiring new ones can be solved by a breakaway. Surrounded by other firms attempting to grow by attracting partners with special skills or desirable clients, firms are vulnerable to the loss of crucial assets. So dissolution may be catalyzed by lateral movement and merger activity and in turn stimulates a new round of lateral movement.

Hiring. As firms have grown and required larger numbers of qualified associates, recruitment activity has intensified. Recruiting visits to an expanding roster of law schools, extensive summer programs, brochures, and expense-paid "call-backs" of candidates have become familiar parts of the big law-firm scene.[121] Starting salaries have increased dramatically, beginning with a great contraction of the supply of associates in the late 1960s. The Vietnam War draft diverted law graduates to other occupations in which they could obtain defer-

117. Smith 1989a.
118. Wise 1987, pp. 1, 32. We use "late 1970s" here to include the few instances in which the data cover years as late as 1981. It is not clear whether these associates arrived in the years stated or arrived later but were assigned to an earlier associate "class." The data presented do not permit us to distinguish between laterals arriving from clerkships and government service and those who were leaving other firms, but it seems safe to assume that there were at least some of the latter.
119. Adams 1989, pp. 1, 6.
120. According to Hildebrandt, Inc., about 100 law firms dissolved in 1987, including about a dozen with more than thirty lawyers (*Wall Street Journal* 1988, p. 17; Abel 1989, pp. 186–87). Although there have been some spectacular breakups of large firms, such as the notable dissolution of Finley Kumble in 1987, the pressure to merge or dissolve was thought to be most severe for midsize firms. In 1988, a Hildebrandt consultant reported that "[i]n the past two years, more than 60 midsize firms—more than 10% of the total nationwide—have either dissolved or merged. . . . Though midsize firms make up 10 percent of all law firms they accounted for 25 percent of the field's mergers and closing in the past two years" (Dockser 1988, p. B1).
121. These efforts have transformed the law school scene by linking law students early and tightly to the world of law practice, a development that has been described by Roger Cramton as "the new apprenticeship."

ments, just when 1960s activism induced disdain for corporate practice among students seeking work in poverty law and public-interest law. The percentage of elite law graduates entering private practice dropped precipitously.[122] Confronted by criticism that their work was unfulfilling and inimical to the public interest, many firms acceded to demands that recruits be able to spend time on "pro bono publico" activities.[123] The *Wall Street Journal* reported that "now it's common for [the big corporate law firms] to permit their attorneys to spend substantial portions of their time in noncommercial work."[124]

Firms responded to their supply problem not only by accommodating their recruits' public-interest impulses but by a sharp increase in compensation. In 1967, the starting salary for associates at elite firms in New York was $10,000, scheduled to increase to $10,500 for 1968. In February 1968, the Cravath firm, breaking with the "going rate" cartel,[125] raised the salaries for incoming associates to $15,000, setting in motion a new competitive system of bidding for top prospects.[126] Firms that wanted to be considered in the top stratum had to match the Cravath rate. The change in New York starting salaries reverberated throughout the upper reaches of the profession. The salaries of more senior associates had to be raised to preserve differentials; the take of junior partners had to be adjusted accordingly; firms outside New York, though paying less, had to give corresponding raises to maintain parity with their New York rivals. Unlike later increases in compensation, the late 1960s increase was not accompanied by pressure to bill more hours; it appears that hours billed were dropping during this period.[127]

In 1986, when the highest-paid beginning associates were getting $53,000,

122. "From 1964 through 1968 . . . the number of Harvard Law School Graduates entering private law practice declined from 54 to 41 percent." Yale graduates entering private practice dropped from 41 percent in 1968 to 31 percent in 1969; the percentage of Virginia graduates entering private practice dropped from 63 percent to 54 percent from 1968 to 1969 (Berman and Cahn 1970, pp. 22–23). "[I]n 1970, none of the thirty-nine law review editors graduating from Harvard expect[ed] to enter private practice" (Green 1970, pp. 658–59). A similar drop among Michigan graduates is documented by David Chambers, who found that those entering private practice dropped from 74 percent in the classes of 1965 and 1966 to about 60 percent for the years from 1967 to 1970. Chambers shows that most of the decrease was due to diversion into teaching and graduate work to secure draft deferments (Chambers, presentation to the annual meeting of the Law and Society Association, Madison, Wis., June 8–11, 1989).

123. Berman & Cahn 1970.

124. Falk 1970, p. 1.

125. See above, page p. 10 n. 30.

126. Observers also saw the move as a response to the declining popularity of practicing in New York, as opposed to other locations, and a Cravath partner attributed the increase to the high cost of living in New York (Zion 1968b, p. 45; 1968a, p. 31).

127. In 1973, Hoffman reported that "the associates' work load has fallen greatly throughout the blue-chip bar. As late as five years ago [1968], associates were expected to produce 2,000 billable hours a year. The target is now down to 1,600 and the actual output is even less. According to one survey, an associate in a Wall Street firm averages only 1,493 billable hours" (Hoffman 1973, pp.

Cravath administered a second shock by unilaterally raising salaries to $65,000.[128] At the time of the first "Cravath shock" the big firm "going rate" referred primarily to a few dozen firms, located mostly in New York; by the time the second shock occurred the big-firm world consisted of several hundred geographically dispersed firms, many national in scope. Long-accepted city differentials have been eroded by branching, especially by recent moves by New York firms into other legal markets, causing some firms in those localities to match the higher New York salaries.

As the number and size of large firms increase, recruitment has become more competitive and more meritocratic, leading to changes in the social composition of the new recruits.[129] The range of law schools from which the big firms recruit has widened and recruitment goes "deeper" into the class.[130] Barriers against Catholics, Jews, women, and Blacks have been swept away. The social exclusiveness in hiring that was still a feature of the world of elite law practice in 1960 has receded into insignificance. Performance in law school and in the office counts for more and social connections for less.[131]

By the late 1980s the population of big-firm lawyers included a significant number of women and members of minority groups. A 1989 survey of the 250 largest firms found that 24 percent of their lawyers were women: 9.2 percent of partners and 33 percent of associates.[132] A 1987 survey of these firms reported that women were "40 percent of the associates hired in the last two years, the same percentage as women in law school."[133] The percentage of women partners has been increasing at almost 1 percent a year throughout the 1980s.[134] These numerical gains have taken place while many women have expressed dissatisfaction with working conditions and career lines in large firms, es-

---

130–31). Hoffman suggests that the reduced hours reflected both interest in pro bono work and an unwillingness of recruits to sacrifice their private lives.

128. Lewin 1986.

129. On increased competition, consider the analysis of Bernstein, who shows that demand for new associates by the 250 largest firms outruns the total production of the "top twenty" law schools, however generously defined (Bernstein 1987–88, p. 20).

130. This is frequently described as a dilution of quality, but it should be recalled that since the golden age law school has attracted a much more talented pool and law school admissions have become more selective (Abel 1989, Table 4).

131. But even without deliberate exclusion, selection on the basis of educational credentials and the candidates' social affiliations, personal preferences, and career expectations will maintain some degree of association between legal roles and the social origins of lawyers. Cf. Heinz and Laumann (1989, p. 332). Abel (1989, pp. 109–10) argues that the inclusion of women and the erection of higher educational hurdles have worked to "narrow the class background of lawyers, whose origins have grown even more privileged." See also Abel (1989, p. 228).

132. Jensen 1990.

133. Weisenhaus 1988, pp. 1, 48.

134. Women were 2.8 percent of partners in 1981 and 9.2 percent in 1989 (Jensen 1990).

pecially as these obstruct and penalize child-rearing.[135] Women are less satisfied than their male counterparts with law practice in general and with practice in large firms.[136]

Blacks remained underrepresented in the world of large law firms: in 1989 2.2 percent of associates and nine-tenths of 1 percent of partners were Black.[137] The ratio of partners had doubled since 1981, but the percentage of Black associates declined slightly after 1981 (from 2.3 percent to 2.2 percent), while the percentages of other minorities rose.[138]

As firms are more openly competitive and more oriented to the marketplace, there is a democratization of manners. Remnants of patrician airs and professional noblesse are dispelled. Lawyers are more businesslike—as one Chicago lawyer observed, "law firms are becoming more like businesses and less like clubs."[139] Paradoxically, the rise of democratic inclusiveness and manners is accompanied by an accentuation of hierarchy within the firm. Rewards, security, prospects, control, and participation in governance are more differentiated, not only between lawyers in the partner-associate core and others, but also within that core.[140] As firms get larger, they are more likely to have specified tiers of partners. An Altman & Weil survey found that 50 percent of firms with more than 75 lawyers had tiered arrangements, while only 29 percent of firms with 41 to 74 lawyers had tiers.[141] In the 1989 *Of Counsel* survey of the 500 largest firms, 40.9 percent had two-tiered partnerships.[142] In some cases lower-tier partnership is not a stage but a destination. In contrast to earlier two-tier arrangements "[i]n the modern version, there is no longer a presumption that once a lawyer is elected an income partner, capital partnership will necessarily follow."[143] Roughly 30 percent of the *Of Counsel* 500 firms had staff attorneys or provisional partners[144] and 20.8 percent had senior attorneys or permanent associates.[145] Use of these categories is increasing rapidly: in 1987,

135. Klemesrud 1985, p. 14; Mairs 1988, p. 1; Kingson 1988, p. 1; cf. Holmes (1988).

136. Repa 1988; Tucker, Albright, and Busk 1989; Hirsch 1985; W. Nelson 1990. The contours of this dissatisfaction remain to be mapped. A study of Michigan graduates of 1976–79 five years after graduation. Chambers (1989, pp. 273–75) revealed that both men and women found the balance of family and work obligations the least satisfactory aspect of their professional lives. But, surprisingly, full-time women lawyers with children reported higher overall career satisfaction and higher satisfaction with the balance of their family and professional lives than did their male counterparts.

137. Jensen 1990.

138. Weisenhaus 1988, p. 50; Jensen 1990.

139. Rottenberg 1979, p. 124.

140. Nelson 1988, p. 275.

141. Altman 1988.

142. *Of Counsel* 1989, pp. 18–20. Percentages are of the 450 firms that returned survey forms.

143. Hildebrandt and Kaufman 1990, p. 19.

144. Staff attorneys refers to nonpartnership track lawyers; provisional partners are lateral hires eligible for full partnership "after further evaluation."

145. Smith 1989c, p. 15.

37 firms reported that they adopted such a category; in 1988, 39 more firms adopted one of them.[146]

Leverage. Firms have become more highly leveraged—that is, the ratio of associates to partners has risen. Using the data from our Group I set of fifty of the largest firms in 1986[147] we calculated the change in associate-to-partner ratios at five-year intervals from 1960, the midpoint of the golden age, to 1985. During that period these firms grew from an average size of 48 to 239, and the ratio of associates to partners increased 28 percent, from 1.15 to 1.47.[148] The associate per partner data are reported in Table 3.[149] The ratio of associates to partners rose consistently during the successive five-year intervals, with the exception of the period from 1965 to 1970, where there is a slight decrease in the ratio. This dip would be consistent with the initial phasing out of permanent associates[150] and the tightening of the labor market, both of which occurred about this time.[151]

Because of the well-known (but less well-explained) difference in the leverage of large New York firms and those elsewhere, we also divided our firms into two groups: those whose principal office is located in New York (NY) and those whose principal office is found outside of New York (ONY).

146. Smith 1989c, p. 15.

147. This data set is discussed in Appendix A.

148. We also used the data from our *National Law Journal* "Two Twenties" data set (described in Appendix A) to calculate the change in associate-to-partner ratios from 1980 to 1987. We found that between these years the associate-to-partner ratio increased 31 percent, from 1.72 to 2.25.

While the trends here are the same as reported in the text, the magnitudes of ratios differ because of the different way that the various sources counted their data (see Appendix A). Our assumption is that the various figures provided by the *National Law Journal,* and the data reported by *Business Week, Juris Doctor,* and Klaw (see discussion of these in Appendix A), are more accurate representations of absolute firm size than those in our data set, based on *Martindale-Hubbell.* For the reasons discussed on page 144, our data set understates the ratio of associates to partners. But because our data set goes back much further and was gathered in a consistent manner, it provides a more accurate representation of trends. In discussing leverage, as elsewhere, we are more interested in the pattern of change in leverage than in the absolute amount at any given time in any given firm. We report the *National Law Journal* data here only to give the reader a sense of the absolute size of the ratios. Once again, the reader is cautioned not to mix data from the different sources (see Appendix A).

149. The absolute numbers of associates and partners can be found in Table 3, below.

150. See above, page 42.

151. This dip appears in another data set that we can derive by combining a report in *Business Week* (1968, p. 79), on the twenty largest firms and a report from *Juris Doctor* on the twenty-five largest firms ("de Tocqueville [pseud.]" 1972, p. 56). These reports, apparently based on information supplied by the firms, list numbers of partners and associates. When we compare the *Business Week* 1968 figures and the *Juris Doctor* 1971 figures, the decrease in leverage is even more pronounced, from an average ratio of 1.99 associates per partner in the 1968 top twenty, to 1.72 associates per partner in the 1971 top twenty-five. The greater decrease might be due to the different dates (1968 and 1971 in the combined set and 1965 and 1970 from our *Martindale-Hubbell* set) or from some inconsistency in the way in which the *Business Week* and *Juris Doctor* surveys were conducted.

Table 3 Associates Per Partner, Group I Firms, 1960–1985

	1960 A per P	1965 A per P	1970 A per P	1975 A per P	1980 A per P	1985 A per P
New York Firms						
Cadwalader, Wickersham & Taft	1.95	2.32	*	2.16	2.09	2.00
Cahill, Gordon & Reindel	*	1.11	1.38	2.15	2.06	1.96
Cleary, Gottlieb, Steen & Hamilton	1.83	2.00	2.40	2.11	2.19	1.75
Coudert Brothers	0.47	0.67	0.74	0.57	1.16	1.43
Cravath, Swaine & Moore	*	*	*	2.84	2.40	2.57
Davis, Polk & Wardwell	*	*	*	*	*	*
Dewey, Ballantine, Bushley, Palmer & Wood	2.66	2.23	1.70	2.65	1.78	1.48
Fried, Frank, Harris, Shriver & Jacobson	1.31	1.62	1.96	1.64	1.95	1.55
Kaye, Scholer, Fierman, Hays & Handler	1.38	1.61	1.33	1.40	1.44	1.90
Kelley, Drye & Warren	1.30	1.00	1.12	1.57	1.86	1.85
LeBoeuf, Lamb, Leiby & MacRae	0.83	1.12	0.88	1.00	1.17	1.39
Milbank, Tweed, Hadley & McCloy	*	1.97	*	1.44	1.62	2.04
Paul, Weiss. Rifkind, Wharton & Garrison	*	1.59	1.57	1.88	1.97	1.97
Proskauer, Rose, Goetz & Mendelsohn	*	*	1.29	1.27	0.93	1.27
Rogers & Wells	1.17	1.07	0.74	0.94	1.20	1.39
Shea & Gould	0.73	0.82	1.09	1.16	1.00	1.40
Shearman & Sterling	1.94	2.58	1.86	2.06	1.64	1.80
Simpson, Thacher, & Bartlett	*	2.38	*	1.59	1.82	1.81
Skadden, Arps, Slate, Meagher & Flom	1.60	0.63	1.90	2.32	2.78	2.31
Stroock & Stroock & Lavan	0.75	*	*	1.08	1.47	1.67
Sullivan & Cromwell	*	1.44	*	1.66	1.75	1.74
Weil, Gotschal & Manges	1.08	1.23	2.13	2.48	1.90	2.86
White & Case	*	1.95	1.48	1.67	1.78	1.78
Wilkie, Farr & Gallagher	*	*	*	*	1.51	1.98
Average, NY Firms	1.36	1.54	1.47	1.71	1.72	1.82
Outside New York Firms						
Arnold & Porter	1.00	1.06	0.85	0.91	1.32	0.87
Baker & Botts	2.16	1.59	1.80	1.28	1.49	1.19
Baker & Hostetler	0.59	0.96	0.80	0.86	*	0.93
Brobeck, Phleger & Harrison	1.12	0.81	1.00	1.05	1.21	1.51
Dechert, Price & Rhoads	0.63	0.94	1.02	1.15	0.99	0.99

Table 3   *(Continued)*

	1960 A per P	1965 A per P	1970 A per P	1975 A per P	1980 A per P	1985 A per P
Outside New York Firms						
Dorsey & Whitney	0.54	1.24	0.51	0.62	0.81	0.89
Dykema, Gossett, Spencer, Goodnow & Trigg	*	0.86	*	1.03	0.86	*
Foley & Lardner	0.85	0.88	1.03	0.89	0.70	0.88
Fulbright & Jaworski	1.55	1.40	1.74	1.47	1.00	1.20
Gibson, Dunn & Crutcher	1.12	0.82	1.05	1.18	0.98	1.31

Hinshaw, Culbertson,
   Moelmann, Hoban
   & Fuller
	1.86	0.93	1.00	0.92	1.62	1.80

Hunton & Williams	0.71	0.95	1.38	1.30	1.32	1.49
Jones, Day, Reavis & Pogue	0.40	0.59	0.59	0.93	1.05	1.36
Kirkland & Ellis	0.75	0.57	0.80	0.85	1.00	1.03
Latham & Watkins	0.90	0.88	1.00	1.52	1.05	1.46
Mayer, Brown & Platt	0.96	0.93	0.54	0.66	0.75	0.77
McDermott, Will & Emery	0.90	1.04	0.70	1.19	0.61	0.59
Morgan, Lewis & Bockius	0.85	0.61	0.88	0.98	1.29	1.25
Morrison & Foerster	0.80	0.57	1.00	1.04	1.47	1.18
O'Melveny & Myers	1.79	1.69	1.63	1.92	1.72	1.79
Pepper, Hamilton & Scheetz	0.76	0.55	0.69	0.87	1.19	1.13
Pillsbury, Madison, & Sutro	*	*	1.36	1.34	1.16	1.24
Reed, Smith, Shaw & McClay	0.59	0.38	0.27	0.78	0.72	0.84
Sidley & Austin	0.86	0.61	0.72	0.80	0.93	1.28
Squire, Sanders & Dempsey	0.94	1.11	1.07	0.98	1.29	1.24
Vinson & Elkins	2.64	3.19	1.31	1.44	1.47	1.10
Winston & Strawn	0.57	0.53	0.51	0.91	0.97	1.03
Average, ONY Firms	1.03	0.99	0.97	1.07	1.11	1.17
Average, All Firms	1.15	1.22	1.16	1.36	1.40	1.47

*No data available.

Between 1960 and 1985 the average size of New York's biggest firms increased almost 375 percent, from an average of 45 lawyers to 214 lawyers. The increase in size of the ONY firms was somewhat greater, growing 425 percent, from an average of 50 to 261 lawyers. But the New York firms continued to be more highly leveraged. In New York the average ratio of associates to partners increased from 1.36 in 1960 to 1.82 in 1985. The firms in other cities, by contrast, had only an average of 1.03 associates per partner in 1960 and 1.16 in 1985.[152] This means that the NY firms are not only more heavily leveraged than

152. Again, comparing the *National Law Journal* data with ours, we see that the trends are basically consistent, though the absolute numbers differ. Using our "Two Twenties" data set (see

the ONY firms, but that the differences are increasing. The average number of associates per partner in the NY firms grew by 34 percent between 1960 and 1985 while for the ONY firms it increased by only 13 percent. Moreover, in 1960 20 percent of ONY firms had associate-to-partner ratios exceeding that of the average NY firm. By 1985 none of the ONY were more leveraged than their average NY counterpart.

At least part of the difference between New York firms and firms elsewhere probably lies in the different meaning attributed to the term "partner" by the NY and ONY firms. If firms designate as partners those lawyers who have been given that title (and a promise of permanent tenure) but not a share of the firm profits, then they would display lower associate-to-partner ratios than if the partner designation were reserved to lawyers who had a share of the profits. There is reason to think that in at least some cities outside New York the partner designation is used more expansively.[153] Since this practice simultaneously reduces the number of associates and increases the number of partners used in calculating these ratios, our comparisons overstate the difference in leverage.[154]

Promotion and Partnership. Over the two decades preceding 1980 the period during which lawyers served as associates before becoming partners had

---

Appendix A), we find that between 1980 and 1987 the associate-to-partner ratio at the twenty largest New York firms grew from 2.16 associates per partner to 2.82. Over the same period the ratio of associates per partner in the outside New York firms jumped from 1.2 to 1.63. The "Two Twenties" data evidence a slight convergence in the ratios of the two samples. According to the "Two Twenties" data the ONY firms have increased their ratio of associates to partners by about 36 percent, while the NY firms have risen by only 31 percent. However, in neither 1980 nor 1987 was any ONY firm more leveraged than the average NY firm.

In addition, Klaw (1958, p. 194) reports the total number of associates and partners at the twenty largest firms on Wall Street in 1957. From this we calculate that the average associate-to-partner ratio at that time was 2.27. The percentage difference between Klaw's lawyer counts (apparently based on information from firms) and ours (based on *Martindale-Hubbell*) is roughly the same as the difference between our counts in later years and those of the *National Law Journal*. On the assumption that both Klaw's and the *National Law Journal*'s counts are roughly equivalent and disregarding the fact that Klaw is counting Wall Street as opposed to New York City firms, we can combine these two data sets to get a rough second approximation of the change in associate-to-partner ratios in New York between the golden age and today. Interestingly, the trends are quite similar to those we report in the text, though again the absolute numbers differ, with an increase of roughly 25 percent in the average ratio of associates to partners in New York firms.

153. Wise 1987.

154. For example, a 218-person ONY firm with a nominal associate-to-partner ratio of 1.18:1 would have 100 partners and 118 associates. But if just 20 percent of those apparent partners are really associates (in the sense of taking out less than they put in), most of the difference from New York firms disappears. If twenty of the nominal partners of the 218-lawyer firm were regarded as associates, the associate-to-partner ratio would be 1.72:1, compared to an average ratio of 1.82:1 in the twenty largest New York firms.

become shorter. Nelson found that the average time spent as associates by those promoted to partnership in large Chicago firms during the 1950s was 7.5 years; this fell to 7.21 in the 1960s; to 6.19 for those promoted between 1970 and 1975; to 5.64 for those promoted between 1976 and 1980.[155] But in the 1980s time-to-partner seems to have stretched out. A study of five large New England firms found that associates had to wait eight or nine years instead of seven.[156] A *National Law Journal* survey of 35 firms in seven localities found that some two-thirds of associates hired in the late 1970s had spent seven to eight "years to partner."[157] Many partners anticipated further stretchout.[158]

Along with increases in leverage, it appears, came lower promotion rates. Nelson studied associates hired by nineteen large Chicago firms from 1971 to 1983 and determined which of them were still with these firms in 1984. If we assume that anyone who was there after nine years had become a partner, we see that less than half of those hired before 1975 had departed by 1984, so that more than half had become partners.[159] But Nelson suggests that "if we project current annual rates [of departure] over a six-year period [the normal period to partnership in Chicago], little more than one-quarter of the lawyers starting with firms would be expected to make partner."[160] But Nelson's figures only indicate that entry-level associates were less likely to become partners at the firm at which they began their careers. Presumably not all associates who left firms before becoming partners changed professions. Many have gone on to become partners at other firms, some at other large firms. In fact the percentage of all associates becoming partners at our Group I and Group II firms has remained remarkably stable over time.[161]

A 1987 *National Law Journal* survey of promotion at the five largest firms in each of seven localities reveals both regional and interfirm disparities. The portion who made partner varied from the lowest range of 10 to 35 percent in New York to the highest of 29 to 64 percent in Los Angeles. The portion making partner at the five largest Chicago firms ranged from 33 to 48 percent, higher than the percentage Nelson anticipates for the coming years, but lower than he reports for the period just past.[162] Similarly, lowered estimates of the percentage who will make partner are suggested by an account of large-firm practice in

155. Nelson 1988, p. 141. For parallel observations regarding the New York firms, see text above, notes 138 and 139.

156. Spangler 1986.

157. Wise 1987. A survey of 150 medium-sized firms found that the median time to achieve partnership had lengthened between 1975 to 1985 from five years to six years. Telephone interview with D. Weston Darby, Jr., of Cantor & Co., August 4, 1989. The survey was reported in Darby (1985, p. 68).

158. Nelson 1988, p. 141.

159. Nelson 1988, p. 139, Table 7.

160. Nelson 1988, pp. 138–39.

161. See below, pp. 103–4.

162. Wise 1987, p. 32.

the southeast, which reported that "[m]anaging partners at many major firms speak openly of their expectations that no more than 10 percent of any incoming class eventually will make partner."[163]

A constriction of promotion to partnership, anticipated elsewhere, seems to have arrived already in New York's largest firms. A *New York Law Journal* survey computed the chances of achieving partnership at 22 of the 30 largest firms in New York City in 1980 and 1989. Some 25.1 percent of the "associate classes" of 1968, 1969, and 1970 (including laterals assigned to those classes) had become partners by 1980; but only 18.8 percent of the classes of 1978, 1979, and 1980 had become partners by 1989.[164] These lower figures seem in the neighborhood of the chances of becoming a partner back in the 1950s.[165]

We noted earlier that in the 1960s firms applied the up-or-out norm with increasing stringency. In the early 1970s permanent associates were described as "a dying breed . . . being phased out by attrition at most firms."[166] But before the end of the decade, the institution was reinvented.[167] Firms modified the "promotion to partnership" model by creating a new stratum of permanent salaried lawyers.[168] This was done under various names: nonequity partner, special partner, senior attorney, senior associate, participating associate, and so on. As a Washington legal headhunter recently observed, "[e]veryone is studying this because everyone is running against the same economic realities. The larger classes of associates are coming up, and there is just not enough room at the top."[169] But permanent associates need not be those who failed to make partner. The managing partner at Cravath recently noted that "[w]e now have about 24 what we call 'permanent associates,' who almost all were specialists in one sort of work or another. Most, but not all, had been hired laterally with their specialties already in hand."[170] After a hiatus of some years, hiring

163. Bellon 1988, pp. 19–20.

164. Adams 1989, pp. 1, 6. These figures should not be overinterpreted. Not only is the time interval for the more recent group one year shorter than for the older group, but the findings are equally consistent with lengthening of time to partnership.

165. As reported by Mayer (1966, p. 334) and Klaw (1958). Cf. Smigel's analysis of Cravath (1969, pp. 116–20). Contemporary associates have their own golden-age myth of a time when young lawyers were trained as generalists rather than being pushed early into a specialty, received intensive mentoring, and "could expect to make partner after a certain number of years" if they "performed well and committed no egregious blunders" (Holmes 1988, p. 20).

166. Hoffman 1973.

167. Bodine 1979.

168. Graham 1983, p. 3; Hallam 1983, p. 1; Galante 1983a, p. 1; Galante 1983b, p. 1; Singer 1987, p. 12; Freeman 1987; Blum and Lobaco 1988. As noted above, the up-or-out norm had rarely been applied with absolute rigor. A Davis Polk partner observed that the new senior attorney program "just regularized what's been the fact for some time in the past" (Graham 1983, p. 3).

169. Griggs and McNeill 1987–88, p. 4.

170. Susman 1987, p. 415.

of permanent associates returned to Sullivan & Cromwell: "[o]f the six-teen . . . in 1987, nine or ten worked in the area of clearing securities registrations, and others in oil and gas taxes, wills, and litigation."[171]

Firms have increased the use of personnel who are not eligible to be partners. This is most evident in the increasing delegation of work to paralegals, that is, lower salaried nonlawyer employees performing routine legal tasks under the supervision of lawyers.[172] The number of paralegals working in law firms increased from 14,000 in 1972 to 32,000 in 1977 to 58,000 in 1982 to 83,000 in 1989.[173] Paralegals work across the spectrum of law firms, but they have become an important and growing presence at big law firms. In 1980 at the twenty largest firms in New York, there were 23.4 paralegals for every hundred lawyers; by 1987 this increased to 30.9 paralegals per hundred lawyers—an increase of 32 percent.[174] In our Outside New York firms, paralegals were almost as numerous: 20 per hundred lawyers in 1980 and 25.5 per hundred in 1987, a 32 percent increase. In short, the paralegal population of the big-firm world seems to be increasing slightly faster than the lawyer population. The presence of paralegals is growing at the same time that the ratio of associates to partners is growing, giving firms additional leverage without additional pressure to create partners.

The search for leverage without "the pressure created by regular associates eager to make partner" is also evident in the hiring of associates on a lower-paid nonpartnership track.[175] Programatic two-tier hiring was initiated by Jones Day in 1984. The second tier was drawn from less prestigious law schools and academic performance was generally lower than that of partnership-track associates. These lawyers are paid less (in 1986 starting staff attorneys at Jones Day received $30,000 per year, as opposed to $52,000 for starting associates). The presence of these low-paid lawyers enables firms to compete for "low end price sensitive business," including routine work that might have been done in-house by corporate law departments.[176] A 1988 survey found that 23 of the 500 largest law firms had added "staff attorney" positions outside the partnership track during the preceding year.[177]

Another device for enlarging capacity without engaging new associates is the

171. Lisagor and Lipsius 1988, p. 258.

172. Simon 1988, p. 1. As Simon points out, definitional problems abound.

173. Census of Service Industries, cited by Sander and Williams (1989, p. 442); Fowler (1990, p. 37). Sander and Williams estimate that almost as many paralegals work outside law firms (Sander and Williams 1989). The U.S. Department of Labor projected paralegal work as the nation's fastest-growing field in the coming decade (Fowler 1990, p. 37).

174. This is drawn from analysis of our *National Law Journal* "Two Twenties" data set (described in Appendix A).

175. Orey 1987, p. 20.

176. Orey 1987, p. 20.

177. Nelson 1989, p. 14.

use of "temporary" lawyers. These "legal temps" are not employees of the firm but are supplied by agencies who screen and certify them. Use of temporaries enables firms to respond to fluctuations in demand (often but not always in connection with litigation) without the increase in overhead to accommodate additional regular employees. Such jobs attract lawyers who wish to work part time or irregularly. Temporaries are used frequently by smaller firms to enable them to handle more business without expanding, but they are another tool for large firms to enlarge capacity without adding to the partner/associate core. The first legal-temp agency opened in 1983; in 1988 there were about a dozen agencies which, between them, operated in about as many jurisdictions.[178] Instead of bringing temporaries in, excess work can be sent out to "satellite firms." And other services, such as "litigation support" can be purchased from outside suppliers,[179] again enabling firms to enlarge capacity without bringing additional lawyers into the core of the firm.

Diversification. In these ways the classic big-firm notion of "promotion to partnership"—that all the lawyers were potentially members of a fraternity of peers—is attenuated. But if all lawyers are no longer potential peers, some nonlawyers are being invited into the core of the firm's operations. Firms feel pressure to provide more services. We have noted the drive to cover more specialities and more locations. The movement to build on successful relations with clients to sell them new kinds of services is not limited to legal services. Since legal services are often consumed in conjunction with other services, some firms have adopted strategies of hiring nonlawyer professionals. "Firms have brought in engineers, teachers, lobbyists, regulatory economists, banking regulators, nurses, doctors, and business managers (MBAs) to help provide client services."[180] In early 1990 the District of Columbia became the first American jurisdiction to permit nonlawyers to be partners in law firms.[181] Some law firms have established coordinate "non-legal" businesses (investment advice, economic consulting, real-estate development, consulting on personnel management, marketing newsletters, etc.).[182] A lawyer whose firm branched out into office-support services said that acquisition of this business was "like a company that makes peanut butter buying a company that makes

178. Labaton 1988, p. D2; Berkman 1988, p. 24; Mansnerus 1988, p. B10. The New York City Bar Association's condemnation of these agencies' fees as offending the ban on fee-splitting chilled their business, drew heated protest, and was withdrawn (Mansnerus 1989, p. B6).

179. Middleton 1984, pp. 1, 26.

180. Haserot 1987, p. 16; Lauter 1984, p. 1.

181. Lewis 1990, p. B10; *National Law Journal* 1990, p. 7; Noah 1990, p. A14.

182. Stille 1985; Saltonstall and Lane 1988; Siconolfi 1985; Marcus 1986; Silas 1986; Lewin 1987; Gibbons 1989.

183. Stille 1985, p. 22.

peanut butter jars."[183] Others project a grander vision of the evolution of law firms into diversified knowledge conglomerates:

> If the railroads had asked themselves what business they were in and had answered "Transportation," they might be in the airline business [today]. . . . We realized we were in the business of selling knowledge, whether we were advising legal clients, giving seminars, doing investment banking, making video tapes, or publishing newsletters.[184]

A partner at Arnold and Porter, which has established three consulting subsidiaries, anticipates that

> by the end of the century . . . large firms will become immensely more diversified in the services they offer. They will become more oriented toward problem-solving than traditional law firms, assemble teams of experts—lawyers and non-lawyers—and offer their clients "one stop shopping." . . . By the end of the century, legal services will be provided broadly in the context of a diversified service firm that will draw upon the talents of many disciplines with financial, economic and scientific resources available within a single institution.[185]

To many lawyers, "diversification" threatens an irreparable breach of professional integrity. Thus, a bar group recently proposed to limit ancillary services to those "solely incidental to (and not independent of) law firms' provision of legal services. . . ."[186] In the meantime it is clear that the notion of the law firm as a repository of exclusively and distinctively legal knowledge and skills is no longer unquestioned.[187]

As the firm copes with the exigencies of its new competitive environment, the situation of the junior lawyers is more precarious and more pressured, although they are more rewarded. But the partnership core is even more affected. Partners are under mounting pressure to maintain a high level of performance— and performance that fits the business strategy of the firm. Many new features of the law-firm world (mergers, lateral movement) amplify the power of dominant lawyers within a firm to sanction their errant colleagues, and the prevalent culture endorses such sanctions. So partners worry about having their pre-

---

184. Stille 1985, p. 20.
185. Fitzpatrick 1989 , p. 465.
186. American Bar Association 1990, p. 3.
187. The shift in perspective is succinctly put by one general counsel reflecting on the change in the nature of professionalism: "Most lawyers think of themselves first and foremost as lawyers, when in reality, they are a very small part of a much larger profession or industry. That industry is the industry of information management." Remarks of Carl D. Liggio (1984, p. 106).

rogatives or shares reduced or even being "de-equitized"[188] or "departnerized"[189] or "pushed off the iceberg" altogether. As with professional athletes, there are real possibilities of downward movement. "[W]ith profits being squeezed and competition on the rise," reported one consultant, "many firms can no longer afford to support these ['unproductive' or 'disaffected'] partners. Firms are trying to 'rehabilitate' these partners, decreasing some partners' incomes and asking others to leave."[190] Thus a long-established 87-lawyer Seattle firm recently dismissed eight partners, along with six associates, on the ground that "the firings were necessary to increase profitability and keep talented attorneys from being hired away."[191] The unassailable security and tenured prerogative of partnership is no longer assured.[192] "Partnership used to be forever, but it is no longer."[193]

As the world of big law firms undergoes these dramatic structural changes, many of its inhabitants experience considerable distress about commercialization, the decline of professionalism,[194] and the loss of the distinctiveness of law practice. To some extent this distress about lost virtue is a constant feature of elite law practice. But what distinguishes current worry about commercialism and professionalism from that of a generation ago is that the latter was combined with stable expectations about the large firm as an institution. If the inhabitants of the golden age thought the large firm was already too big,[195] they harbored few doubts about its durability. They confidently anticipated a future much like that present. But now the expectations of those in large firms about what firms and law practice will be like in the future are strikingly different. Talk—and presumably consciousness—too has changed. We turn now to these changes in the discourse within and about the world of the large law firm.

The "New Information Order" of the Law

The lament that lawyers have declined from an earlier virtue, their lofty professionalism abandoned for pursuit of commerce, has been a recurrent com-

188. At least eight partners in a 238-lawyer Chicago firm had their equity interest taken away (Samborn 1989, p. 2).

189. Fisk 1988, pp. 49–50.

190. Heintz 1983, pp. 15, 19–42.

191. *National Law Journal* 1989a, p. 2. Cf. the report that in the early eighties, "[d]issatisfied with the performance of some of its partners, Willkie, Farr and Gallagher of New York has asked about a half dozen to leave" (Bernstein 1982, pp. 84, 100).

192. Cf. Steven Brill's observation that the single transcendent change in large-firm practice in the 1980s is "The End of Law Partnerships as We Once Knew Them" (Brill 1989a, p. 3).

193. Bernstein 1982, p. 100.

194. See, e.g., American Bar Association (1986b).

195. Smigel reports that in the early 1960s most lawyers in firms of one hundred or more lawyers "feel they have reached or passed their optimum size" (Smigel 1969, p. 367).

panion of the big firm since its beginnings.[196] Is it different this time? Is the wolf really here? We argue that this time *is* different in at least two ways. First, the exponential character of growth means that the magnitude of the inevitable structural changes will be far greater than earlier adjustments. Second, changes in the state of knowledge, information, and belief about the legal system make it more difficult to avoid challenge to long-accepted models of professional life. In the past, the system of information about law helped to assuage elite discomfort; now it aggravates that discomfort.

Large-firm law practice was once shrouded in confidentiality. When Smigel studied Wall Street lawyers in the late 1950s he encountered a massive institutionalized reticence.[197] Information about partnership agreements, finances, relations with clients, even their identity, was taboo. Older and conservative lawyers, he reported, "thought of their organizations in much the same manner as clergymen think of the church—as an institution that should not be studied."[198] Even among big-firm lawyers, much of their world was, by preference, left opaque. "Talking about clients and fees just isn't done, not even when lawyers gather among themselves."[199]

Tom Goldstein, one of the pioneering figures in the new legal journalism, recalled that in the early 1970s

> when I began reporting on legal topics in the *New York Times,* law firms were reluctant to part with even the most harmless information. I remember when I spent several hours just finding out how many lawyers worked at Rogers & Wells. . . . After finally reaching a lawyer at the firm who would talk to me, I was told to count up the names listed in the Martindale-Hubbell Law Directory. When I complained that, for journalistic purposes, the directory was out of date, I was told I was out of luck.[200]

Such reticence was supported and enforced by the Canons of Professional Ethics, originally adopted in 1908, which condemned as "unprofessional"

196. See *The American Lawyer* (1895, p. 84); Dos Passos (1907, p. 46); Stone (1934); and additional sources cited in Gordon (1988).

197. Smigel 1969, p. 18–20.

198. Smigel 1969, p. 19.

199. Hoffman 1973, pp. 71–72. But, as Smigel observed, the Cravath starting-salary shock of 1968 (see text above, p. 56), helped dispel the earlier reticence, resulting in "a more candid exchange of information on an intimate level. One lawyer said, 'Everyone knows what everyone else is getting' " (Smigel 1969, p. 374).

200. Goldstein 1983, p. 1353. Cf. the irritation of *Forbes* when its attempt to obtain interviews with "two powerful and influential law firms" for a 1971 article on the "top of the profession" met with refusal as "a matter of ethics" (*Forbes* 1971, pp. 30–31).

various forms of advertising, solicitation, and getting business through agents. Canon 27 concluded with the admonition that:

> Indirect advertisement for business by furnishing or inspiring news-paper comments concerning causes in which the lawyer has been or is engaged, or concerning the manner of their conduct, the magnitude of the interests involved, the importance of the lawyer's positions, and all other like self-laudation, defy the traditions and lower the tone of our high calling and are intolerable.

Over the years the wording had been changed in detail but "furnishing or inspiring newspaper comments" was still "reprehensible."

In the 1970s, the new Code of Professional Responsibility provided in Disciplinary Rule 2-101:

> A lawyer shall not prepare, cause to be prepared, use or participate in the use of, any form of public communication that contains professionally self-laudatory statements calculated to attract lay clients; as used herein, "public communication" includes, but is not limited to, communication by means of television, radio, motion picture, news-paper, magazine, or book.[201]

Breaches of these standards, at least highly visible ones, were likely to attract condemnation. In 1963, four partners in a small New York City firm of impeccable respectability were censured for violating Canon 27. Their offense was cooperating with *Life Magazine* reporters in publication of a magazine article that portrayed the firm and recounted some of its cases.[202] In 1976, Tom Goldstein's *New York Times* profile of Paul Weiss led to the filing of "several complaints . . . with the grievance committee of the Association of the Bar of the City of New York, accusing Paul Weiss of unethical self-promotion. An investigation lingered for several months. Paul Weiss partners were required to sign affidavits as to whether they knew [Goldstein] or had talked to [him] before the article was published."[203]

A few years later the interested reader could find an abundance of information about firm organization, finances, relations to clients, office politics, and so forth. The suddenness of the change is epitomized in the observation of a journalist who wrote two books about elite New York lawyers, contrasting talking to lawyers in the early 1980s with talking to them ten years before. "What a

---

201. American Bar Foundation, Code of Professional Responsibility, Disciplinary Rules 2-101(A) (as amended February 1975).

202. The censure was imposed by the Appellate Division, which found this objectionable self-promotion even though the article was "an example of well-written legitimate journalism." *Matter of Connolly*, 18 A.D.2d 466, 477, 240 N.Y.S.2d 126 (1963).

203. Goldstein 1983, pp. 1351, 1354.

difference a decade makes! In contrast to the [earlier] research, no law firm slammed the door in [my] face, no lawyer stonewalled."[204]

The turnabout came quite abruptly in the late 1970s.[205] This dramatic opening was a curious by-product of the Supreme Court's 1977 *Bates* decision, ruling that sweeping restrictions on lawyer advertising violated the First Amendment.[206] *Bates* liberated lawyers to talk to the press about their practices, for they no longer feared being accused of advertising. This new access to lawyers combined with a new curiosity about law and lawyers to make possible the new legal journalism.[207] Reporting about lawyers in general publications like the *New York Times,* the *Wall Street Journal,* and the newsweeklies became more frequent, detailed, and intrusive.[208] In 1978 a new kind of trade press suddenly appeared within the legal world.[209] National publications like the *National Law Journal, American Lawyer,* and *Legal Times* provided a steady diet of detailed backstage information about firm structure, hiring policy, marketing strategies, clients, fees, and compensation.[210] Contemporary observers noted that the new legal press was "[i]nvading the inner sanctums of the nation's law firms";[211] and that "law and lawyers are becoming demystified. The rites of secrecy have passed."[212] Information that just a few years earlier would have been available only to a few insiders now circulated freely.

Michael Powell summarizes the way that the new trade press both reports and celebrates the new competitive legal marketplace:

> The new legal press . . . portrays the practice of law as a highly competitive business, fosters a market orientation, emphasizes the

204. Hoffman 1982, p. 340.

205. A significant part of the prehistory may be found in the magazine *Juris Doctor,* published by MBA Communications, New York, from 1971 to 1979 (vol. 9, no. 3 is dated May 1979).

206. *Bates v. State Bar of Arizona,* 433 U.S. 350 (1977).

207. This curiosity reflected the sharp increase in the number of lawyers (see above, p. 39) and was manifested in the advent of the first prime-time TV shows about noncriminal law and lawyers, including "The Paper Chase" (1978–79) and "The Associates" (1979), and culminating in "L.A. Law" (1986–). On lawyers on TV, see Stark (1987); the various contributions to *Yale Law Journal* (1989); Rosen (1989). On lawyers in movies, see Chase (1986); Mastrangelo (1985–86).

208. For a sketch of the new era of legal journalism, see Sherman (1988, p. 32).

209. See Goldstein (1983, p. 1351); Powell (1985). These did not displace the "legal newspapers," focusing on court calendars and legal notice advertising, that flourished in most sizable cities.

210. Several local publications in this new style included *Chicago Lawyer,* which commenced publication in November 1978, under the aegis of Chicago's "counter" bar association, the Chicago Council of Lawyers (see Star 1981, p. 16) and *Manhattan Lawyer,* published since 1987 by *American Lawyer* publisher Steve Brill. In 1986, Brill bought *Legal Times* and eight local legal papers, linking them to the coverage of the new legal journalism (Oliver 1987, p. 1).

211. Kiernan 1979, p. C-1.

212. Goldstein 1979.

development of rational [firm] organizational structures, encourages
the adoption of new technologies and modern management techniques, and promotes the awareness of [participation in a]
national . . . [legal community.][213]

As firms faced a more competitive setting, "the image the new legal press fostered was that of an aggressive, business seeking firm consciously developing
new speciality areas and expanding its offices."[214] To navigate these uncharted
waters, firms have relied upon management consultants to advise on organization, compensation, recruiting, training, marketing, mergers, computers, and
other matters.[215] These consultants, in turn, generate and disseminate new information about firm practices and performance.

Firms are not only the subjects of this new flow of information, but in large
part they are its source. They respond to surveys. And, more importantly, they
have become more aggressive disseminators of information, both in connection
with clients' matters (with press releases, conferences, interviews with reporters), but also on behalf of the firm itself. It is lawyers in the profession's other,
"individual," hemisphere who go in for television advertisements, newspapers
and billboards; big firms produce brochures,[216] send out newsletters, conduct
seminars,[217] and retain public-relations firms to present themselves to potential
clients.[218]

The new connection between the media and law firms was part of a wider
change that we might call the legal-information explosion. Over the past twenty-five years, the development of new lines of scholarship about the law in action made available a profusion of information about the working routines of
courts and judges, about the work of lawyers, the structure and politics of the
bar, the impact of legal regulation, and so forth. Although calls for this kind of
scholarship go back many decades, it was only in the mid-1960s that an inter-
disciplinary research community emerged, actively and continuously pursuing
such inquiries in a cumulative way.[219] "Law and society" scholarship was
joined in early 1970s by "law and economics" scholarship and by other schools
of thought that attempted to understand law through philosophy, literary theory,
or feminist theory. All of these agreed that the legal world could not be under-
stood in its own terms but required the application of some method provided by

213. Powell 1985, p. 22.
214. Powell 1985, p. 21.
215. Granelli 1980, p. 1; Hayes 1989a, p. 90. In addition to firms that specialize in consulting on
law firm management, some Big Eight accounting firms supply consulting services to law firms.
216. Galante 1985, p. 1.
217. On the origins and growth of the law-firm seminar, see Vilkin 1982, p. 1.
218. On firm use of public-relations specialists, see Zlokower 1981, p. 19; Barnett 1982, p. 42;
Schenkman and Ross 1985, p. 15.
219. On the course of such inquiry, see Galanter (1985).

another discipline, although there was disagreement about the discipline to be applied. Legal activity was to be explained by exogenous forces. The long-challenged but resilient faith that law was an autonomous realm that could be known by study of authoritative legal texts was no longer dominant.[220] A comparison of law reviews in 1985 with their predecessors in 1960 found that a greater portion of the 1985 reviews was devoted to articles that were theoretical rather than practical. In 1985 the reviews were far more critical of existing doctrine. In 1960 more articles defended doctrine than criticized it; in 1985 there were "more than two and a half articles criticizing doctrine for every article defending it."[221]

In tandem with the new legal journalism, these new lines of scholarship penetrated into previously off-limits backstage areas of legal life. They analyzed the strategems of litigants, they revealed the propensities of judges, they interviewed jurors about their deliberations, they detailed the politics and economics of law practice, they revealed the deployment policies of police and prosecutors. As scholarship and journalism examined its workings more closely, the legal world became more accessible to their scrutiny. Not only are law firms more open, but the operations of courts (including the Supreme Court)[222] are less shrouded and many core legal activities are more accessible—as dramatized by the Freedom of Information Act, by open-meeting laws, by courtroom television, by interviewing of jurors.[223]

In the old regime of restricted information about the law in action, the legal order could be perceived in terms of its esteemed frontstage qualities: as formal, autonomous, rule-determined, certain, professional, learned, apolitical, and so forth. Everyone knew it was not exactly that way in his or her own corner, but private and fragmented knowledge of local deviations did not challenge the received picture of the system as a whole. Professionals could maintain favorable images of the legal world and the profession even while dealing with lots of information about what the dominant paradigm labeled deviant, atypical instances. But as this picture of what the legal process is like has lost its power to command assent, it has become more difficult to dismiss politics, discretion, bargaining, and improvisation as extraneous appendages, alien to the law.

220. See Posner (1987).
221. Saks 1989, pp. 5–6.
222. Dramatically marked by the publication of Bob Woodward and Scott Armstrong's *The Brethren* (1979), but embodied in disclosures by the judges themselves (Wermiel 1986; Taylor 1988).
223. The new openness of the law world is exemplified by the turnabout in the willingness of prosecutors and police officials to discuss enforcement policies. When one of us first became interested in such matters in the 1960s, inquiries to officials about priorities and how they were set met with adamant refusal to acknowledge the existence of such policy-making. "We enforce all the laws; we don't decide which laws to enforce" was the stock reply. Now police chiefs and prosecutors may be found justifying their enforcement priorities to the public on television.

The relatively stable and comfortable consensus about law has been shattered. The world of law is far more intellectually diverse than it was in 1960. By 1960 there was no longer significant disagreement with the notion that law is not a self-contained realm of transcendent values but takes meaning from its effects in the wider world. For the most part legal intellectuals and professionals shared a view of law as "a rational technical apparatus which is continually transformed in the light of expediential calculations, devoid of all sacredness of content."[224] There remains wide agreement that law is an imperfect instrument to be wielded to control or improve that world. But within this "secularized" instrumental view of law, schools and movements of legal thought, displaying a variety and disagreement unimaginable in 1960, flourish in the law schools and through conferences and journals. Law and society, law and economics, Critical Legal Studies, alternative dispute resolution, the Federalist Society, feminist legal theory—all have substantial followings in the legal academy and some have adherents on the bench. None of them were visible in 1960.[225] For the most part these bodies of thought, which are not built on legal categories, are remote from the views of practitioners. But in other ways at least some of them are closer than rarified analysis of doctrine, paying more attention to the practitioner's quotidian world of tactics, fees, and compromises.

The increased diversity of legal thought is manifest among judges and practitioners as well as in the legal academy. More of the decisions of appellate courts, both federal and state, are accompanied by concurring and dissenting opinions.[226] Until recently debates within the organized bar on central professional issues involved a narrow and homogeneous group of elite lawyers, and controversy, though often vigorous, was among a restricted range of views. When in 1964 the organized bar set out to reformulate its 1908 Canons of Ethics, the president of the American Bar Association, Lewis F. Powell, Jr., appointed a committee

> consisting of two law professors, two former judges, and eight men whom their chairman, Edward L. Wright of Little Rock, described as "general practitioners." Two of these were former presidents of the ABA, one a chairman of the ethics committee. All of these "general practitioners" were members of substantial law firms; most concentrated their efforts on corporate clients. No women served on the

---

224. Weber 1978.

225. On the diversification of legal thought, see Posner (1987). On the various conservative movements, see McConnell (1987). On the law and society movement, see Galanter (1985). On critical legal studies, see *Stanford Law Review* (1984); *Cardozo Law Review* (1985).

226. The United States Supreme Court concurring and dissenting opinions were 51 percent of all opinions in 1959 and 60 percent of all opinions in 1982. Posner 1985, p. 237. A trend toward a higher percentage of dissenting opinions in state Supreme Courts is reported by Glick and Pruet (1986).

committee, or blacks, or Jews. Most went to top-ranked schools. None was then serving in the government, although some has served previously. None had been legal aid attorneys. . . . In short, all were members of the bar's elite.[227]

The new Code of Professional Responsibility was adopted in 1969. Yet just seven years later ABA president William Spann established a new group to review "all facets of legal ethics." The makeup and the history of the Kutak Committee (later Commission) reflected a new diversity within the legal profession. The members included women, Jews, a black, a prominent critic of the adversary system, government policy-makers responsive to the legal-services community, and eventually several nonlawyers; only three of the nine original members were in private practice. The commission "sought out the opinions of some of the profession's harshest critics"[228] and engaged a great number of constituencies and specialty groups within the profession, provoking in the process two full-blown rival codes. Passage of a much modified version of its Model Rules came after unprecedented, spirited, and well-recorded controversy.[229] One observer who carefully traced the course of these proposals was "struck by the heterogeneity of ethical views in today's profession."[230]

Conventional and celebratory views about law still command the allegiance of some lawyers all of the time and most lawyers some of the time. But they coexist with a host of views that challenge the authority of legal learning. The intellectual moorings that once enabled the higher reaches of the profession to dismiss disturbing information as deviant and exceptional are subverted. Legal elites, awash in information that discredits the received picture of the legal world, must address more informed, cynical, and critical publics without the armor of science or the mantle of altruistic professionalism. In this pluralistic and demystified legal world, the problem of reconstructing a viable sense of professionalism is daunting.

Thus in the early 1990s we find that the big firm of the first two-thirds of the century is becoming something else. The large agglomeration of specialist lawyers organized around the "promotion to partnership tournament" is still there—indeed it is much larger. But a cadre of permanent salaried personnel (paralegals, second-tier associates, and permanent associates/senior attorneys)

227. Lieberman 1978. Chairman Wright's account of the work of this "broad spectrum of the profession" may be found in Wright (1970).

228. Schneyer 1989, p. 697.

229. In contrast to the voluminous documentation of the work of the Kutak Commission, the predecessor Wright Committee (see Wright 1970) "intentionally compiled no record of its discussions and deliberations." (American Bar Foundation 1979, p. xi).

230. Schneyer 1989, p. 735.

now surrounds that promotion-to-partnership core. Within the core, promotion comes to fewer entry-level associates and it often comes later. For those who achieve promotion, the meaning of partnership has changed. The prospect of an orderly procession to unassailable eminence has been replaced by entrance to an arena of pressure and risk amid frenetic movement. In the next chapter we offer an explanation of the transformation from the classic big law firm into what we might call the late big law firm. We argue that this is the result of a conjunction between the growth imperative inherent in the big firm's organizational form and a set of changes in the business and legal environment.

5 Explaining Big-Firm Growth and Change: The Promotion-to-Partner Tournament

We now turn our attention to some of the reasons for the transformation of the large law firm. We believe that focusing on rapid firm growth—and the resulting struggle to accommodate increased size, new sources of labor (especially entry-level labor), and new and greater revenue requirements—yields significant insight into this complex battery of changes. In our view as firms have grown they simply have outpaced earlier methods of monitoring and coordinating personnel, recruiting associates, and generating revenues (to compensate the larger staff). To survive, firms have adapted by slowing growth, generating new sources of income, remolding existing governance structures, or accepting decreased or at least different profit distributions.

To understand why firms have restructured requires inquiry into why they have grown so fast and why staffing and revenue constraints have begun to impose restrictions on growth. Here too the answer is complex. Our explanation encompasses changes in corporate clients' demands of law firms, the supply of young lawyers, and the underlying structure of the large law firm. This last issue particularly intrigues us and captures a substantial portion of our attention. By emphasizing the structural component of the growth we do not mean to imply that other factors do not play a major role in the rapid increase in the size of the big firm. Other analysts have largely ignored the pressures for growth inherent in the structure of law firms, thereby overemphasizing the role of other variables in explaining the transformation. We attempt to correct the past emphasis on nonstructural variables by exploring in depth the organizational basis of law-firm growth.

The Pattern of Growth

To build a model of why law firms grow, we first quantify the nature of that growth.[1] We propose to begin by examining the growth patterns of the indi-

---

1. Unless otherwise noted, growth refers to growth in the size of the firm as measured by the number of attorneys associated with the practice. For a discussion of the complexities of that measure. see Appendix A.

vidual big firms found in our Group I and Group II data sets. The reader can grasp the character of the growth patterns by looking at the data reported in Graph A (top left corner) of the ten representative firms pictured in figures 1–10.[2] Figures 1–5 graph the growth of five representative Group I firms while figures 6–10 graph the growth of five representative Group II firms. Figures 1 and 6 may be found in the text, and the entire set of figures 1–10 is in Appendix A. Even a cursory glance at these graphs indicates that the total number of attorneys and the number of partners at each firm has grown substantially since each firm's inception. The data also indicate, and the graphs confirm, that much of this growth has occurred since 1970.

Many observers subscribe to a "shock theory" of recent firm growth. Until the early 1970s firm growth curves (of both partners and total lawyers) could be viewed, so the description goes, as straight lines sloping gently upward. The firms were viewed as having grown by constant, but unremarkable, absolute amounts over time. Suddenly, sometime around 1970, some "external shock" caused growth to increase dramatically, thereby increasing the steepness of the growth line. Thus the "shock" theory posits constant, though different, absolute amounts of growth (slopes) and implies decreasing rates of growth both prior to and after 1970.

We can see how well the traditional story approximates the actual data by estimating the intercept and slopes of the kinked linear function (KLF) that best fit the growth history of each of the law firms in our sample. Visual comparisons of the representative curves drawn from these estimates and simple statistical tests of goodness of fit can give us some gross indicators of how well the kinked linear model performs as an estimate of individual law-firm growth patterns. The rows identified as "KLF" associated with each firm listed in tables B1 and B2 in Appendix B present the estimated intercept and slope of the kinked linear functions.[3] Where the data are available, results are presented on

2. The entire data set is reported in Galanter and Palay (1990a). The data are available for a small charge by writing the Director, Disputes Processing Research Program, The Law School, University of Wisconsin, Madison, Wis. 53706.

3. To compute the estimated kinked linear function, we use ordinary least squares to regress size of firms against time. To account for the structural break around 1970 we use a dummy variable to account for shifts in either the slope or intercept after that point. Thus the model we estimated is

$$Y_t = A + B_1T_n + B_2(T_n - T^*) D$$

where Y = the number of attorneys in the firm at time t, T_n represents the time periods from 1 to n, T^* is the year in which the external shock occurs, and $D = 1$ if $T_n > T^*$ and $D = 0$ otherwise. B_1 is the slope of the function to the break and $B_1 + B_2$ is the slope afterwards. Because we are dealing with time series data, serial correlation problems are assumed to affect the efficiency of the ordinary least squares regression estimators, making them appear more precise than they really are. We could easily correct for the bias in the precision of our estimates by employing generalized least squares. But because we are not really interested in the precision of the estimators and because we do not want to ascribe undue sophistication to our results we have chosen not to do so. In any event,

both the size of the firm and the size of the partnership. Because adequate data on associates are sometimes unavailable, several of the firms are described in terms of the partnership data alone. Graph B (upper right corner) in figures 1– 10 depicts the estimated kinked linear function superimposed on the actual growth curves of representative firms and partnerships. Visual inspection of the graphs indicates that the kinked linear function in fact seems to fit well much of the actual data. In addition, we can use the R^2 statistic to make an informal assessment of the goodness of fit of the model.[4] The high R^2's are evidence that the KLF model does a good job of describing the actual data.

Closer inspection of the actual curves, however, reveals the possibility of a more complex growth history for many of the firms. Look again carefully at any of the graph A's in figures 1–10. While the curves are everywhere steeper after 1970 than before, the slope—or the absolute amount of growth for a unit in- crease in time—appears to increase, not to remain constant, even before 1970. Similarly, post-1970 rates of growth also appear to increase over time, not re- main constant. Firms, *both* before and after 1970, grew at increasing rates.

We propose an alternative explanation to account for this pattern of growth: The constant percentage increase from 1922[5] onward implies an exponential growth pattern in which the firm's early growth will appear—in absolute num- bers—quite unremarkable. After all, a firm that began with one person in 1920 and grew by 10 percent per year would still have only six lawyers in 1940. But eventually, as the 10 percent increase is applied to an ever larger base, the expo- nential character of the firm's growth would assert itself. The same firm that grew to six attorneys prior to World War II would have forty-five attorneys in 1960 and three hundred five lawyers a mere twenty years after that.

We fitted a curve representing an exponential function (EF) to the actual growth patterns of the big firms in our study.[6] The rows labeled "EF" in tables B1 and B2 present the results. A representative sample of these curves, dis- played in graph C (bottom left corner) of figures 1–10 shows that the EF model is not a bad approximation of the actual data, especially in the earlier years.

---

the R^2's tend to be quite high using ordinary least squares, and the basic results are unlikely to change substantially even if the serial correlation were eliminated.

4. R^2 is the proportion of the total variation in the dependent variable explained by the regression of the dependent variable on the independent variables. Thus it is a measure of how closely the estimated function approximates or resembles the actual function (Pindyck and Rubinfeld 1981, p. 79).

5. We use this date only because 1922 is the earliest volume of *Martindale-Hubbell* available to us at the University of Wisconsin Law School.

6. To estimate f(t) we take the natural log of both sides of the exponential equation which results in

$$f(t) = Ln(Y_t) = Ln(Ae^{Bt}) = A + Bt$$

We then used ordinary least squares to estimate f(t) and again ignore serial correlation problems.

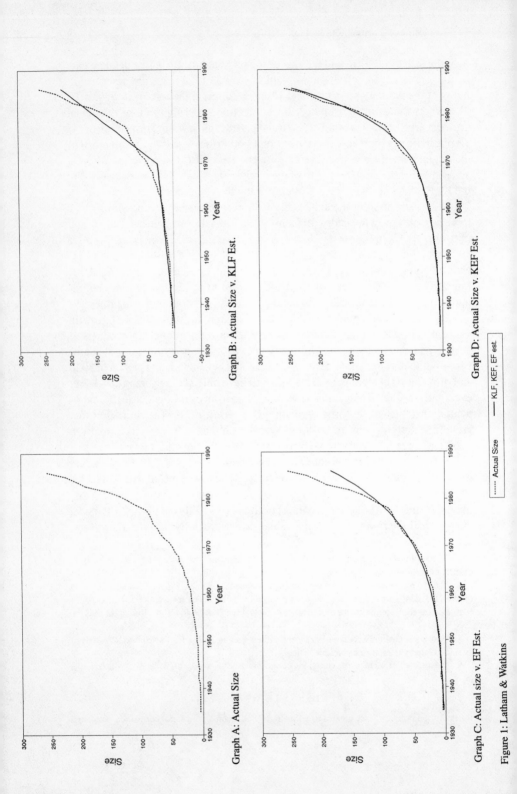

Graph A: Actual Size

Graph B: Actual Size v. KLF Est.

Graph C: Actual size v. EF Est.

Graph D: Actual Size v. KEF Est.

Actual Size .... KLF, KEF, EF est. ─────

Figure 1: Latham & Watkins

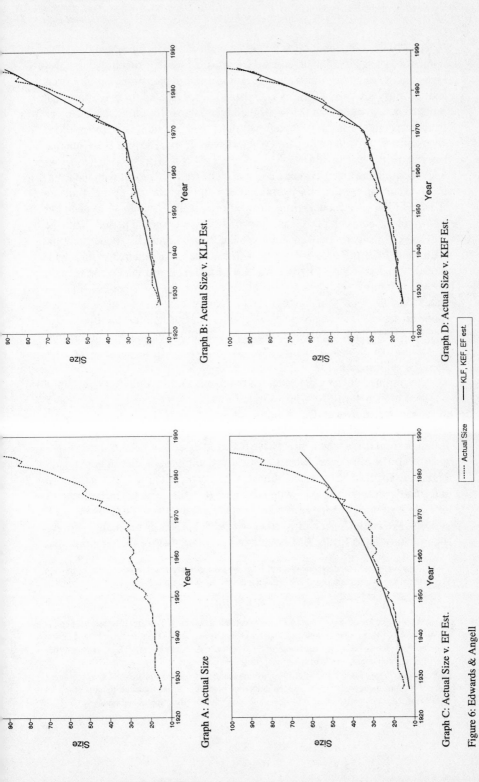

Graph A: Actual Size

Graph B: Actual Size v. KLF Est.

Graph C: Actual Size v. EF Est.

Graph D: Actual Size v. KEF Est.

Actual Size   —— KLF, KEF, EF est.

Figure 6: Edwards & Angell

After 1970 the exponential function often underestimates the actual data. The impressions left by the data tend to be confirmed by R^2's that are reasonably high, though rarely as high as the KLF model. Of the thirty-six Group I firms and the thirty-six Group II firms with data to report, the R^2 for the exponential function was greater than the R^2 of the kinked linear for only twelve and six firms respectively. Similar, though not quite as dramatic, results were found when only the growth of the partnership was examined. The results are summarized in the top half of table 4.

Combining the external shock component of the KLF model with the exponential function results in a hybrid model—the kinked exponential function (KEF). In the KEF model, firms grow at exponential rates to 1970 and after 1970, but the constant percentage growth differs during each period. With the KEF model we get a marked improvement over the pure EF model, and the KEF model fits the data at least as well as, and often better than, the KLF model. The data in the KEF rows in tables B1 and B2 and graph D (bottom right corner) in figures 1–10 depict the results of merging the two theories.[7] To illustrate, look at graph 4 in figure 1. Here the predicted curve for Latham and Watkins depicts a firm growing exponentially both before and after 1970. Around 1970 something changed the steepness of Latham and Watkins' ascent, as well as that of most of the firms examined, but not by as much as the KLF model would suggest.

Determining which model better fits the data is a more complex issue. While one can compare the R^2's of the respective equations, the results in this instance are somewhat equivocal. On the one hand the R^2's produced by the two models are often so close that we do not know whether the differences are significantly different from those which might have occurred randomly.[8] On the other hand, even if all the differences were statistically significant, neither model unambiguously fits the firm-size data better. When comparing two models one can informally say that the model with the higher R^2 "fits" better. The bottom half of table 4 summarizes the results of comparing the R^2's of the KLF and KEF models. We are interested in whether one model produces the higher R^2's for significantly more firms. At first glance it appears that for the Group I Total

7. To estimate the kinked exponential functions we use a dummy variable to account for shifts in either the slope or intercept after 1970. Thus the model we estimated is

$$LnY_t = A + B_1 T_n + B_2 (T_n - T^*) D$$

where LnY = the log of the number of attorneys in the firm at time t, T_n represents the time periods from 1 to n, T^* is the year in which the external shock occurs, and $D = 1$ if $T_n > T^*$ and $D = 0$ otherwise. B_1 then is the estimate of slope of the function to the break and $B_1 + B_2$ is the slope after 1970. Again no attempt was made to correct for serial correlation.

8. Ideally one would like to test this proposition using a test of significance. However, because the residuals of the models are in different units (one in units of Y and the other in units of log Y) direct statistical comparison would be like comparing the proverbial apples and oranges.

Table 4 Comparison of Number of Times Alternative Growth Models
Produced the Higher R^2

	Total Lawyers		Partners	
	Group 1	Group 2	Group 1	Group 2
R^2 KLF > R^2EF	24	30	31	28
R^2 KLF = R^2EF	5	2	4	4
R^2 KLF < R^2EF	7	4	15	5
R^2 KLF > R^2KEF	10	17	21	25
R^2 KLF = R^2KEF	10	6	10	6
R^2 KLF < R^2KEF	16	13	19	7

Size data the KEF model produces the greater number of higher R^2's and that
for the Group I Partnership Size, Group II Total Size, and Group II Partnership
Size data the KLF model yields the greater number of higher R^2's. But a careful
analysis indicates that the differences between the number of higher R^2's generated by the two models is significant for only the Group II Partnership data.[9]
For the Group I Totals, the Group I Partnership and the Group II Totals, the
results indicate that we cannot reject, even at reasonably low levels of significance, a null hypothesis that there is no causal significance to the difference

9. To reach this conclusion we first counted the number of times the R^2's from the KLF and the
KEF models fell into the KLF > KEF and KLF < KEF categories. We then compared these to the
expected value for these categories under the null hypothesis that the proportion of cases falling into
each category is the same and calculated a simple chi-square statistic. The results are as follows:

	Total Lawyers		Partners	
	Group I	Group II	Group I	Group II
R^2 KLF > KEF	10	17	21	25
R^2 KLF < KEF	16	13	19	7
Expected in each category	13	15	20	16
Chi-Square	1.3846	.533	.1	10.125
Probability of occuring under H_0	(.3 − .2)	(.5 − .3)	(.8 − .7)	(.01 − .005)

The chi-square statistic is used to test whether a significant difference exists between an observed
number of objects or responses falling into a given category and the number expected to appear on
the basis of some null hypothesis (Siegel 1956). If the observed values in each category closely
approximate the expected results, then the chi-square statistic will be small. Given our null hypothesis that there is no significant difference between categories, the smaller the chi square the more
likely the difference between the expected and observed results occurred purely by chance. The
numbers in parentheses below the chi-square statistic are the probability of the chi-square value
occurring under the null hypothesis. Thus we cannot reject the null hypothesis at significance levels
below these probabilities. Most researchers will generally not reject a null hypothesis which generates a probability greater than a significance level of .1.

between the number of observations in each category. This means that we are unable to say with much confidence that either model of total firm size produces a greater number of higher R^2 values. From the R^2's alone we can only say that the KEF model of firm size works as well as the KLF model.

We can attempt to get a better sense of the strength of the rival models by comparing their ability to predict the future growth of the firms. Because our data set was originally constructed with data through 1986 we can use each of these models to roughly predict the size of the firms in 1988 and then compare the estimates with the actual[10] size of the firm as derived from the 1988 *Martindale-Hubbell* directory. The results of this comparison are displayed in tables 5 and 6 and figures 11 and 12. (Figures 11 and 12 are found in Appendix C.) In tables 5 and 6 the first three columns after the firm's initials present the 1988 size estimates derived from the respective models. The fourth column displays the actual size of the firm in 1988. Figures 11 and 12 translate into bar graphs the data in tables 5 and 6. The horizontal axis displays the initials corresponding to those of the firms listed in tables 5 and 6. The vertical axis presents the number of lawyers (predicted and actual) working for each firm. For example, on the first page of figure 11 one finds the firm of Dorsey and Whitney represented by the initials DW. Above DW are four bars. The first, second, and third bars depict, respectively, the KLF, EF, and KEF predictions of the firm's 1988 size. The fourth bar represents the actual size of the firm in 1988. As can be seen, the KEF model proves to be the best predictor of Dorsey and Whitney's 1988 size. Moreover, for all of the Group I and Group II firms the kinked exponential model is a better predictor of actual size than either of the other two models in 67 percent (24 of 36) and 63 percent (22 of 35) of the cases, respectively. Together, the kinked exponential (KEF) and the pure exponential (EF) models come closer to the firm's actual 1988 size than the kinked linear (KLF) model in 83 percent (30 of 36) of the Group I and 74 percent (26 of 35) of the Group II comparisons.[11] Thus from these rough predictions it appears that the exponential model yields better forecasts of 1988 size than does the kinked linear model.

We see, then, that both the KLF and KEF models do a reasonable job of describing the same underlying data, while the KEF model is a better predictor of

10. Of course, by "actual" we mean "as published in *Martindale-Hubbell.*" As we discuss in Appendix A, our data are based on their information, which may or may not represent the true "actual" size of the firm at a specified point in time.

11. Interestingly, all three models tend to underestimate the 1988 size of the firm. Of the best estimates of 1988 size, 26 out of 36 cases of the Group I cases and 20 of 35 of the group II cases underestimates the 1988 size. This might indicate that the underlying process is one in which firms grow by an increasing percentage each year, that there has been a new shock to accelerate growth at a slightly different rate, or that 1988 was just one of those years. We find this issue intriguing and intend to pursue it more carefully at some future point.

Table 5 Comparison of 1988 Actual Size and Estimated Size Based on Alternative Growth Models, Group I Firms

	Firm Initials	1988 Estimate			1988 Actual
		KLF Model	EF Model	KEF Model	
Arnold & Porter	AP	194.41	361.41	190.57	233
Baker & Botts	BB	300.26	272.05	325.71	331
Baker & Hostetler	BH	237.16	186.05	348.97	360
Cahill, Gordon & Reindel	CGR	197.25	200.14	199.54	216
Coudert Brothers	CB	219.99	199.94	223.18	272
Dechert, Price & Rhoads	DPR	237.66	342.75	226.11	296
Dewey, Ballantine, Bushley, Palmer & Wood	DB	193.08	204.38	198.54	238
Dorsey & Whitney	DW	250.04	200.14	314.19	306
Dykema, Gossett, Spencer, Goodnow & Trigg	DG	197.05	155.71	271.78	268
Foley & Lardner	FL	241.97	177.51	291.20	292
Fried, Frank, Harris, Shriver & Jacobson	FF	257.10	298.87	318.94	306
Fulbright & Jaworski	FJ	381.69	448.54	374.65	414
Gibson, Dunn & Crutcher	GDC	360.29	254.17	447.20	458
Hinshaw, Culbertson, Moelmann, Hoban & Fuller	HC	147.92	128.51	174.51	236
Hunton & Williams	HW	278.14	169.69	374.28	363
Jones, Day, Reavis & Pogue	JD	410.65	315.77	506.23	736
Kaye, Scholer, Fierman, Hays & Handler	KS	233.50	384.91	213.58	252
Kirkland & Ellis	KE	293.88	262.17	320.86	294
Latham & Watkins	KW	237.82	218.33	303.38	358
LaBoeuf, Lamb, Leiby, & MacRae	LL	214.41	171.06	268.81	339
Mayer, Brown & Platt	MB	271.17	234.63	317.98	365
McDermott, Will & Emery	MW	266.20	295.01	302.48	341
Morgan, Lewis & Bockius	ML	401.28	361.41	470.13	576
Morrison & Foerster	MF	240.99	197.75	353.19	302
O'Melveny & Myers	OM	340.30	287.44	371.67	378
Pepper, Hamilton & Scheetz	PHS	228.85	178.93	267.74	283
Shea & Gould	SG	204.00	280.34	263.49	347
Sidley & Austin	SA	454.83	334.96	614.62	543
Simpson, Thacher, & Bartlett (BOOK)	ST	331.07	325.71	335.63	354
Skadden, Arps, Slate, Meagher & Flom	SAS	370.71	386.84	640.98	472
Squire, Sanders & Dempsey	SS	324.95	255.70	392.68	332
Stroock & Stroock & Lavan	SSL	212.72	233.69	253.92	271
Sullivan & Cromwell (BOOK)	SC	343.73	238.17	426.67	338
Vinson & Elkins	VE	370.56	346.89	420.73	420
Weil, Gotschal & Manges	WG	287.65	252.40	401.42	357
Winston & Strawn	WS	216.46	134.16	259.30	241

Table 6 Comparison of 1988 Actual Size with Estimated Size Based on Alternative Growth Models, Group II Firms

| | Firm Initials | 1988 Estimate | | | 1988 Actual |
		KLF Model	EF Model	KEF Model	
Bond, Schoeneck & King	BSK	100.232	104.8992	102.5141	102
Briggs & Morgan	BM	100.228	112.1683	119.3428	119
Calfee, Halter & Griswold	CHG	106.425	91.37757	129.5413	110
Choate, Hall & Stewart	CHS	114.972	95.10676	120.6628	108
Curtis, Mallet-Prevost, Colt & Mosle	CMCM	103.846	87.35672	111.1633	96
Dilworth, Paxson, Kalish & Kaufman	DPKK	127.414	124.9608	141.5991	126
Edwards & Angell	EA	97.296	68.51139	108.202	123
Fennemore Craig	FC	77.073	47.751	96.06259	95
Foley, Hoag & Eliot	FHE	112.703	139.491	126.2167	119
Fox, Rothschild, O'Brien & Frankel	FROF	85.234	73.33221	91.92748	103
Haight, Brown & Bonesteel	HBB	78.348	90.28759	83.68	125
Hinckley, Allen, Snyder & Comen	HAS	67.955	49.45188	73.1857	111
Ice, Miller, Donadio & Ryan	IMDR	113.978	98.8892	125.4616	122
Jackson & Kelly	JK	81.679	46.20093	99.08717	122
Lane, Powell, Moss & Miller	LP	103.903	69.47729	136.4557	123
Lewis & Roca	LR	86.453	117.0967	83.01323	108
Luce, Forward, Hamilton & Scripps	LFH	95.981	85.54136	115.3533	107
Miller, Nash, Wiener, Hagar & Carlson	MNW	88.645	105.8476	90.64946	110
Mintz, Levin, Cohn. Ferris, Glovsky & Popeo	MLC	88.388	71.8083	105.6361	117
Mitchell, Silberberg & Krupp	MSK	111.137	97.61196	127.8682	106
Palmer & Dodge	PD	103.898	68.64855	124.4619	121
Parker, Chapin & Flattau	PCF	98.922	108.8532	110.2775	111
Patterson, Belknap, Webb & Tyler	PBW	110.113	100.5847	126.0905	125
Patton, Boggs & Blow	PBB	91.387	132.8207	128.8952	90
Phelps, Dunbar, Marks, Claverie & Sims	PDM	102.967	74.81	123.34	122
Pitney, Hardin, Kipp & Szuch	PHK	85.584	55.81262	98.10124	108
Preston, Thorgimson, Ellis & Holman	PT	99.048	43.5104	158.6975	111
Robinson & Cole	RC	88.258	66.88669	102.5141	123
Ross & Hardies	RH	76.72	73.77353	75.48999	92
Shook, Hardy & Bacon	SHB	78.389	76.86111	87.61919	129
Schwabe, Williamson & Wyatt	SWW	82.8766	117.566	130.7125	115
Steel, Hector & Davis	SHD	89.785	56.65612	106.9114	109
Sullivan & Worcester	SW	119.165	107.5547	158.5389	123
Taft, Stettinius & Hollister	TSH	117.592	107.5547	129.2825	141
Webster & Sheffield	WS	97.403	101.0889	112.0561	112
Weinberg & Green	WG	111.034	153.3925	105.9535	104
White & Williams	WW	93.36	80.7211	106.6977	113
Whiteford, Taylor & Preston	WTP	66.089	52.56235	83.68	112
Wyman, Bautzer, Christensen, Kuchek & Silbert	WBC	107.278	142.0246	116.9797	124

1988 size. The distinction between constant absolute levels of growth (linear model) and constant percentage rates of growth (growth model) is more than a technical mathematical issue. This distinction highlights a key difference between competing theories of firm growth. In contrast to those who see law-firm growth in terms of a line with a sudden, one-time change in slope—and, therefore, as fully accounted for by an early 1970 shock—we view the size of firms as the result of continuous growth of an exponential nature. To us, the consequences of constant percentage increases in the number of lawyers associated with the firms at least partially explains the jumps in the size of firms during the 1970s. All agree that firms are much larger today than they were even twenty years ago. But in our view, they did not get that way by a sudden change alone. Law firms have moved steadily toward the gargantuan since the inception of the modern firm around the turn of this century.

Simply seeing some pattern in the existing data is of little value if no credible theory accompanies it. In the next section we offer an explanation of why law firms appear to grow by a constant percentage each year. In our view law firms do not grow exponentially by accident. Instead, structural features inherent to the big law firm fundamentally influence their growth patterns.

Toward a Theory of Exponential Growth

For those who conceive of law-firm growth curves as kinked lines, a theory is needed principally to explain the reason for steady absolute growth until 1970 and the steeper angle of ascent of that growth after 1970.[12] Indeed, if the underlying growth process was linear, then, on average, 85 percent[13] of the growth between 1970 and 1986 would not have occurred but for the 1970 kink. To put it another way, a firm that actually grew from 2 attorneys in 1930, to 65 in 1970, and to 250 by 1986 would have grown to only 90 attorneys by 1986 if the pre-1970 growth rate had continued.[14]

12. The theory would, of course, also have to explain the upward slope of the underlying growth patterns.

13. We obtained the estimate of 85 percent by first using the KLF regression results to project the 1986 size of each firm in Group I, based on the assumption that it had continued to grow after 1970 at the same rate as it had until that year. This number would then represent the estimated size of the firm had there been no kink. Subtracting each firm's 1970 size from this estimate gives us G, the post-1970 estimate of growth without a kink. Dividing G by the actual growth after 1970 gives us an estimate of the percentage of each firm's total growth that is not attributable to the 1970 kink. We then computed the average (15 percent) over all firms in the sample for which there was sufficient data. The balance of firm growth (85 percent) is attributed to the 1970 kink.

14. To arrive at this result we subtracted the hypothetical firm's 1970 size (65) from its 1986 size (250) to arrive at the firm's post-1970 growth (185 attorneys). Our argument is that the KLF model implies that only 15 percent of these attorneys would have been added had there been no kink. Fifteen percent of 185 equals roughly 28; adding these 28 attorneys to the 65 working for the firm in 1970 gives us the approximately 90-person law firm we project in the text.

A theory that seeks to account for kinked exponential law-firm growth, as ours does, must explain not only the "kink" but the underlying nonlinear growth pattern as well. In the kinked exponential model the change in growth rates after 1970 accounts for no more than 50 percent of the growth in recent years.[15] Fully half of the post-1970 growth would remain even if the percentage growth rate had remained unchanged. With an inherently exponential model, the 65-attorney firm that grew to 250 between 1970 and 1986 would have grown to 160 lawyers in 1986 even without the 1970 "kink."

Thus, the rapid growth of the large law firm has two components: one exogenous to the structure of the firm, accounting for the kink in the curves; the other endogenous, explaining the underlying shape of the curves. While we briefly discuss the external changes below, we concentrate most of our attention on the internal pressures for growth. We allocate our discussion in this manner not because we doubt the existence and importance of an external "shock."[16] Instead, we suggest that whatever changes occurred in the early 1970s to make law firms grow faster do not, and probably cannot, entirely explain the growth witnessed either before or after 1970. We argue that one cannot fully understand the growth of the big law firm without recognizing the role of the internal growth imperative created by what we term the "promotion-to-partner tournament." The reader who prefers to take up the reasons for the growth kink before examining the internal growth mechanism, is referred to pages 110–20 below.

Exponential Growth

Our general argument proposes that the big law firms, as presently structured, have a built-in "growth engine" responsible for a significant share of the growth "spurt" witnessed since 1970.[17] In particular, we contend that roughly half of the growth is a by-product of the mechanisms used by law firms to govern the sharing of human capital. In order to maintain their existing organizational structure, these firms *must* grow exponentially; that is, the number of

15. To compute the estimate of 50 percent, we followed the procedure in footnote 13 but substituted for the KLF projections the KEF-based projections of post-1970 size, given the assumption that the firm had continued to grow after 1970 as it had until that year.

16. Indeed, we are engaged with our colleagues Stewart Macaulay and Joel Rogers in an intensive analysis of changes in the use of law by American businesses. See Business Disputing Group 1989; Galanter and Rogers 1988.

17. Alternatively, one might argue that the law-firm growth curves simply mimic the growth in demand for big law firm services. That is, law firms might have grown exponentially because the demand for their services has grown exponentially. This is an intriguing hypothesis but one whose exploration is hampered by a lack of available data. General census data on the demand for big law firm services go back only as far as 1967 and are gathered only at five-year intervals. Thus it is impossible to determine whether the growth in general demand has been exponential. Data on the demand for specific firms' services are almost totally nonexistent.

At first glance the data that do exist give some credence to the hypothesis. From 1967 to 1982 law-firm receipts from businesses rose from roughly $20 billion to just over $166 billion. This

lawyers working for a firm inevitably will increase by a constant (or possibly increasing) percentage.

If a firm's required growth outpaces either the relevant supply of labor or the firm's revenue base, further growth becomes impossible without changes. A firm that does not or cannot grow must restructure—that is, transform itself— or face failure. The transformation we have documented in chapter 4 above reflects precisely these changes. We discuss below the implications of a "gap" between growth in size on the one hand and the availability of new labor and the growth in revenues on the other. We also will address various ways of coping with the revenue shortfall.[18] But first, we want to trace the sources of this gap back to their roots in the firm's growth imperative.

The Underlying Transaction. We begin by attempting to understand the basic transaction that underlies the big firm.[19] The discussion here relies on certain assumptions about human rationality and its social setting, which we attempt to reveal and clarify, at least in the footnotes, as we go along. To understand why attorneys organize their firms as they do, we must explain why they associate in the first place. Attorneys may enter into cooperative associations for various reasons, but we are interested in those combinations based upon an exchange of human capital for labor.

An attorney, like any other producer, combines labor with the capital she has accumulated over time. The lawyer's capital, unlike that for an automobile manufacturer, consists mainly of human assets.[20] Her human capital combines four types of assets. First, she possesses her pre-law-school endowment of intelligence, skills, general education, and the like. Second, she invests in her legal education and experience-dependent skills. She attends law school, per-

---

growth can be viewed as steady (15 percent per year) and as having the characteristics of an exponential function.

But, for several reasons, the rapid growth in receipts hardly provides conclusive proof of an exponential growth in the demand for business legal services. First, the time period over which the sample on receipts is taken is quite short (fifteen years) and the number of observations (four) is quite small. Second, the data on receipts are consistent with both a kinked linear and a kinked exponential function. Third, and perhaps most important, an increase in receipts is indicative only of an increase in revenues, and not necessarily of an increase in demand. Revenues could increase just as easily from a growth in the supply of services, which in turn lowers price and increases purchases. The available evidence suggests that the growth in revenues is probably attributable to both increased demand and increased supply. Clearly demand has increased, but whether that demand has grown exponentially since 1967 is far from clear (Sander and Williams 1989, pp. 444–52). Whether the demand has grown exponentially since 1922 is unknown and virtually unknowable.

18. See below, pages 116–20.

19. Many of our observations about the basic transaction underlying the law firm are equally applicable to other professions as well. Medical practices, investment banking houses, and large accounting firms face many of the same issues and dilemmas.

20. Gilson and Mnookin 1985, p. 324; Palay 1986.

haps goes on to a clerkship, and participates in continuing legal-education programs in order to acquire the basic skills of the profession. She also may acquire significant information and skills from more senior practitioners. Eventually, she acquires the experience-dependent skills that distinguish a practicing attorney from a "kid" just out of law school. These skills include, for example, the knowledge necessary to understand and evaluate a law or regulation, to decide which rules a regulator likely will enforce, or to anticipate where a client most likely will run into trouble. She does not acquire practical knowledge of this nature in a classroom. Acquiring experience-dependent skills requires significant learning-by-doing and the time and resources to do it.

Third, and perhaps more important, an attorney invests in her professional reputation. Through her reputation an attorney disseminates information to clients and other attorneys about her qualifications, skills, temperament, legal philosophy, honesty, and integrity. Reputation also acts as an *ex ante* indicator of the quality of service a client can expect from an attorney. To the extent that an attorney values her reputation, it will act to bond her future conduct. For if she behaves contrary to her reputation, she risks tarnishing or losing it.

Finally, an attorney makes human capital investments in developing relationships with her clients. A lawyer must familiarize herself with the personnel, procedures, history, finances, and goals of the client. She also must develop a cooperative working relationship and degree of trust to enable her to give better service to the client. The process of eliciting client cooperation and trust often consumes significant time and energy. Such attorney-client relationships also help to attract new clients, retain old ones, and perpetuate the lawyer's reputation.

We assume that at least some attorneys will have surplus human capital—that is, more capital assets than they can productively use by themselves.[21] Fittingly, the historian of the Shearman and Sterling firm begins his narrative with the fortuitous first meeting of Thomas Shearman with David Dudley Field:

> Shearman was then twenty-five, and Field fifty-six; Shearman had just been admitted to the bar . . . and had no clients and nothing to do, while Field was a famous lawyer with more clients, and would-be clients, and more of their business, than he wanted or could possibly have handled.[22]

21. We could as easily approach this problem from the opposite perspective, excess labor. We believe it will become apparent why it is preferable to examine the implications of excess human capital.

22. Earle 1963, p. 1. In 1933, Karl Llewellyn neatly stated the complementary roles of seniors and juniors in the big firm: "The young man learns, makes contacts, gets opportunity, hopes for a partnership, and sweats twelve hours a day. . . . The old man, if he has survived the killing apprenticeship, cashes in on his own experience, recorded (the forms in the files!) or trade-secret in his head, on his own good will, and on the young man's labor. He plans. He guides. He worries. He may still slave. He often makes final decisions. He always is responsible. But above all, he is, and

An attorney may find herself with surplus human capital as a result of the constraints on her personal supply of labor, which is ultimately fixed by the working hours in the day. Once she reaches the limits of her labor, she can only increase her output by adding to her capital stock. But eventually, for a fixed quantity of labor, the additional output resulting from another unit of capital will diminish to zero. At this point, she has the potential for "surplus" capital. Her reputation or expertise, for instance, may increase the demand for her services, but she simply does not have the additional hours to accept more work.[23]

The amount of capital available to her is a function of her initial endowment and investment, as well as the nonrival character of her assets. Capital is non-rival if its employment by one user does not prevent other users from simultaneously receiving the identical benefit from the same asset. Highways or the national defense are the examples of nonrival capital most often used in introductory economics courses. A highway, up to the point of congestion, can support multiple users at one time. Where an asset is nonrival then, the opportunity cost of sharing the capital is zero up to the point of congestion. In this sense, attorney human capital is nonrival to a significant extent. Sharing client relationships and reputation with, or transferring experience dependent skills to, another attorney does not diminish the benefit the "owner" or other lawyers can derive from those assets. An attorney's capital, though producing no additional value from her own efforts, still might have productive value if simultaneously lent to someone else. Thus even an attorney who has the optimum amount of capital for her own supply of labor may have "surplus" capital if she also can lend her assets to another attorney to use simultaneously.

We assume an attorney's ability to share at least some, though not necessarily all, of her human capital. The owner of certain assets—innate intelligence, aptitude, intuition, or physical presence—cannot transfer them to others. Unique assets of this nature have no separate market value because they cannot be detached from the original owner. For instance, a renowned trial attorney cannot share her courtroom presence or sixth sense about jurors with her associates. But most attorneys possess a mix of shareable and unshareable assets. For in-

---

he is valued as, a *business-getter*. The measure of him is the business he can summon from the vasty corporation deep. He is to attract more orders for services than he or twenty like him can supply. . . . He cashes in, then, as an enterpriser, putting his own label on the work of others" (Llewellyn 1933, p. 177).

23. Of course, if the client's demand for the attorney's work product is perfectly inelastic, the attorney could simply raise her price because no matter what the price the client would demand the same level of services. We assume that competition (before specific client relationships develop) and potential competition (even after specific client relationships develop) prevent attorneys from raising their rates above the prevailing market price. A lawyer who does otherwise risks losing the client in the short run and gives other lawyers the long-run opportunity and incentives to develop the client relationships necessary to exert competitive pressure.

stance, while our trial attorney cannot lend her courtroom presence, she still can share her experience-dependent skills, such as knowledge of how to pick a jury or take a deposition. Similarly, while an attorney specializing in takeover defenses can lend to others her approach and past experience in fending off hostile takeovers, she cannot lend her unique intellect and problem-solving skills.

All attorneys have some human capital. Some have more than they productively can combine with their own labor to produce additional income. We refer to these attorneys as having surplus human capital. When an attorney can share her human capital, she can increase her income by lending these assets to other attorneys. On the other hand, attorneys with no surplus human capital are either self-supporting or net borrowers. Net borrowers of human capital typically obtain access to sufficient capital by selling their labor to those who have a surplus.

Imagine, for instance, a sole practitioner, P, who has shareable surplus human capital. She would like to lend or rent these assets to A, an attorney with little human capital of his own, but a full complement of labor. For convenience, one can think of P as a "partner" and A as an "associate." P might contract with A to produce an output, using his labor and her capital, which one of them then would sell to a client. If A resells the product, typically he would pay P a "rent" equal, in theory, to the marginal product of the capital,[24] keeping the remainder for himself both as a "wage" and as a return on his own assets. If P markets the product to the client, as is typically the case, she would pay A the marginal product of his labor and capital (as a wage and as a return on his human capital investments, if any), retaining the remainder—minus overhead and other support costs—as compensation for her capital.[25]

"Contracting" with anyone, even an attorney, while conceptually straightforward, often presents difficulties in practice. Assume for convenience that P, the lawyer with surplus capital, retains control over the output. The contract may require enforcement, monitoring, or adaptation as conditions change. We refer to the institutional arrangement for conducting these activities as a governance mechanism. We can imagine two extreme possibilities. On the one hand, P could depend entirely upon markets. She could remain a sole practitioner, rent her capital to A, and agree to purchase his output for a price or to forward it to the client, who in turn will compensate A. Markets and their prices then

---

24. The marginal product of capital refers to the unit of output produced by the last unit of capital.

25. As with the compensation of any component of labor, the ability to pay A his marginal product is independent of how the services are sold to the client. In particular, it is unrelated to hourly billing. The price charged for the output can be determined in any number of ways including a flat fee for the service, an hourly rate, or a percentage of the value of the underlying deal. While the common practice over the last thirty years has been to charge by the hour, this has not always been so, and there is evidence that hourly billing is once again falling into disfavor for certain types of transactions (telephone interview with Mary Ann Altman of Altman & Weil, Inc. August 7, 1989). Altman & Weil is a long-established firm in law-firm consulting.

would regulate P's behavior.[26] On the other hand, P could organize the sharing of her capital as a firm. She could hire A, the lawyer with extra labor, combine his labor with her assets, sell the additional output to her client, pay a wage to A derived from the proceeds of this sale, and retain the remainder as compensation for her capital. In fact, attorneys tend to use internal organization—the firm—to govern the sharing of their human capital. We discuss why attorneys organize into firms in the next section.

Organizing the Sharing of Human Capital: Why (Law) Firms? So far we have argued that an attorney might want to enter into an association with another lawyer to share human capital. We have said nothing about why this association ultimately must result in the creation of a big law firm. We approach this question by comparing the transaction costs of producing legal services in a firm with those incurred in producing the same services through markets.

In a world without transaction costs, there is no a priori reason a law firm—large or otherwise—must result from contracting among attorneys. Any form of coordination—a big law firm, an association of smaller practices, or a network of individual practitioners tied together by spot contracts—would yield an identical result. The attorneys would agree to maximize joint product and to divide the revenues in proportion to their marginal contribution to its production.[27]

We interact, however, in an economy replete with transaction costs. Transaction costs refer quite literally to the "costs of running the economic system,"[28] including such tasks as gathering information, monitoring performance, negotiating and communicating agreements, and protecting against opportunistic behavior. These costs are "the economic equivalent of the friction in physical systems"[29] and they reflect the human[30] and environmental[31] conditions that

26. Obviously, we could complicate the model yet further by adding a third-party arbitrator—e.g., courts—to the market governance scheme.

27. We adopt the convention of describing this maximizing in terms of monetary gain, but "more" can be more of anything.

28. Arrow 1969, p. 48.

29. Williamson 1985, p. 19.

30. First, human decision-makers are only limitedly rational. People act purposively and whatever goals they seek they generally prefer more attainment to less. However, they have only a restricted capacity for gathering, evaluating, and storing information. They cannot see the future and they have only limited problem-solving capabilities. In short, they possess what Professor Herbert Simon terms "bounded rationality" (Simon 1957, p. 199; 1976, pp. 38–41, 80–81, 240–44).

Second, human decision-makers can and do act opportunistically. On the one hand, they attempt to exploit the advantages that they may attain from the making of "false or empty, that is, self-disbelieved threats and promises" concerning future conduct (Goffman 1969, p. 105). On the other hand, they distort or selectively disclose information (Williamson 1975, p. 32).

31. Because of the uncertainty and complexity of the environment in which these actors interact, they effectively reach the limits of their capacity to receive, interpret, and use information.

In addition, the world of contract often is populated by only a small number of potential buyers

make contracting (potentially) costly. Parties to complex, long-term contracts, like those necessary to lend human capital, face a variety of impediments to smooth exchanges. The parties must create a governance structure to monitor behavior, to adapt the agreement to changed circumstances, and to ensure that the parties actually perform agreed-upon exchanges.

Our argument reduces to this: in a world with transaction costs attorneys attempting to lend shareable human capital will require internal organization—that is, a firm—in order successfully to govern the transaction. Understanding why lenders will organize this way requires a careful examination of those elements of the sharing arrangement that give rise to transaction costs.

To begin with, long-term agreements render the parties vulnerable to the opportunistic conduct of their trading opposites. P, as the lender of human capital, has three[32] potential concerns.[33] First, A might "grab" assets she lends to P. For instance, A might depart with a client in tow. Second, the prospect of A's prematurely "leaving," or at least threatening to leave, with firm-specific skills and information for which P has paid, but not amortize fully, may trouble P. While the investments are generally worthless to A if he leaves, P's inability to recover the unamortized portion of her investments makes her vulnerable to his departure. Third, A might "shirk," that is, either fail to make the expected (and already paid-for) human capital investments that A must make to further P's future interests or that he will fail to employ borrowed assets to their full potential, thereby depriving P of her expected returns.

A's opportunistic conduct alone, however, will not impede efficient contracting. The existence—before and after contracting—of a large number of substitute sources of supply and demand will render problems of this sort negligible. Where these conditions prevail markets generally will act as adequate safeguards for the parties' investments.[34] Unfortunately markets most likely will not govern effectively the underlying transaction that concerns us. Where

---

and sellers. Where the participants are few, either markets cannot be relied upon to work correctly or situations akin to monopolistic competition develop. Of special interest to transaction-cost economists are those circumstances in which a large number of buyers and sellers exists at the outset but is reduced substantially once initial bargains are set. In this process, a situation that initially appears to have the requisite buyers and sellers for a well-functioning market devolves into some form of monopolistic or "small numbers" bargaining environment (Williamson 1975, pp. 22–23).

32. Gilson and Mnookin (1985, pp. 330–39) distinguish three distinct types of opportunistic conduct. We have found their distinctions quite useful and have retained them. We want to make clear, though, that to us "grabbing" includes not only extortion—as could be implied from their description—but also encompasses walking off with human capital in general and clients in particular, without providing adequate renumeration.

33. We discuss A's concerns below, pp. 96–97.

34. If markets were available, an attorney unhappy with the performance of an associate could simply replace him with a more adequate substitute, just as another damaged asset would easily be replaced from off-the-shelf alternatives.

assets are either transaction-specific or unique, substitutes will not readily exist.[35] Markets require a large number of readily available substitutes to perform their governance function. Asset specificity makes it difficult to find those substitutes without cost. Hence, markets will not suffice to protect contracting attorneys from opportunistic conduct.

Much of the human capital lent by P is specialized, which makes sharing it with others risky. For instance, transferring experience-dependent skills (typically along with other advanced skills) to A requires P to make significant transaction-specific investments. To the extent that the transferred skills relate directly to P's unique knowledge or relationships, she cannot find comparably trained associates in the open market. Once P undertakes to train A, the associate will become costly to replicate. To fire and replace A entails a willingness on P's part to sacrifice, and then reproduce, her investments in him.

P also makes transaction-specific investments in client relationships. P does not make these investments to further directly the sharing arrangement between herself and A. Instead, the investments are unique to the transaction that exists between P and her clients. For instance, P may have spent many years developing a relationship of reliance and trust with the top managers of a client corporation. However, when P "lends" this asset to A and permits him to do some of the client's work, she places these past investments at substantial risk. A, in a sense, now (at least partially) controls an asset specific to P's relationship with her client. Even though A did not make the initial investments to develop the asset, he has as much opportunity as P to destroy it. A might produce inferior work, breach the client's confidence, or cause P to lose a case. Such behavior might result in the deterioration of the trust and reliance that the client has placed in P. Alternatively, A may gain the client's trust and then demand more money from P by threatening or attempting to leave with the client in tow. P's simply ending the association with A will prove an idle threat if A really can leave with the client. Threats of termination do not penalize a person who wants to leave, especially if he can take some of your capital with him. If in fact A takes the client, then P will not realize a return on either her past investments in the client or her recent investment in A.

P's investments in her reputation are similarly unique. Once created, P encounters great difficulty in changing, replicating, or replacing her reputation. As with investments in client relationships, P places her general reputation at substantial risk when she lends it to another attorney. A might, under P's auspices, provide services of unsatisfactory quality. Alternatively, A might damage irreparably P's reputation for honesty by improperly disclosing confidential information while under her supervision.

---

35. A transaction-specific asset is one whose value is significantly reduced outside of the immediate transaction.

Any delay in the return on transaction-specific investments increases the asset's vulnerability. P might not expect a return from either the client relationship or the capital lent to A until well after making the investment. Where the payback comes long after the investment, P risks losing significant out-of-pocket expenditures.

Moreover, the extent to which transaction-specific assets are nonrival makes their protection all the more important. That is, taking advantage of the nonrival aspects of surplus human capital results in interdependencies that create substantial risks for the lender. Possessing a nonrival asset allows the owner to earn multiple returns on her investment by simultaneously lending the same asset to more than one borrower. But such concurrent uses create a system of interdependencies that makes the entire value of the asset dependent upon the actions of all who use it. Opportunistic behavior by any one participant can destroy not only his marginal contribution but, potentially, the entire asset. The threat of opportunistic conduct prevents the lending attorney from relying upon the borrower's promise to act honestly during execution or renegotiation of the agreement.

The mere fact that human capital is nonrival does not create the threat of opportunistic behavior, but it potentially multiplies the effect one actor can have. As P lends her capital to more participants, she increases its value and her return, but she also increases the risk that one of the other attorneys will grab it or destroy it completely.

Thus, in order to take advantage of her nonrival assets, P requires an effective method of monitoring the performance and behavior of other lawyers. Markets will prove ineffectual in the governance role because the underlying assets are unique; hence, parties seeking to lend human capital will search for alternative governance mechanisms to regulate their exchanges.

A, too, has concerns about potential opportunistic conduct. He needs assurance that P will fairly compensate him for his labor and for any human capital he brings to or develops on P's behalf. Where part of A's compensation involves a possibility of promotion to an ownership interest in P's business, A also seeks assurance that, if he meets implicit conditions, P actually will promote him. In theory, P should be able to devise a contract specifying that A will receive rewards based on his productivity. For the contract to be effective, however, both parties must be able to obtain inexpensive and reliable indicators of A's effort or output or, at a minimum, both parties must have identical information about A's productivity. Otherwise, both parties cannot verify compliance with the contract terms. But monitoring output in the provision of legal services to clients is difficult and costly. While P can measure the number of hours A puts in, she has a more difficult time assessing how many "quality" hours A has worked. Ultimately, the assessment of A's output comes down to a subjective evaluation of performance by those charged with observing him. Because of the inherent subjectivity of the assessment, A cannot costlessly verify it. He cannot, for instance, go and look up his performance and say "Hey, you miscalculated my contribution." In addition, neither P nor A can easily separate one individual's contribution to the production of legal services from that of other participants. This problem especially arises where P, the supervisor, is one of the contributors (as she generally is) and therefore has an incentive to understate A's contribution.[36] Thus, no monitoring system can assure the honest reporting of A's contribution—an assurance essential to accurate compensation under an output-based or piece-rate compensation scheme—because A cannot independently verify (prove) his precise contribution.

When monitoring is costly or information is asymmetric, A has the opportunity to produce less-than-promised effort or output because detection is unlikely. P has the opportunity to reduce her compensation costs by purposely undervaluing A's effort. A cannot independently verify whether P has evaluated him correctly, but he recognizes P's incentive to cheat. Consequently, he will hesitate to produce a maximum effort for fear that P will not reward him accurately. Under these circumstances, P most likely will not extract more than minimal effort from A.

The realization that many of the human capital investments he has made are specific to P's business compounds A's concerns. Where he has found a client for P or has developed a detailed understanding of the business of one of P's clients, A's assets are of less value outside his present employment relationship. Even if P agrees to pay for the assets, the limited alternatives to which A can put his assets leave him concerned that once he has made these investments, P will renege on the agreement. Thus P has significant bargaining advantages in establishing the value of and the return on these assets. A's inability to use the assets elsewhere confers on an opportunistic P the ability to confiscate almost the entire return on A's new capital. Similarly, P's firm might refuse to promote an otherwise qualified A, who has developed large amounts of human capital specific to P's business, because so long as P pays A *something* for his capital, he has no better alternative than to employ these assets for P.

Professor Oliver Williamson contends that parties with significant investments in firm-specific or nonredeployable assets will attempt to govern their exchanges with "specialized," transaction-specific mechanisms.[37] He reasons that the more specialized the investment, the lower its value in its next best use. Consequently, even if a large number of potential buyers and sellers exist at the outset, first-mover advantages will greatly reduce competition once initial contracts are awarded. This reduction in alternative uses can raise problems during the performance or renegotiation stages by heightening the risk of opportunistic

36. Malcomson 1984, pp. 486–507; Holmstrom and Tirole 1989, pp. 111–15.
37. Williamson 1985, p. 75.

behavior. Both sides, therefore, make increased expenditures *ex ante* to protect themselves against the possibility that the other party will attempt to exploit its *ex post* bargaining advantage. These expenditures take the form of governance mechanisms that are bilateral and unique to the parties.[38] The firm in general, and the law firm in particular, is one such specialized governance structure. Conversely, as investments become more standardized, the parties have less incentive to make extra expenditures on governance because by definition they have alternative sources of sale or supply. Consequently, the parties more willingly use generally applicable governance mechanisms like courts or markets.[39]

Excludability problems reinforce P's choice of a firm to govern her transaction with A. So long as P does not share her human capital with others, she has a simple mechanism for assuring that others do not unwarrantably use her human capital. She simply announces for all to hear that no one may claim the use of her human capital. Once she allows others to employ her human capital, however, she faces two problems. First, other attorneys may claim falsely to have access to her human capital. Second, because the opportunity-cost of sharing her capital is zero, A's possible attempt to relend P's capital to other attorneys, without paying her the appropriate return, will cause P concern. branding provides a reasonably inexpensive method of letting the world know who has the right to use her capital. But rather than burning her initials into A's forehead, P simply makes him part of an organization. She then must communicate to the world that those who cannot prove membership in her firm have no access to her capital. In this context, P simplifies communication by using the convention that lawyers are not affiliated unless they demonstrate that they are—by letterhead or office location, for example. P's potential clients will not use an attorney who cannot prove his affiliation with P because of uncertainty as to whether they are getting legitimate or counterfeit goods.

Organizing the Sharing of Human Capital: Why Large (Law) Firms?

To this point we simply have adapted the transaction-cost-asset-specificity argument to the problem of sharing human capital. This argument explains, in part, the *existence* of law firms, but not their size. We argue that the rapid growth we currently observe relates directly to the specific governance structure used by law firms to protect shared human assets from opportunistic conduct. Throughout this section we assume that revenue or labor-supply constraints will not hinder a firm's growth. Clearly this assumption is unrealistic, but we make it here for expositional convenience and then relax it below, in the last section of the chapter (pp. 116–20).

---

38. Williamson 1989, pp. 72–78.
39. Williamson 1979, pp. 239–41, 250–53.

We posited above an attorney P with lots of surplus human capital to share. Now that she has started a law firm to serve as a governance mechanism for the sharing of her human capital, she confronts two competing incentives. On the one hand, she has an incentive to hire as much labor as possible to use her capital.[40] So long as the marginal demand for her output supports the marginal cost of the hired labor (one of P's variable costs), P can make money by hiring additional units of labor to use her capital. On the other hand, she has a strong incentive to monitor carefully any attorney she hires. Each additional unit of labor increases the probability that someone opportunistically or inadvertently will destroy or remove P's stock of capital. Thus either she must closely monitor the actions of her associates or eventually accept ruin. We argue that the mechanism chosen in most firms to monitor performance (and to reconcile conflicting incentives) has lead *inevitably* to a pattern of exponential growth. We analyze the problem in two stages. First we discuss why firms grow and then we explain why they tend to grow exponentially.

Why Firms Grow. Law firms, like many professional firms, employ a complex monitoring scheme to protect themselves from opportunistic associates.[41] At least initially, partners carefully watch over associates, amending and supplementing their work as needed. During this period, partners closely evaluate the work-product and behavior of their newly hired associates and act as quality-control supervisors. But the law-firm monitoring scheme goes beyond mere supervision and includes significant structural components.

First, to assure the partners that they will receive the proper return on the investments they make—whether those investments are in client relationships, reputation, or the skills they impart to associates—the firm must induce associates not to grab or leave prematurely. The partner worries that the associate might walk off with the firm's clients or, often more realistically, depart with skills—or clients of his own—that the firm has paid the associate to develop. The partners want to ensure that the associate has an incentive to remain with the firm until it fully amortizes those investments. Deferring payment of some percentage of the associate's salary creates part of that incentive.[42] The firm fires those associates who act opportunistically thereby preventing them from

40. We assume that the marginal product of capital does not decrease very quickly as P adds additional units of similarly skilled labor. Either a large reservoir of human capital or its nonrival nature would validate this assumption.

41. Large accounting firms, physician groups, investment banks, and consulting firms often include some form of deferred compensation in their compensation package. Regardless of its specific form, the firm will pay the deferred compensation only if the prospective recipient meets certain performance criteria. Both physician groups and accounting firms use promotion to partnership as a potential bonus for correct behavior. Investment banks combine potential promotion with sizable year-end bonuses.

42. Gilson and Mnookin 1989, p. 573.

receiving this deferred income. Those who do not grab or leave prematurely receive the deferred salary in varying forms of promotion and bonuses.

While deferred compensation partially alleviates problems related to grabbing and leaving, partners still must find some method of motivating associates not to shirk. The firm cannot use simple productivity-based compensation schemes because associates cannot verify the partners' observation of associate productivity. Therefore, the firm cannot assure the associates that a maximum effort will receive a maximum reward.[43]

To provide both the necessary assurances and incentives for maximum effort the big law firm typically ties the payment of its deferred bonus to the outcome of what we call the "promotion-to-partner tournament."[44] The rules are simple. For a fixed period of time (six to ten years) the law firm pays a salary to associates who neither grab nor leave. At each successive stage in the hierarchy, part of the associate's salary increase includes a deferred bonus for nonopportunistic behavior in the earlier years. In addition, during this period the firm implicitly tells its associates that it constantly evaluates them for a "super-bonus," consisting of promotion to partner. In effect the firm holds a tournament in which all the associates in a particular "entering class" compete and the firm awards the prize of partnership to the top α percent of the contestants.[45] The firm evaluates associates on their production of two goods: high-quality legal work and their own human capital. An associate's final standing in the tournament, measured subjectively, not mechanistically, will depend upon the size and quality of the "bundle" of both goods. In most instances a winner essentially must accumulate significant amounts of both high-quality legal work and human capital, though of course amassing extremely high levels of one or the other might prove sufficient. After a specified period of time, the firm ranks the players in a particular class, and declares the top α percent "winners." Though it has been the typical practice, there is no intrinsic reason that the firms must fire the losers. So long as losers receive total compensation substantially less than winners, the incentive effects of the tournament will remain.[46] Thus,

43. See above, pp. 96–97.

44. There is an interesting economics literature on tournaments and contests. The seminal work was done by Lazear and Rosen (1981). Interesting variations and extensions are developed by Nalebuff and Stiglitz (1984); O'Keeffe, Viscusi, and Zeckhauser (1984); Malcomson (1984); and Rosen (1986). Dye (1984) identifies several difficulties with using tournaments. The articles developed out of the labor economics literature, but have wider application to questions of structure and hierarchy in firms, and competitive relations between firms.

45. The economics of a general contest in which a firm announces at the outset that a fixed percentage of contestants will be winners is described by Malcomson (1984).

46. Gilson & Mnookin (1989, pp. 578–81) take the argument one step further. They assert that the firm must fire all those it does not promote, to allay associates' concerns that at the time of the promotion decision the firm might act opportunistically by refusing to promote even qualified associates. This assures the associate that the firm will not attempt to retain the associate's firm-specific

the firm either may tell the losers that they can remain as associates, but will never become partners, or it may fire them and give them a consolation prize (such as help finding another job or severance pay) or give them nothing.

The tournament provides the assurances and incentives required by both the associates and the partners. Associates now have an incentive to produce the maximum combination of legal work and human capital. By declaring in advance that, on average, it will promote a fixed percentage of the associates after a period of time, the firm has obligated itself to distribute a fixed amount of compensation to the winners of the tournament. Regardless of who wins the tournament the firm must pay out the same prizes. This point is essential to the firm's compensation scheme because it communicates to associates that it is in the firm's own interest to award the prize of partnership to those who have produced the largest combined bundle of output, quality, and capital. To award the prize on other grounds would saddle the firm with less productive attorneys at no savings in prize money.[47] Moreover, the associate easily can verify that the firm pays out the agreed-to prizes by observing how the present and preceding classes fare and whether the firm continues to recruit new classes of associates.

---

human capital investments without paying for them. We find their argument to be thoughtful and interesting but are uncertain as to its applicability to all firms that employ the up-or-out promotion system. First, as we noted above in Chapter 3 the up-or-out promotion system has been more a paradigm than a hard-and-fast rule. Its administration, except for a period during the 1960s and 1970s, has not prevented firms from having a cadre of well-paid permanent associates. We also suspect a visibly kept promise to promote a certain percentage of associates each year provides enough observable information to associates for them to know that partners have not acted opportunistically.

We suspect that the up-or-out system developed on the one hand from a desire to economize on monitoring costs. If the firm cannot promote the associate, then the prospect of advancement cannot be used further to discipline opportunistic conduct. Thus, protecting the partners' investments from this associate will take more monitoring resources than protecting them from one who has a real prospect of an ownership interest. Consequently, once the prospect for promoting an associate no longer exists, the firm likely will release him. Permanent associates, then, are more than associates who were unable to develop sufficient human capital for promotion; they are ones who are particularly trustworthy and predictable.

On the other hand, firing associates who had been passed over, in some sense contributed to the overall morale of the firm. The classic large law firm combined two often conflicting ideologies—meritocratic screening and fraternal equality. All attorneys were considered peers or potential peers. But once an associate was passed over for partner, he could never become a peer and the sense of institutional fraternity would be destroyed. The up-or-out promotion system allowed the firm—at a cost—to maintain the dual ideologies of meritocracy and equality.

The breakdown of the up-or-out system might stem from several sources. First, firms have faced in recent years a seller's market for elite law-school graduates. They simply cannot find enough good associates. Second, as firms become "taller" organizations with more hierarchic distinctions, the breach in the peer ethos resulting from the retention of unpromotable associates is relatively less.

47. Malcomson 1984.

If the firm intends to continue recruiting new associates, current associates may safely assume that the firm will continue to adhere to the implicit contract rather than risk the adverse reputational and motivational effects associated with breaching.[48] By promoting some but not all of the associates the firm communicates to them that it will reward productivity but not shirking; therefore, the associate will exert a maximum effort to win the contest.

Firms can conduct the tournament in various ways, so long as in the end they promote a fixed percentage of associates and they offer a total compensation package competitive in the market for associates.[49] Some firms may eliminate associates at given intervals (say, yearly); others may make decisions more randomly; while still others, at least in theory, might wait until the end of the tournament to notify the losers. The precise rules are dependent upon the incentives the firm wants to maintain, the structure of its compensation package, and firm culture. But by eliminating some associates early on, the firm improves the chances for partnership of the surviving associates, thereby increasing, for a given money wage, the expected value of the survivors' total compensation.

The promotion-to-partner tournament, originally instituted as a mutual monitoring device, contains an internal dynamic that explains why firms must grow. Growth occurs because, at the end of the tournament, the firm must replace not only the losing associates who depart, but also all those who win and are promoted. If the firm did not hire associates to replace its newly promoted partners, then the pretournament partners would share their surplus human capital with fewer associates and, therefore, make less money. To maintain at least a constant ratio of pretournament associates to pretournament partners, the firm must hire new associates to take the place of those who won the tournament. By replacing promoted attorneys the firm grows by the number of promotions. If the firm fires the losers, then it must also replace them, but their replacement has the effect of maintaining firm size, not increasing it. Allowing losing attorneys to remain as permanent associates also contributes to size maintenance, not growth.

Why Firms Grow Exponentially. The last section provides one reason why firms hire associates and why these firms grow. Our argument goes further and asserts that a by-product of the promotion-to-partner tournament is that the firm

48. Gilson and Mnookin (1989, p. 580 n. 38) attribute to Professor Steven Shavell a similar observation about the importance of reputation and the ability of associates to verify firm promises by witnessing the firm's behavior towards others.

49. The expected value of an associate's compensation depends upon his money wage, his chance of becoming a partner, and, if offered, the value of a partnership share. In general, the lower the overall chance of becoming a partner, the higher must be the associate's money wage or the rewards of becoming a partner.

very likely will grow by more than the number of newly promoted partners. The tournament, with its fixed promotion percentage, not only provides incentives for associates to work hard, but also usually guarantees that the firm will grow at least exponentially. From one year to the next the firm's growth rate will depend upon the ratio of associates to partners in the base year, the percentage of associates promoted, and the number of associates that it must hire the next year to replace the newly promoted partners *and* to meet the next period's associate-to-partner ratio.[50] If the promotion percentage remains constant over time, the firm will grow at an exponential rate (constant percentage growth rate) if the associate-to-partner ratio remains constant. If the associate-partner ratio rises, the percentage growth rate will increase.

Thus our claim that firms will tend to grow (at least) exponentially depends upon our argument that each firm's promotion percentage remains reasonably constant and the ratio of associates to partners either remains constant or increases. Empirically, there is evidence supporting both propositions. From our sample of 100 of the largest firms we calculated both an indicator of the direction of the firm's promotion rate over time and the firm's associate-partner ratio.

We are careful here to state that our calculations are an indicator, not a measure, of stable promotion rates. Our tournament story is one in which the firm promotes a constant percentage of each class to partner at the end of a fixed period of time. However, to be precise, we can only calculate from our data the net increase in the size of the partnership as a percentage of all associates at the firm in a given year. But our calculation accurately indicates the stability of promotion rates per class so long as (1) on average the percentage of all new partners who began at the firm as associates remains reasonably stable and (2) the relative distribution of partnership promotions over all associate classes remains reasonably fixed. In essence, we assume that each year the percentage of

---

50. Algebraically, in year t the firm's size will be $A_t + P_t$ and in year $t + 1$ it will be $A_{t+1} + P_{t+1}$. If the firm hires no lateral partners and has a net (of retirement) promotion rate of α, then its size in $t + 1$ can be written as $A_{t+1} + (P_t + \alpha A_t)$. Furthermore, if τ represents the firm's yearly percentage growth rate then

$$(1 + \tau)(A_t + P_t) = A_{t+1} + (P_t + \alpha A_t) \tag{1}$$

If we define the associate-to-partner ratio as $n_t = A_t/P_t$ then with enough manipulation, (1) can be rewritten as

$$\tau = [\alpha n_t (n_{t+1} + 1) + n_{t+1} - n_t]/(n_t + 1) \tag{1'}$$

which indicates that the firm's growth rate is a function of its net promotion rate and its associate-to-partner ratio. The net promotion rate implicitly incorporates partnership attrition, but a yet more sophisticated version of the model could easily factor in explicitly the firm's partnership attrition rate or such practices as the lateral hiring of partners and the lateral hiring of associates.

all promotions from each class remains stable, with the most senior classes having the largest percentage and the least senior classes the smallest percentage (usually zero). We have found no evidence to contradict this assumption.

When we look at each firm's associate promotion rate we observe no obvious upward or downward trend for 44 of 49 (90 percent) of the Group I firms and for 42 of 49 (86 percent) of the Group II firms.[51] We also compared the average promotion rates of the Group I and Group II firms during the four decades since 1950. For Group I the rate rose from 5.34 percent (1950–59) to 5.44 percent (1960–69), to 5.71 percent (1970–79), to 5.85 percent (1980–86). Despite the apparent upward trend, no statistically significant difference exists between the mean promotion rate of the 1950s and that of the 1980s. For Group II the rates were 5.55 percent (1950–59), 7.98 percent (1960–69), 7.89 percent (1970–79), and 8.19 percent (1980–86). Certainly a significant increase in the promotion rate occurs here after the 1950s. No statistically significant difference exists, however, between the average rates of the 1960s, 1970s, and 1980s. Finally, we compared the average promotion rates of firms during the golden age, 1956–65, to the firms during the transformation, 1976–85. For Group I firms the rates were 4.99 percent and 5.5 percent, while for Group II firms the rates were 7.15 percent and 7.92 percent. For both sets of firms no statistically significant difference exists between the two means.[52] Similarly, the associate-partner ratios for the Group I firm ratios increased or showed no trend for 37 (76 percent) of the 50 firms. For Group II firms the ratio either remained constant or demonstrated no trend for 38 (78 percent) of 49 firms.

One widely shared assumption is that recently more partners than in the past have joined firms laterally, becoming partners without first playing in the firm's promotion tournament. Assuming that attrition rates have remained constant, then the stability of our estimates would mean that a smaller percentage of the firm's entering associates are becoming partners.[53] We want to make clear, though, that the perception of a decline in the promotion rates of the entering

---

51. To reach this conclusion we regressed promotion rates for each firm on time and examined the sign of the coefficient (Galanter and Palay 1990b, tables I and II).

52. Somewhat more formally, the conclusions to this point can be stated as follows. First, for Group I firms we cannot reject the null hypothesis that the mean promotion rate for the 1950s is equal to that of the 1980s (t = .6265). Second, for Group II firms we cannot reject the null hypothesis that the mean promotion rate for the 1960s is equal to that of the 1980s (t = .1478). Third, for Group I firms we cannot reject the null hypothesis that the mean promotion rate for the golden age is equal to that of the transformation period (t = .6863). Fourth, for Group II firms we cannot reject the null hypothesis that the mean promotion rate for the golden age is equal to that of the transformation period (t = .6446) (Galanter and Palay 1990b, tables III, IV, V, and VI). For each of the four comparisons, a value of t less than 1.29 means that it is reasonable to infer that there is only a negligible probability of a statistically significant difference between the means.

53. Adams 1989, p. 6.

class need not be inconsistent with the story we tell. Recall that our complete story is one in which firms grow exponentially for a considerable period, then something shocks the system to make them grow at a different rate, but that new percentage growth-rate remains stable for a considerable period of time. We have focused our discussion on why the law firm's tournament produces this stability. But we acknowledge that periodically something might shock the entire industry so as to permit one-time changes in promotion (or growth rates). So long as there is a return to stable growth at these new rates our story is consistent with the known facts. Promotion rates will be stable, but kinked, and the pattern of firm growth will be exponential, but kinked. Exactly how the changed promotion rate will impact on the kinked growth rates depends on the changes in a number of additional variables as well, including changes in promotion rates, associate-to-partner ratios, attrition rates, and the length of the tournament.

Why should the promotion percentage remain constant and the associate-per-partner ratio show no trend or increase? The number of associates per partner that a firm can hire depends upon two factors: the monitoring resources of the firm and the amount of human capital each partner in the firm possesses. Because risk increases with the number of users sharing the assets in question, the ability to monitor places real limits on the number of associates to whom a partner can lend capital. But for any given level of monitoring, a firm can hire more associates per partner the more human capital each partner has. Put succinctly, the bigger each partner's reputation, the more secure and broader her client relations, and the more valuable are her experience-dependent skills, the more associates she can sustain. In addition, the more human capital the firm has, the more resources per partner the firm can afford to spend on monitoring associates and, again, the more associates it can hire. Thus whether a firm can increase the number of associates per partner from one period to the next depends upon whether the human capital per partner has increased. Conversely, the firm must reduce the associate-partner ratio if capital per partner declines.

For most large firms, and in fact for any firm with substantial recruiting experience, choosing the promotion percentage effectively chooses the firm's future level of capital per partner. As a firm gains sophistication and knowledge about the quality of the associates it recruits, especially as the number of recruits becomes large, the firm will predict more accurately the quality of the winners of its tournament. While the firm might not know the ultimate winners' identities, the firm will know what it will take—in terms of current output and future human capital—to win. For a given level of overall associate quality, a lower promotion percentage at a specified firm (that is, tougher selection criteria) will increase the average productivity and average human capital of the winners of the firm's tournament; a higher promotion percentage (less-demanding selection criteria) will have the opposite effect. In setting the promotion percentage, the firm essentially establishes the amount of human capital it will require new partners to bring to the firm. The amount of human capital the new partners bring to the firm, in turn, influences both the amount of human capital per partner and, consequently, the associate-to-partner ratio in the post-tournament period. If the firm sets the promotion percentage too high, the firm's average capital per partner will decrease, and the firm's associate-to-partner ratio will fall. If the firm sets the promotion percentage low enough, average capital per partner actually might increase, thereby allowing the firm to hire marginally more associates per partner.

The associate-to-partner ratio tends to remain constant or to increase because firms generally establish a promotion percentage that will leave it with partners who have at least as much human capital as the average of the existing partners. To do otherwise would not be in the interest of the existing partners. First, existing partners have an incentive to deny promotion to attorneys with less human capital than the average of the existing partners. This incentive derives from a concern (eminating from envy, greed, or ideology) that less-endowed partners would attempt to "tax" the wealthier existing partners. Second, and probably more important, firms rarely can compensate partners solely on the basis of their individual contribution. The costs of measuring productivity makes it prohibitively costly to do so,[54] and the benefits of risk-sharing make it undesirable.[55] Consequently, the firm bases at least some percentage, and often a significant percentage, of a partner's income on the average productivity of the firm. A firm that promotes associates with less capital than the average partner will lower the firm's future average productivity. This in turn likely will lead to lower profits per partner. Thus, because firms will hesitate to allow associates with less human capital than the average partner to win the tournaments, the average amount of capital per partner tends not to decline over time. Because the associate-to-partner ratio is a function of the capital-to-partner ratio, if the latter remains constant or increases, the former tends to follow suit.

The promotion percentage—whether set to raise average firm productivity or, as a lower bound, to keep it constant—tends to remain generally constant, for once established, the firm will find the promotion percentage costly to change. The integrity of the firm's compensation package depends upon the associate's ability to observe the promotion percentage. By its actions toward preceding classes, the firm implicitly tells the associates what percentage can expect to win promotion. Each year, the associates can observe who actually wins and determine whether this corresponds to the promotion percentages they have come to expect. If associates see the promotion percentage decline, they

54. Gilson and Mnookin 1985, pp. 346–52.
55. Gilson and Mnookin 1985, pp. 321–29.

likely will not develop strong expectations about its ultimate level as their tournament draws to a close. Moreover, a firm that (implicitly) advertises one promotion percentage, but then unpredictably lowers it at the end of the tournament, will have difficulty recruiting in the future. Potential recruits will not trust the firm to award as many prizes as it initially promises. Thus, assuming adequate information and holding all other variables constant, prospective employees will downgrade the value of the firm's compensation package. This downgrading will place the firm in an inferior competitive position vis-à-vis other recruiters. This phenomenon does not require a firm to adhere strictly to a given promotion percentage, but rather suggests that, on average, the promotion percentage cannot decline over time without the firm experiencing adverse morale or recruiting effects.[56]

If the promotion percentage is constant and the associate-to-partner ratio is not decreasing, a firm will grow exponentially. As the firm promotes the designated percentage of associates, it must replace them and *must also hire enough new associates to keep the associate-to-partner ratio from falling.*[57] The firm needs these additions to the associate pool to support the new partners by using the new partners' shareable human capital. So long as the number of promotions exceeds the number of departures from the partnership, each promotion to partner will lead to net increases in both the number of partners and the number of associates at the firm. Because the promotion percentage is constant and the associate-partner ratio is constant or increasing, the firm's percentage growth rate will be constant (exponential) or increasing (faster than exponential). We emphasize this point because a firm that grows exponentially will eventually exhibit large jumps in membership quite apart from external shocks. We argue, therefore, that these sudden spurts in law-firm size actually result, in significant part, from the inevitable product of a long-term, historic process begun on the day the firm institutionalized its promotion tournament.

Thus, the law firm can be viewed as an internal market for the lending and borrowing of human capital. In order to retain the winning lawyers' skills as well as their investment in them, the firm (that is, the partnership) agrees to purchase from the winners their surplus human capital and monitoring services. The firm will compensate new partners by paying them a wage for their services and a return on any human capital that is loaned, minus any payment new partners must make for use of other partners' capital, and, perhaps, a handling charge. In return the firm will broker the new partners' assets to associates and

56. In some respects, then, the best news that a senior associate can receive is that last year's class did not produce as many partners as usual. A firm could then be expected to promote more associates than usual the next year to maintain a constant average promotion percentage.

57. Allowing the associate-per-partner ratio to decline would invariably reduce per-partner profits. Firms do, of course have this option, but we suspect they will resist it.

partners who can use them. The firm will also arrange for the monitoring of the assets and assign partners (perhaps the new partners themselves) to watch over them.

Besides gaining a financial share of the firm's assets, newly promoted partners can integrate their monitoring activities and human capital into the larger monitoring economy of the firm, thus availing themselves of any economies of scale in monitoring. The team structure of big firms, for instance, appears to subdivide monitoring activities to create monitoring economies. In addition, new partners can use the economies associated with the already existing partnership incentive structure to further safeguard their capital. That is, the incentive of becoming a partner helps increase the number of associates that the firm can monitor effectively at one time. Moreover, the incentives associated with an ownership interest, the tiering of the partnership,[58] and the informal grievance structure of a firm also provide mechanisms for protecting new partners' capital from other *partners* that borrow it.

New partners gain another advantage in that they now can plug their human assets—many of which are already firm-specific—into a well-developed internal capital market. Significant information- and signaling-cost savings may accrue to the new partners because the other partners and associates will know of both the existence and quality of the new partners' capital. In addition, new partners have the opportunity to mix their human capital with that of other partners in beneficial ways. Not inconceivably lawyers might find it advantageous to exchange a significant portion of their human capital for the capital of other partners in the firm.

Firms That Do Not Grow. The continued existence of small firms is not inconsistent with our argument.[59] We can imagine at least three types of small firms coexisting in our world of big firms. First, there are the incipient big law firms. These small firms have structured themselves so that over time they will grow exponentially.

Second, some firms have made a conscious decision to remain small. In general, these firms have declined to use fixed-percentage promotion tournaments as a mechanism for monitoring and protecting their human capital. Firms that neither expand their monitoring resources through promotion (or lateral hires)

58. For instance, many firms now have tiers of partners (junior and senior, equity and nonequity) and various management groups that hold varying levels of formal and informal power.

59. For that matter, we also have not attempted to describe every conceivable big firm, only the promotion-to-partnership firm based on the promotion-to-partner tournament. Firms can be large without being promotion-to-partnership firms. Examples include the national multibranch law firms such as Hyatt Legal Services and Jacoby & Myers, which have an administrative hierarchy and large numbers of salaried lawyers, and which market standardized legal services to individuals. See Seron forthcoming; Jensen 1989, p. 1; Snider 1987, p. 29.

nor screen and filter associates will find that their existing monitoring resources place absolute limits on the size they can achieve. For instance, a firm that promotes only occasionally and unpredictably will have limited success in using the possibility of becoming a partner as a mechanism for protecting human capital, monitoring associates, and reconciling incentives. Small boutique law firms often follow promotion patterns of this nature. Often, associates remain associates throughout their tenure with the firm. As associates develop desired skills and human capital, the likelihood of their leaving increases.

Similarly, a firm that follows a zero-growth promotion policy (ZGPP), whereby the firm promotes associates only as partners leave, will be able to remain small. In theory a firm could set the promotion rate so that the number of promotions exactly equals the number of retiring partners. In order to maintain the tournament structure necessary to motivate associates, the ZGPP firm would need to require regular and consistent retirements. For instance, the firm might require partners to retire at a particular age or after specified years with the firm. But so long as the age distribution of the partners was such that enough retirements occurred each year to permit a positive promotion rate, the firm could have both a tournament and a ZGPP. Of course, maintaining the necessary age distribution might conflict with conducting the tournament purely on the basis of productivity. And if the zero growth promotion policy resulted in a promotion rate lower than that of the rest of the market, the firm would need to compensate by offering entering attorneys either higher money wages while they remained associates or greater rewards if they became partners.

Third, some firms—probably the vast majority—remain small simply because they have no surplus, shareable human capital. On the one hand, some firms have attorneys with just enough reputation, client relationships, skills, and experience to support themselves. Such firms rarely hire associates who expect to become partners. Instead, if they hire anyone, they hire an occasional clerk to handle low-profit, relatively menial tasks. On the other hand, some attorneys have substantial human capital, even surplus human capital, that they cannot share. Plaintiffs' litigation firms provide an example of this type of small firm. The attorneys who populate these firms are often highly skilled, with substantial reputations. Because their human capital is so highly idiosyncratic, however, they cannot effectively lend it to others.[60] For instance, a topflight plaintiffs' litigator has the majority of her human capital tied up in her courtroom and other trial skills and reputation. Thus while she can use other lawyers and investigators to prepare aspects of her cases, clients will generally insist upon her presence at important depositions, negotiations, trials, and the

---

60. Professor John Coffee explains that plaintiff's firms remain small because "reputations of plaintiff's attorneys are personal and portable, [so that] plaintiff's firms lack the 'firm specific' capital that serves as the social cement in institutional firms" and the nature of the cases produces more severe monitoring problems (Coffee 1986, pp. 707–08).

like. She cannot lend that presence to associates and therefore cannot share her human capital. Instead she attempts to increase the return on her capital through selectivity in taking cases. Of course, her success at increasing her income in this manner depends upon her ability to set her own price by differentiating her services from those of other practitioners.

Some Alternative Theories of the Kink in Post-1970 Growth

We acknowledge that the available evidence suggests that something "shocked" law firms into more rapid growth after 1970. We argue, however, that the shock theories are both under- and over-inclusive: under-inclusive because alone they fail to explain why firms grew prior to 1970 and why, after 1970, their growth patterns have the shape that they do;[61] overinclusive in that they attempt to account for too large a portion of big-firm growth. Though our premise of exponential growth explains pre-1970 growth and partially accounts for post-1970 growth, our fully specified model also requires an external shock. Therefore, we want briefly to examine some of the characterizations of the external shock that accelerated growth after 1970. Because our overall objective has been to explain the portion of growth not accounted for by this shock, we only survey the leading theories put forward to account for the kink in the growth curves. We discuss briefly some of the more important shortcomings of these theories, but our analysis is hardly exhaustive.[62]

Supply of Lawyers. Some have attributed the growth of large law firms to the general lawyer boom. One such argument assumes that large law firms simply have received their proportionate share of the growing number of lawyers and law school graduates. Between 1960 and 1970 the supply of lawyers increased by 26 percent, but between 1970 and 1980 it almost doubled, increasing from 274,000 to 522,000.[63] Similarly, between 1960 and 1970 the annual volume of law school graduates increased by 60 percent, while the volume increased almost 140 percent between 1970 and 1980.[64]

Another argument emphasizes that while the nation's law schools graduated almost 300 percent more lawyers in 1980 than in 1960, the most prestigious

---

61. In fact, to explain pre-1970 growth most of the conventional theories say little more than that firms grew because the demands of their clients grew. This is akin to saying that the dinosaur was large because there was once an abundance of the necessary vegetation. Any such account fails to explain why there had to be relatively few large dinosaurs instead of lots of smaller ones.

62. A theory that focuses on the increased slope of the growth curves after 1970 must explain, not why the firms got big, but why their growth rate accelerated. Theories concerned with economies of scale, economies of scope, and minimum scale are generally concerned with growth, not accelerated growth, and are not discussed here.

63. Sander and Williams 1989, p. 433, Table 1.

64. Sander and Williams 1989, p. 445, Table 8.

schools did not maintain that same pace.[65] Large law firms traditionally had done the bulk of their recruiting at these schools. As the number of students available from the elite schools failed to keep pace with the needs of the big firms, they recruited deeper into the classes of these schools and more heavily from the less prestigious schools. The firms assumed, whether correctly or not, that as they recruited from nontraditional sources they risked hiring less productive young lawyers (in terms of both the quantity and quality of their output). Firms could either accept the lower quality and quantity of expected output, demand more hours from attorneys, or hire more law school graduates than before to compensate for lower average production. Apparently, so the argument goes, firms have chosen some combination of the second and third options.

Increased Merger Activity. Rapid growth often is traced to the extensive law-firm merger activity witnessed in recent years. Four possible reasons usually are given to explain the increased number of mergers.

First, some theories base their explanations of increased merger activity on the firms' desire for market (that is, monopoly) power. But these theories usually ignore the vertical or conglomerate (not horizontal) nature of most merger activity and the fact that large law firms control only about 10 percent of the legal services market.

Second, an attempt by attorneys to diversify their risks by developing a full "portfolio" of specialties—their reaction to increased business uncertainty— can explain increased vertical integration.[66] The data here are weak and in general proponents often overplay risk-aversion explanations for vertical merger activity.[67] In addition, between 1949 and 1969 income inequality within the legal profession appeared to decrease—just what one would expect to find with lawyers trying to diversify their portfolios of law-related income. If income diversification drove the merger activity after 1970 this trend should have continued. During the period from 1969 to 1979, however, income inequality actually increased.[68] Moreover, an increase in the use of productivity-based partner compensation plans accompanied the rise of merger activity. Compensation packages based on productivity defeat the entire purpose behind risk diversification.[69]

65. In 1980, eight of the nation's most prestigious law schools granted only 38 percent more J.D.s than in 1960 (Sander and Williams 1989, p. 462).

66. Gilson and Mnookin 1985, p. 322.

67. Victor Goldberg (1985), for instance, argues that price-adjustment problems in private contracts can be explained without resort to a discussion about attitudes toward risk.

68. These conclusions were derived from an examination of the ratios of median to mean lawyer income. The lower the ratio the more unequal the income distribution. Using this method, it is altogether possible that income inequality in a particular stratum of the profession will be invisible because of a greater increase in inequality in other strata (Sander and Williams 1989, p. 20).

69. Gilson and Mnookin 1985.

Third, mergers often are explained as mechanisms for building internal referral markets and "one-stop-shopping" law offices. Attorneys faced with the problem of becoming known to clients combine with attorneys who want to provide additional services. We can understand why attorneys attempting to become better known might want to find places in firms with good reputations. But given that this incentive always should have existed, why would it have lead to a surge only in post-1970 mergers?

Finally, law firms are sometimes described as reflecting, or "mimicking," their clients. Many clients of big firms engaged in merger activity during the post-1970 period. Like their clients, lawyers began to look for the same alleged benefits in acquiring, or being acquired by, other firms.

Each of these explanations has some plausibility. But none of the merger stories explains why percentage increases in law-firm growth began in the early 1970s, before the firms accelerated their merger activity.

Increased Demand for Legal Services. Beginning with the observation that sometime after 1970 the demand for all legal services increased, some contend that large law firms simply received their proportionate share of this growing demand and expanded their operations to meet it. Some evidence exists to support this theory. For instance, between 1970 and 1985 the volume of legal services nearly tripled.[70] Over roughly the same period, the receipts of the twenty largest law firms grew at a nominal rate of 17 percent per year, while the average receipt for all firms increased at a nominal rate of roughly 11 percent per year.[71] Moreover, while the inflation-deflated receipts of the top twenty law firms quadrupled, the market share of the large firm less than doubled, rising from 5 percent to nearly 8 percent between 1972 and 1980. This combination of statistics further indicates that the industry as a whole grew.[72]

At least two weaknesses exist to the "more demand" argument. First, the impressive industry-wide growth of 11 percent accounted for only 65 percent of the growth of big firms, which grew significantly faster than the rest of the industry. Second, even assuming that the theory of general growth in the profession seems to move in the same direction as the limited data on big firms, the theory neither explains the acceleration of their growth after 1970 nor specifies any plausible model of cause and effect.

Increased Demand for Big-Firm Services. A more sophisticated variant of the demand-based expansion argument suggests that, after 1970, the demand for *corporate* legal services increased. Between 1967 and 1982, business cli-

---

70. Sander and Williams 1989, p. 435.
71. Sander and Williams 1989, p. 437.
72. Sander and Williams 1989, p. 437.

ents became an increasingly important source of revenues for law firms, growing in absolute terms from $5 billion to $34 billion and as a percent of total law-firm receipts from 39 percent to 48.6.[73] Furthermore, big firms provided a disproportionately large percentage of the services purchased by the corporate sector. Thus, as the demand from the corporate sector increased, the size of big firms increased correspondingly. While this argument has some obvious merit, it fails to distinguish between the need for more corporate lawyers and the demand for larger law firms. The growth of corporate demand will certainly support the former, but does it require the latter as well?

To answer this question affirmatively, some have argued that corporations not only required more services, but that they now require more services per legal matter. In this scenario, legal matters are assumed to have become more complex: laws are more intricate and enigmatic, corporate clients are more geographically dispersed, and the stakes in outcomes have magnified. Servicing clients with new, sophisticated, large scale, tight deadline problems requires a greater mix of specialties, disciplines, and law office locations. Clients desire larger firms because they assume that a single big firm will minimize the transaction costs of coordinating large projects more effectively than will multiple smaller firms. Thus, the client presumes that a dollar spent for a big firm's work will buy more legal (as opposed to coordinating) services. Assuming that clients prefer more services per dollar, clients with large-scale work will want big firms to handle it.[74] While this argument appears plausible, it is little more than pure surmise. Beyond the speculative ruminations in the press and in the corridors of law firms and law schools, little objective evidence of the changing scale and complexity of law-firm work exists. For example, we have found no evidence that the size of work teams or the complexity of the work product within the firms has grown. This lack of evidence does not show that legal work is not changing, it merely indicates a need for further investigation to document the trend adequately.

The Rise of In-House Counsel. A refinement of the internal-referral-market story credits the rise of the in-house counsel with accelerating law-firm merger activity and, hence, the growth of recent years. Increased corporate reliance on their own internal legal departments to handle routine and advisory functions, so the argument goes, forced outside law firms to develop methods of coping with the increased uncertainty of maintaining, and possibly losing, traditional sources of work. In addition, in-house counsel became more aggressive in shopping for legal services. Rather than choose a law firm to marry for life, corporate counsel now increasingly choose particular lawyers or firms for spe-

73. Sander and Williams 1989, p. 441.
74. Sander and Williams 1989, pp. 472–73; Tullock 1980; Tullock 1975.

cific projects. An increasing proportion of the big-firm workload shifted to litigation and rapidly changing, complex areas of the law.[75] Getting clients and marketing the firm's specialized skills became ever more significant, thus adding to the importance of referrals.[76] Transaction-cost considerations made the development of internal referral markets within the law firm attractive[77] and led to the vertical mergers[78] of diverse law firms. Larger firms resulted.[79]

Though we find congenial the introduction of transaction-cost theory to the discussion, we remain only partially convinced. First, the loss of business to in-house counsel should not lead a priori to a law firm getting bigger. Usually when a producer's market shrinks it must cut back on the size of its operation. Second, a murky relationship between the rise of in-house counsel and the need for internal referral markets undergirds the internal-referral-market argument. But one might plausibly imagine that a law firm's need to fashion its own referral market would decrease as the skills of the client's purchasing agent increased. In choosing an outside attorney for a specific task, a corporation without able and experienced in-house counsel will need to look for simple, familiar signals of quality and capacity such as the size or reputation of the law firm. But where the client possesses an expert purchaser of legal services, the expert can delve more deeply into the quality of prospective outside attorneys. The in-house counsel who merely relies on the reputations of outside firms hardly qualifies as an expert.[80]

The in-house counsel who is an expert shopper should find good lawyers wherever they practice and despite the size or reputation of their firm. At worst she ought to be better at finding them than the nonexpert purchaser of legal services. In either case, the increased prominence of in-house counsel does not lead necessarily to the consolidation of law firms. Such a conclusion would imply that less talented attorneys have used law-firm mergers to hide in good firms and insulate themselves from careful examination by in-house counsel. We do not intend completely to dismiss the internal-referral-market argu-

---

75. Nelson 1988, pp. 51–56; Chayes and Chayes 1985.

76. Nelson 1988, pp. 51–56.

77. Nelson 1988, pp. 66–69.

78. Vertical mergers are those between firms with complementary specialties and expertise, for instance, the merger of a firm that specializes in tax and estate planning with one whose expertise and client base is in corporate finance.

79. Nelson 1988, pp. 59–60.

80. The situation is similar to that of finding a "good" restaurant in an unfamiliar city. Like the corporation without an expert purchaser of legal services, a foreign diner might look for familiar signals of expected quality: association with a good hotel, costliness, recommendations of casual acquaintances. But a diner who knows the town well—an expert—would bring to bear additional information: multiple opinions from people she knows well and trusts, her own past experiences, and her ability to sample and review the restaurant's fare. From the native's perspective, the information that the restaurant is in a good hotel or is very expensive is of less value.

ment, but to question the role the corporate counsel played in stimulating it. Either the in-house counsel performs her duties well, in which case internal referral markets are redundant; or, she consumes legal services only slightly better than her corporate bosses, in which event law firms should not have made radical changes to accommodate her shopping ability.

Changes in the Business Use of Law. A yet more sophisticated version of the increased-demand argument maintains that during the early 1970s businesses significantly changed their use of law and lawyers. This version explains the change as produced both by an increase in the number of important business disputes and by a breakdown in conditions that foster nonlitigious forms of dispute resolution.[81] According to this view the business world of today is more complex than the business world of a generation ago: there are many more players, more products, more intense competition, more fine-grained calculations made about the distribution of risk, and more uncertainty about the rewards of risk. Profound changes in the American and world economies accompany, and partially account for, this increased business complexity. These changes include increased integration of American product and capital markets into increasingly competitive global markets; floating exchange rates; liberalization and integration of world capital markets; declining American economic performance; increased economic importance of service industries, particularly finance; and tremendous growth in governmental regulation.

Because of these changes the number of potentially important business disputes has increased. Further, the informal mechanisms traditionally used to avoid and resolve disputes in the American economy no longer resolve these potential conflicts adequately.[82] Clients now bring lawyers into transactions earlier, more often, and in greater numbers. Lawyers play a more active role in helping to avoid or prepare for the myriad disputes and complications associated with the new competitive and unstable business settings. Moreover, the transactions themselves foster litigation as a strategic device, and the parties to transactions now resolve greater numbers of their disputes by litigation. Thus

81. The argument is that, other things being equal, both the number of business disputes and the tendency of businesses to use lawyers to help resolve or avoid such disputes will vary directly with: (1) competition among firms; (2) product specialization and need for "specific performance" of product agreements; (3) increased turnover of parties to deals; (4) the number of parties to and complexity of deals; (5) spatial and cultural (including international) dispersion of parties; (6) instability in prices; (7) relative stakes of parties in any single deal; (8) the rate of economic change, which by itself disturbs governance mechanisms (Business Disputing Group 1989). Increases along these dimensions have given rise to a vast increase in the number of potential disputes and have eroded the structures of continuing relations and their characteristic opportunities for sanction (e.g., exit threats and reputational harm) that permitted the less contentious or more "noncontractual" dealing and dispute handling in earlier periods as described by Macaulay (1963).

82. Business Disputing Group 1989.

the complexity of legal problems has changed the amount and character of the work required of the lawyer. Handling any particular matter—both litigation and "deal making"—may require larger numbers of lawyers (though not necessarily more total lawyer-hours) because of short time lines, issues crossing specialties, and the enormous sums at stake. Consequently, the increase in the size of law firms has as much to do with changes in the methods of handling clients' problems as it does with increased demand for legal services.

At the risk of seeming indecisive, we suspect that factors emphasized in each of the above explanations of the shock have contributed something to the growth of large law firms. Precisely how they have done so, and in what proportion, we leave to future research. Intuitively, the changing business use of corporate legal services and the need for new methods of combining inputs (primarily labor and human capital) to provide these services strike us as providing the most fertile ground for future exploration.[83]

Confronting the Constraints on Exponential Growth

Earlier, we examined the growth incentives associated with large-law-firm organization. We have argued that, as traditionally organized, the big law firm must grow. We have essentially ignored the question of whether the firm *can* grow by assuming that the firm faces no constraints to becoming bigger.

While useful above, the assumption of unhindered growth is clearly unrealistic and, for our argument, unnecessary. We do not propose that law firms will grow forever. We accept that real constraints to growth exist, and we examine some of these below. In fact, the distinction between a firm's need to grow and its ability to do so is at the root of our broader argument. As the firm grows, it converges upon a series of binding constraints. In confronting these constraints, big firms either must accept change or face failure. We refer to these changes cumulatively as the transformation of the big law firm.[84]

Many of the changes in big law firms can be explained as responses to three different constraints. First, the firm faces a revenue or budget constraint. Second, the ability to find associates to fill its ever-increasing needs further hinders law-firm expansion. Third, as firms grow larger, their ability to maintain quality control diminishes. We discuss these three constraints in turn.

---

83. Along with our colleagues in the Business Disputing Group, Stewart Macaulay and Joel Rogers, we have begun to address the question of the changing role of law in corporate dispute resolution. See Business Disputing Group (1989).

84. Changes in one firm makes changes both easier and more necessary in other firms. Easier because if firm X stretches out the years-to-partnership it becomes easier for firm Y to do so. Necessary, because having done so, firm X can now pay its partners more and lure productive attorneys away from a nonresponsive Y.

A firm always must generate enough revenues to cover its costs.[85] As growth becomes so rapid that the firm can no longer generate new revenues sufficient to cover the costs of adding new attorneys, a "revenue gap" develops. Of course a "revenue gap" simply implies that new income has not kept up with new costs. The gap might exist in any firm at any stage of growth. Business might simply fail to grow at the requisite pace, diseconomies of scale might develop, or costs might escalate beyond expected levels.

But an environment where clients have become more willing to shop for lawyers presents especially acute problems. As they gain additional leverage, clients will reduce any pre-existing monopoly rents that would have accrued to attorneys in the less competitive days when clients used a single firm. This additional bargaining power can translate into lost revenues for the law firm. The large practice faces the additional potential complication of having to adjust to a change in its historic returns to scale. The firm probably realized any economies of scale during the earlier years of the practice. As the returns to scale disappear, adding new attorneys changes the firm's historic cost structure, forcing the firm to adjust.

When this revenue gap develops, the firm must change to survive. Both in theory and in practice the firm has three alternatives from which to devise a strategy. First, it can stretch existing income to cover more attorneys, and the partners can either make less money or ask associates to bill more hours with no increase in compensation.[86] Assuming the firm wants to remain competitive in the pursuit of associates, belt-tightening generally requires that partners accept smaller distributions from existing residuals. Evidently some firms have accepted this strategy. While big-firm revenues have increased appreciably in recent years, partners have not necessarily benefited proportionally. Between 1972 and 1987, the receipts of the twenty largest firms quadrupled in constant-dollar terms.[87] But while receipts have grown dramatically, per-partner profits over the last twenty years have remained quite flat, increasing by only 20 percent, or an average of 1 percent per year in constant dollars. In contrast, associate incomes have risen by over 60 percent, or roughly 3 percent per year in constant dollars.[88] This implies a significant redistribution of firm income from partners to associates. While firms might choose self-sacrifice as an appropriate short-run strategy, over the long-term this approach will lose partners (and human capital) to firms willing to pay for them.

85. A firm's "costs" must include a reasonable return on a partner's investment in human capital. Much of what law firms refer to as "profits" are in fact returns on a lawyer's human capital.

86. Associates are being asked to work more hours, but salaries are also increasing. In fact, in constant dollars associate salaries are increasing faster than partner incomes (Sander and Williams 1989, p. 453).

87. Sander and Williams 1989, p. 439.

88. Sander and Williams 1989, pp. 474–75.

A second strategy suggests that the firm attempt to reduce its growth rate. Presumably this suggestion means that the firm must align its growth more accurately with the rate of increase in the demand for its services. For any given per capita partnership income, the growth rate of the firm is generally a function of four variables: (1) the ratio of associates to partners, (2) the percentage of associates becoming partners, (3) the length of time between joining the firm as an associate and becoming a partner, and (4) the number of partners leaving the firm. For a specific number of partners in a particular year, the associate-to-partner ratio will determine the absolute number of associates the firm will employ. The percentage of associates promoted to partner will determine how many new associates the firm must hire to replace and support any new partners. The length of time it takes to become a partner will influence when the firm can expect to add the associates necessary to support and replace the newly promoted attorney. The number of partners leaving the firm, assuming they take no associates with them, will determine how many associates the firm can reassign to use the capital of other partners.[89] Changing any of these variables results in an adjustment in the growth of the firm. If, for instance, the firm reduces its ratio of associates to partners, then for a fixed number of partners the absolute number of associates would decrease. Even if the firm promoted the usual percentage of associates to partner, it would grow more slowly as a fixed percentage of a smaller base was added to the firm over time. If, alternatively, the firm decided to reduce the historic percentage of associates declared winners in its tournament, but left all other variables constant, the firm's growth similarly would slow. In a particular year the firm would promote a smaller percentage of associates, which would necessitate the hiring of fewer new associates to maintain the constant associate-to-partner ratio.

Adjusting any of the first three variables also implies a change in the underlying structure of the firm—such adjustments, that is, portend the transformation of the practice. In fact, as we discussed above, we presently witness substantial efforts in this area. For instance, the percentage of associates becoming partners seems to be declining in some firms and the years to partnership have lengthened. In addition, law firms now make wider use of nonequity partnerships, paralegals, "temporary" attorneys, "second-tier" associates with no expectation of making partner, and the practice of retaining as permanent associates those passed over for partnership. But each of these adjustments conflict to some extent with the purpose and goals of the firm's tournaments. Slowing a firm's growth potential in this manner creates difficulties in recruitment, compensation, motivation and retention of productive young associates.

Hiring fewer associates in a given year is an alternative means of slowing

---

89. If for instance, a firm only promoted a qualified associate to replace a partner who had left, the firm would have no need to grow. The firm would simply replace the promoted associate and reassign the departing partner's former associates to support the new partner.

down growth. But this strategy likely will lead to reduced partner income. Remember, the firm hires new associates to replace and support the newly promoted partners. Failure to hire enough associates to both replace and support the new partner will mean that either she or her more senior colleagues must forgo income. This strategy might work in the short run, but it likely will prove unsatisfactory over time.

A third strategy for addressing a revenue gap calls on the firm to increase the demand for its services. This strategy essentially translates into greater competition for clients, more marketing of services, less inhibition about advertising and soliciting, the movement into nonlaw businesses, and other methods for expanding the firm's markets. Ever greater numbers of firms seem to prefer this strategy.

Besides its potential for causing a revenue gap, exponential growth poses an additional set of problems for the large law firm: where will it find the ever-increasing number of associates it requires? Traditionally, the large law firm hired most of its associates right out of elite law schools. Presumably the firms believed that they could more easily find associates of a particular quality and productivity at these schools. But as firms have grown at ever increasing rates, these schools have lost the ability to provide the necessary pool of associates.[90] To make up for the shortfall of new associates graduating from elite schools, firms can respond in three ways.

First, firms can expand the pool of potential recruits. Rather than interviewing only those students in the top quarter of their class, the firms might examine those ranked lower. Alternatively, the firm might begin to hire from less prestigious law schools. A firm that follows either strategy may think that it should anticipate a higher attrition rate among junior associates. To make up for the expected attrition, the firm actually might hire more associates than it would have hired through traditional sources. Thus one might expect to see higher associate-to-partner ratios today than in the past.

Second, the firm might attempt to hire away more experienced associates from other firms. Lateral hires and raiding of this nature, almost unheard of twenty years ago, are becoming commonplace.

Finally, the firm might attempt to purchase productive associates from other firms. Firms do not trade associates like National Football League teams. Instead, they can accomplish much the same thing by merging with firms that have surplus labor. We suspect that at least some of the observed merger activity between law firms has as its underlying goal the correction of unbalanced capital-to-labor ratios. Firms with unproductive surplus human capital will attempt to merge with firms with excess labor, and vice versa. Mergers, then, become a method of capturing labor or capital from other firms.

The firm's capacity to maintain quality output as it grows places a third con-

90. See Sander and Williams (1989, p. 476).

straint on growth. That is not to say that the big firm cannot maintain quality control; after all, we base our transformation story on its attempt to do so. But as with increases in scale in any manufacturing operation, the methods of ensuring the requisite caliber of performance change along with the scale of the operation. When a firm has fifty securities lawyers working in one office, no longer can a senior partner personally know and observe them all as was possible when the firm had but two.

Attempting to monitor and enforce the performance of partners presents especially acute problems. As part of the solution to this monitoring problem, firms require attorneys to post a hostage upon becoming a partner. That is, a new partner must commingle her assets with those of the other partners, thereby subjecting her capital to retaliation if problems arise. In addition, the development of a firm culture[91] through social control[92] and prospective monitoring[93] will play an active role in mitigating opportunistic conduct. Finally, the firm will look for structural solutions as means of mitigating the diseconomies involved in monitoring partners. The division of the firm into functional subgroups—for example, litigation, banking, corporate—and the use of the same tournament-based monitoring scheme employed to control associates represent the principal structural solutions available to the firm. Thus, the firm will have junior partners, senior partners, members of the executive committee, managing partners, and the like. In short, the firm will become increasingly hierarchical and will take on the characteristics of the proverbial "corporate ladder."

91. Gilson and Mnookin 1985, pp. 371–80.

92. Social control refers to "those processes in the social system which tend to counteract the deviant tendencies" (Parsons 1951, p. 297).

93. Prospective monitoring refers to the initial careful selection of associates so as to reduce the need to monitor actual contract performance. By finding a group of attorneys with a reasonably homogeneous set of characteristics and motivations, the firm can reduce the need for explicit monitoring in the future. These characteristics will have been developed in complex ways through family life, schooling, training, and past employment. It is impossible to specify exactly what qualities a particular partnership should look for.

6 Metamorphoses? A Brief Inquiry into the Future Shape of Law Practice

For a long time, those who inhabited the world of the big firm could expect that the coming years would not be terribly different from those just past. In this they resembled the inhabitants of universities. But this sense of stability has been shaken. What lies ahead, many feel, may be very different. For individual careers and for firms as such there is a sense of uncharted seas and an unknown destination. In levels of change, uncertainty, and anxiety big law firms resemble the world of gender relations more than they do universities.

We have argued that the big firm, by choosing the "promotion to partnership tournament" as a form of governance, committed itself inadvertently to a dynamic of exponential growth. The environment allowing, growth will come in ever-larger increments that will eventually change the character of the firm and, by the conjoint growth of its companions, of the legal world in which it is situated. This is not to say that the classic "promotion to partnership" firm is doomed to extinction. Undoubtedly, many firms of this type will continue to exist. But we think that the world of large business-law practice will be characterized by greater diversity and experimentation in the organization of firms, at least in the near future. It seems unlikely that new kinds of firms will entirely supplant the existing sorts of firm. But some of the most successful and enduring firms of the future are likely to look and behave quite differently from the firms of the recent past.

Those who cannot manage exponential growth or who seek to avoid its unattractive accompaniments will seek to devise other institutional forms more to their liking. We would expect that some of these would flourish, changing the mix of firms that populate the corporate hemisphere of the legal world in the near future. We make no claim that the future course of legal practice is fated and known to us. We foresee a period of fluidity and experimentation. What will emerge from such a period remains unknown and unknowable. But, taking off from existing forms, some old and some innovative, and from current trends, we would like to speculate about the near future of the big firm, its variants, companions, and rivals in the corporate hemisphere.

The first set of options share a tendency toward market orientation, rationalization of incentives, and accentuated hierarchy.

The "Later Big Firm." In such firms the "promotion to partnership" core would be reduced (in relation to the total mass of the firm) by some of the host of devices for slowing the effects of the promotion-to-partner tournament described above: two-tier hiring, permanent associates, paralegals and technology, contracting out, and a general stretching out of the time to partnership.[1] There would be various levels of partnership and partners' performance would be continually tested. The tournament, already pervasive for associates and of some import for partners, would be greatly extended and intensified during the partnership phase. Partnership would become less of a plenary and permanent reward, necessitating the design of additional incentives for performance and loyalty.

The "Big Six" Firm. A variant on the Later Big Firm is suggested by the observation that the coverage-driven push toward greater size, more locations, and greater range of services might lead to giant national (or international) firms that bear some resemblance to the "Big Six" accounting firms in size, structure, and market concentration.[2] But to fully mimic the Big Six, a law firm would have to further modify its traditional promotion-to-partnership core. The Big Six are generally characterized by taller hierarchies and considerably more associates per partner than the traditional big law firm. For example, in 1989, one of the Big Six (Arthur Andersen) had 40,136 professional personnel, of whom 2,405 (6.0 percent) were partners.[3] Thus in addition to utilizing more bureaucratic systems of control the law firm that attempts to evolve in the direction of the Big Six would need to increase the ratio of associates to partners, and reduce the rate at which associates are made partners.

We are somewhat skeptical that big law firms will eventually look like the Big Six accounting firms. First, the big law firms must travel a considerable distance before their market shares are anywhere nearly as concentrated as the accounting profession's. As table 7 indicates, law is still remarkably unconcentrated compared to other suppliers of professional services to businesses. Moreover conflict-of-interest problems might set more restrictive upper bounds on law-firm concentration.

Second, we remain skeptical of the Big Six option for the very reason that the big accounting firm is based upon a relatively high associate-to-partner ratio. Law firms which attempt to emulate this model would be required to increase their associate-to-partner ratio and to reduce their promotion rate. On the one

1. Steven Brill foresees the emergence of firms that liberate themselves from the "growth inertia trap" of "exponential growth generated from the supply side" and learn to conform growth to increases in demand (Brill 1989b).

2. Mergers in 1989 reduced what were once known as the "Big Eight" to the "Big Six."

3. Arthur Andersen & Co. 1990, Firm Growth Table. The highest partner ratio among the Big Eight was 11 percent.

Table 7 Concentration in Law Compared to Other Service Industries: Percentage of Total Receipts of Largest Firms (1982)

	Share of Receipts of Largest			
	4 Firms	8 Firms	20 Firms	50 Firms
Law	0.9	1.7	3.6	7.1
Accounting	16.9	28.3	34.0	36.3
Engineering, Architecture, and Surveying	10.9	16.4	25.6	34.6
Advertising	9.2	16.3	30.2	42.8
Management Consulting and Public Relations	6.4	8.9	12.8	17.8

Source: U.S. Department of Commerce, 1982 Census of Service Industries—Industry Series (1985) Table 6a.

hand, this would in effect reduce the expected value of being an associate. Therefore, without a dramatic change in the market for associates the firm would have to pay a premium by providing greater compensation up front or by increasing the value of a partnership. A failure to adjust associate salaries or partnership value would result in a reduction in total compensation. On the other hand, as we argued above, the number of associates per partner a firm can afford is related directly to the amount of human capital per partner possessed by the firm and the constraints on the firm's ability to monitor associates. To increase the associate-to-partner ratio the firm would have to dramatically increase the value of its human capital per partner. We are unable to see where that increased value will come from. In addition, monitoring costs also limit the size of the law firm's associate-partner ratio. There is no indication that the firms have so substantially overcome the difficulties in monitoring associates as to allow them to significantly increase these ratios.

To say that law firms will not take the Big Six path is not to say that the Big Six might not enter the market for supplying corporate legal services. With their very substantial resources, their large legal departments, and their enormous network of clients, one could easily imagine a scenario in which accounting firms decided to compete directly with large law firms in providing business-related legal advice. Much of the debate about law-firm diversification is couched in terms of law firms incorporating other sorts of professionals. It seems improbable that boundaries between professions would be relaxed in one direction only. As law firms increasingly offer a wider range of services, they will face competition from other business advisers like accounting firms, management consultants, and investment bankers who will include legal services in *their* multidisciplinary packages. As the bar relaxes its claims that lawyers cannot share control of their work and firms with nonlawyers, it will find it more difficult to maintain that the diversified entity must be devoted exclusively to producing legal services or be under the overall control of lawyers.

The "Multidisciplinary" Firm. Of course the multidisciplinary trend will run in both directions. Not only should we expect accountants and other professionals to offer legal services, but we anticipate that more so than today the Later Big Firm will stress a multidisciplinary or "diversified" law practice. The firm oriented in this direction will incorporate the labor of other professionals and will supplement its legal services with management consulting, investment counseling, lobbying, and so forth. We noted above the move of some aggressive law firms into such arrangements already.[4] Some foresee that firms will become diversified-service firms deploying teams drawn from many disciplines, "more oriented to problem-solving than traditional law firms."[5] Something like this is already happening in accounting firms, where the accounting and auditing core forms a decreasing portion of the firms' work and consulting services an increasing portion.[6]

Is the multidisciplinary thrust another device for adding employees outside the partner-associate core? Or is it a device for changing the character of that core by including nonlawyers within it? So far most hiring of nonlawyer specialists has been in subsidiaries or on an ad hoc lateral basis.[7] Bar rules forbidding partnerships with nonlawyers have obviated the promotion question.[8] But the recent authorization of nonlawyer partners in the District of Columbia seems to portend an erosion of such barriers.[9] We can imagine a world in which such nonlawyer workers become common and some are invited to participate in the partnership. Firms will have to hire senior people who have developed their expertise elsewhere or will have to hire junior people to cultivate their skills under the supervision of seniors. Some juniors might be hired to remain supervised staff. But presumably some junior hires would be talented people with the potential to develop their own human capital. Would such nonlawyers be hired on the associate's "promotion to partner" deal or on some other basis? How would a firm provide incentives to induce people to

4. See above, pp. 66–67.

5. Fitzpatrick 1989, p. 465.

6. For instance, accounting and audit fell from 66 percent of Arthur Andersen's revenue in 1975 to 49 percent in 1985.

7. The same argument from professional symmetry arises in connection with subsidiaries. If law firms can own nonlaw subsidiaries, can't nonlawyers have a law subsidiary? Corporations are allowed to have legal departments that supply legal services to themselves. Why can they not supply legal services to their customers?

8. Andrews 1989.

9. On March 1, 1990, the District of Columbia Court of Appeals adopted a rule that permits partnerships for nonlawyers who are involved exclusively with helping lawyers to provide legal services (Lewis 1990, p. B10; Samborn 1990, p. B1). Nonlawyers would work in firms whose "sole purpose" is the provide "legal services" to clients. Hence, the use of subsidiaries will continue for the provision of services that cannot be readily characterized that way.

work hard and to develop their human capital in such specific multidisciplinary forms? How could the work of these nonlawyers be monitored? Because the problems of monitoring and motivating other professionals are quite similar to the problems of monitoring and motivating lawyers, it is likely that these problems will be solved by "tournaments" not unlike those used by current law firms. Will the nonlawyers participate in the same tournament as lawyer associates? Or will firms organize parallel tournaments—like the separate tenure competitions in neighboring departments in universities?

So long as such nonlawyers are rare, relatively immobile, and hired on individualized deals, their presence may enlarge profits for partners without any threat of expanding the partnership. But where the inclusion of nonlawyers becomes common and these professionals have opportunities to move to other employment, there will be pressure on firms to reward the nonlawyers at levels sufficient to retain them. The most accomplished professionals are not likely to be content to remain in a subordinate tier. So even if the multidisciplinary move seems tempting as a device to shrink (relatively) the promotion-to-partner tournament, we would expect its widespread and extended use to require the enlargement or duplication of the core promotion tournament. Even if diversification succeeds in shrinking the proportion of lawyers competing for ownership interests, the number of professionals involved in one promotion tournament or another is unlikely to decrease substantially as a proportion of the total firm.

In a second set of options, firms might attempt to retain the specialization, rationalization, and marketing themes of the later big firm but either abandon hierarchy, coverage, and size or modify the relatively uniform structure of rewards.

Boutiques. The term "boutique" has come to refer to highly specialized small firms residing in the corporate hemisphere.[10] These firms cultivate their comparative advantage in selected specialties and suppress any push to more general coverage in order to maintain their attractiveness for referral work from big firms.[11] Despite their size, such firms compete with big firms for lawyers. Typically, though, the ratio of associates to partners is lower than in big firms.

Though commentators are not always careful to do so, it is important to dis-

10. Schept 1980, p. 1; Crossen 1981, p. 27; Schaeffer 1981, p. 6B; Appleson 1983, p. 1; Coyle 1987, p. 1.

11. The market for highly specialized services is in large part a referral market and referral is encouraged where the referring firm has no fear that the referee firm can compete with it for general representation of the client.

tinguish the boutique from the incipient big law firm.[12] The boutique combines small size, intense lawyer and firm specialization, and a commitment to remain small.[13] The incipient big firm may contain the first two elements but never the last. Unlike big firms, where a major part of the partners' return is from renting capital to associates, it appears that partners in boutiques increase their income by using associates and other resources to maximize return on the sale of their own time.[14] But recognizing the difference between the large law firm and the boutique simply raises a host of yet unanswered questions.

For instance, what incentives do high-quality young attorneys have for joining and remaining with a boutique? Certainly the boutique must pay well. But presumably some of the compensation is paid in the currency of collegiality, absence of the competitive pressure of the tournament, working with senior attorneys as a protégé, and so forth. The very closeness, personal relationships, increased loyalty, and desire for regard from seniors provides the control over shirking that is provided by the tournament in the big law firm. But if all the compensation is paid up front, what incentives are there for the associate to remain with the firm once he has learned all he can from the present partners? Will the young lawyer find it undiminishingly rewarding to be the protégé of a senior attorney? If an associate who masters the skills of the partners is promoted, how does the firm remain small? If that associate is replaced, can the top of the pyramid grow without the bottom growing? If associates typically leave and build their own specialized practices, how does the boutique maintain its comparative advantage and the correspondingly high prices it previously commanded? Just how big can a specialized firm get? Are the services the boutique provides inherently different from those of the big firm? Is there a commitment to confine income gains to those that can be had by cultivating comparative advantages and specialization rather than by increasing the base of the pyramid? Would this be a viable strategy—given that specializations fall as well as rise in favor?[15] These are all questions which must be confronted by any lawyer contemplating a boutique practice. That they do not have easy answers explains in part why the true boutique is seldom observed. Will the boutique form become widespread? We tend to doubt it, but it is likely to continue to occupy an

---

12. And from other kinds of firms that remain small because they have no shareable human capital. See pp. 109–10 above.

13. From the point of view of associates, a branch of a large firm may have appealing boutique-like qualities of small size, personal relations combined with a large-firm credential, less travel, and more transfer possibilities that may facilitate moves for a two-career family.

14. As one not necessarily typical boutique manager put it: "we have got to make our profit off making more money on a case per hour. . . . Contingent fee work primarily. That is what allows us to get sufficient profit so we don't have to add a bunch of associates on who we are leveraging and making money." (Susman 1987, p. 133).

15. See, e.g., Ranii (1981, p. 1), on the attrition of various administrative law specialties in the era of deregulation.

important niche as a supplier of legal services to the business and legal communities.

Mixed-Compensation or "Life-Style" Firms. By the "mixed-compensation"[16] firm we refer to firms in which there is a commitment to reduce the traditional big firm's heavy dependence on monetary compensation and instead to facilitate a mixture of pecuniary and "life-style" rewards such as child-rearing leaves, flextime, part-time work, sabbaticals, time for political or pro-bono work.[17] The lawyers in such firms are willing to take returns in the form of these amenities rather than higher cash income. The emphasis might be on overcoming the separation of work from home that characterizes modern life (child care, flextime, electronic cottage). Or lawyers might be eager to take returns in terms of less hierarchy on the job, submergence in political movements, or other "communal" forms. In its various versions, the mixed-compensation firm represents an attempt to harmonize professional work with other valued aspects of life.

We may easily imagine a mixed-compensation boutique. Could there be a mixed-compensation big firm? Why couldn't a large firm attempt to maximize not just monetary returns to its lawyers but their total fulfillment? Among the hundreds of big firms there are some that pursue such aspirations. Informal inquiries generated a list of half a dozen. One was Anderson, Russell, a 76-lawyer New York firm that has reduced hierarchy (including partner/associate titles), discourages internal competitiveness, and emphasizes participation and equality.[18]

16. Of course compensation in the strictest sense is almost always "mixed" and includes not only cash but *implicit* values for satisfaction, personal fulfillment, prestige, and the like. What we want to distinguish here are those firms where the value placed on the nonmonetary elements of the package is no longer implicit and is not assumed to be the same for all members of the firm.

17. The term "life-style" has emerged as a descriptive tag referring to the whole collection of preferences for other sorts of fulfillment over more income (and the work satisfaction associated with obtaining it). (See, e.g., Carter (1989a, p. 4) ("Stanford Law School's placement office recently sent a questionnaire . . . with a laundry list on lifestyle issues."); Carter (1989b, p. 4) (". . . NALP has made a major lifestyle concession of its own; Executive Director Jamienne S. Studley is moving from the association's Washington, D.C., office to follow her husband to San Francisco, and she will still be executive director of the D.C.-based NALP."); Brill 1989b. We use the more cumbrous "mixed-compensation" tag because the term "life-style" is difficult to separate from connotations of self-indulgent consumption. In particular, it suggests an equation of parental responsibilities with very different kinds of preferences. We do not affirm these preferences as being of equal value; nor do we affirm that they are entirely distinct. One might, for example, imagine distinct "parenting" and "other" types of "mixed-compensation" firms. But we doubt that such types would remain distinct, since parenting responsibilities tend to be concentrated during the first half of lawyers' tenure with their firms.

18. Stuart 1986, p. 10. In a more elaborate account in June 1987, the firm was reported to have 85 lawyers (*Susman* 1987).

Holland & Hart, a profitable 220-lawyer Denver firm, founded in 1947, is recognizably a big law firm, organized around the promotion to partnership and responsive to the pressures of the market.[19] It has brought in several small firms by merger; it has eight branches; lawyers receive "a business getting reward of 10 percent of the fees they bring in the door."[20] But at the same time the firm has institutionalized an unusual degree of egalitarianism (in titles, offices, votes, personal relations), a heavy commitment to pro bono work (5 to 20 percent of each lawyer's time), as well as periodic sabbaticals and other human enrichment policies. As cynics might anticipate, paradise is not without some murmurs of dissent. A senior partner observed that "[t]he bottom-line movement gained momentum. . . . The collegial aspect has fallen off and emphasis on productivity and profits has gained."[21]

Is it foreordained that the party of the bottom line will prevail? Our expectation that firms would keep growing (if they could) rests on the assumption that partners would prefer not to decrease income. Are we saying that they are single-mindedly determined to have more cash? Not necessarily, only that they want "more." But why not take rewards in other forms? Why do big-firm lawyers insist on taking the gains of firm growth in the form of more money income rather than as sabbaticals, time for child-care, political involvement, greater work satisfaction, or whatever? Presumably some lawyers would trade the next increment of cash for an increment of one of these. Why is this only dimly reflected in the way large firms are organized? Instead, they are organized as if everyone were trying to maximize take-home income. Firms have successfully created internal markets for their human capital. Why is it apparently so much more difficult for them to create a companion internal market in amenities?

We believe that there are at least two problems which lead firms to emphasize monetary rewards beyond all else. First, there is the transaction-cost problem of attempting to value the nonmonetary benefits. Money is not all that partners want. But as firms get bigger, securing and monitoring agreement about the priority ordering, the value, and the mix of "goods" they want as their return from practice becomes ever more complex. Since "money" is high (even if not first) on everyone's scale, it is almost always possible to get agreement on more money over any other competing good. As firms get larger, agreement becomes more difficult. This is especially so when firms at the same time become more diverse in terms of gender, ethnicity, class origin, and educational background—and when lateral hiring and mergers reduce opportunities for differences to be smoothed out by early socialization in the firm culture. The problem of getting agreement that we would all like sabbaticals rather than more money becomes insurmountable. So we fall back on money as the medi-

19. Jensen 1988c, p. 1.
20. Jensen 1988c, p. 23.
21. Jensen 1988c, p. 23.

um of exchange which can be used as a second-best solution, a summation of the diverse priorities of the members. Reputation and prestige, insofar as they are instrumental to securing more money, are also relatively easy to get agreement on.

Our transaction-cost/governance argument about the increasing difficulty of agreement on nonmonetary forms of reward as firms grow is reinforced by changes in the market. The ready availability of lateral movement permits the partner who wants money instead of, e.g., sabbaticals, to leave if her partners insist on the latter. A concentration of partners who wanted sabbaticals or more independence could overcome problems of pluralistic ignorance and negotiate the package they want. But then those who preferred money could leave and go elsewhere with disruptive effects. Hence, even if they are in the majority, and even if they know it, the "mixed rewards" party are not likely to impose their will.[22] Mixed-rewards dissidents, in contrast, are not as mobile, since they would have to find new firms that have a schedule of rewards that approximates their own. Such firms are rare and usually small and their reward schedules are not readily known. So the transaction costs of such a move for mixed-rewards dissidents are very high.

Second, mixed-compensation firms tend to emphasize monetary rewards because even firms with a significant concentration of lawyers seeking nonmonetary compensation must face the problem of assuring those who receive alternative forms of payment that they are not being exploited. The problem stems in part from the suspicion of those receiving mixed-compensation packages that they are not being fully compensated for the value they add to the firm. Whether true or not, the perception exists. Perhaps the perception originates in the sense that the market for those wishing to sell their services for alternative compensation is more limited than for those wishing to work for traditional pay. The concern is that an attorney, once he has declared his attention to receive mixed compensation, is no longer fully mobile and has no less costly alternative than to sell his services to his existing firm. Consequently, he believes that his firm gains monopsonistic[23] power over his services and has the ability to extract a rent from him when he attempts to buy back his time for alternative pursuits or obligations. This leads to feelings of vulnerability, exploitation, and exposure to additional pressures.

A third set of options pursue the benefits of size—visibility, economies of scale and scope, capacity to take on large matters—not by enlarging firms but by establishing linkages between them.

22. Both of the instances of successful consensus described above seem to rely heavily on strong leadership, embodied in firm "tradition" and selective recruitment. How enduring this proves in the large-firm setting remains to be seen.

23. A monopsonist is the demand-side equivalent of a monopolist. Unlike the monopolist, who is a single supplier of a particular output, a monopsonist is the only consumer of some good or service.

Networks or Affiliation-Groups. Smaller firms may seek to obtain the benefits of the big firm by linking themselves to other firms for sharing of clients, training facilities, or information about management, practice-development strategies, tactics, support services, and experts for litigation. In many respects the linkage of smaller firms mirrors the structure of the big-firm which is in a sense a network of working groups, departments, and regional offices. But the small-firm network achieves coordination without formal integration. Thus the work of a number of law firms in a set of related matters might be supported and coordinated without creating an elaborate internal organization. The practice of in-house legal departments or outside firms serving as national litigation coordinator, for example in defense of a particular product, can produce such networks without organizations. Such a coordinator may select local counsel, provide technical backup, and set litigation policy with an eye to maximizing the integrity of the product.[24]

By affiliation-groups we are referring to a variety of organizational forms that are more inclusive and less integrated than the conventional law firm and more integrated than these ad hoc support arrangements. Some of these groups are regional, some national and international. Some are electronic networks with little organizational superstructure; others have separate headquarters and staff.[25] They share the aspiration to achieve some of the advantages of pooling capital while retaining local autonomy and avoiding the governance problems that follow from merger.[26] Affiliation-groups pool human capital; the sharing is inter-, not intra-, firm. They represent a different form of pooling than the partner/associate deal that is at the heart of the big law firm. Such pooling obviates the need for a tournament within the affiliation group but not the need for parallel tournaments within the component firms.[27]

Subcontracting. Extra-firm collaboration need not be prearranged or continuing. Firms might enlarge their capacity by subcontracting to other lawyers

24. Alperson 1983, p. 10 (a New York firm serving as national counsel to one asbestos manufacturer set up a document center and devised a two-way communication system to coordinate the activities of counsel in forty different jurisdictions); Warshauer 1984 (the attorney in charge described the role of this kind of coordinating counsel).

25. Jensen 1988b, p. 1.

26. The appearance of such networks invites the question of whether we might expect to find the related but distinct two-level solution of franchising, in which the parties contract for an exchange of capital in a standardized form. One might imagine a national law firm's brand name and package of tested procedures being exchanged for a smaller firm's local reputation and client contacts. Some law-firm branching may approximate this.

27. Each of the member firms may be built around such a deal and tournament, but the intrafirm tournaments are not integrated but remain parallel. We might imagine scenarios of disintegration in which a firm decomposes its tournament into several parallel ones—for example, for separate departments, regional offices, or nonlawyer professional groups.

or firms.[28] For example, it was reported that Seattle firms involved in the massive litigation about WPPSS "are tending to use contract lawyers rather than letting themselves balloon with the extra business."[29] Firms may have a strategy of seeking very large matters and meeting staffing needs by contracting with smaller firms. Thus a dynamic Houston firm of some thirty lawyers was able to take on the Hunt Brothers massive litigation: "we go to small firms around the country and . . . we pick the lawyers we want to work on the case. . . . It's great for referrals in the future. It assures that we aren't going to have to expand too quickly."[30] Subcontracting strategies are facilitated by the growth of firms supplying temporary legal workers, both lawyers and paralegals.[31] And outside suppliers provide firms with "litigation support services" that include not only computerized document retrieval but can extend to "taking over case management, tracing the whereabouts of defendants and witnesses, writing briefs and researching issues, providing expert witnesses and making visual presentations for trial."[32] Firms can use these products to achieve enlarged capacity while avoiding a commitment to growth that might be unsustainable.

Finally in our list of alternatives, we should consider providers of business-law services who have not chosen the law firm as a vehicle for organizing these services.

In-House Law Departments. Corporate law departments have grown rapidly at the same time that there are more and larger big firms. There are now groups of salaried lawyers in corporations, governments, and other organizations who are undertaking more and more of the range of things done by the big law firm. In some instances this means displacing the large law firm; in other instances it means enhanced control over outside law firms. Corporate departments may model themselves on the big firm[33] or adopt organizational structures that depart sharply from that of the big firm.[34]

In-house law departments are very different kinds of creatures that deserve

28. Granelli 1978, p. 1.

29. Cox 1987, pp. 1, 34.

30. Susman 1987, pp. 130–31. Farming out work has always been a part of the big-firm repertoire. What seems to be new is its elaboration as an alternative way of being a contender for the most profitable legal work.

31. Berkman 1988, p. 24; Mansnerus 1988, p. B10.

32. Middleton 1984, pp. 1, 26. The recent growth of contract research services is recounted in Hayes (1989b, p. B1).

33. The attempt to organize General Foods' law department as a firm with associates, promotion to partner, and collegial governance is described in Stevens (1987, p. 80–94).

34. See the general counsel of Arthur Young and Co.'s description of his office of nine lawyers and sixty support staff (Liggio 1984).

more detailed analysis. They do not enjoy the autonomy of free-standing firms; their size is linked to the needs of a single client; the prosperity of seniors is not connected to the number of juniors. If the in-house law department wished to incorporate the promotion to partnership tournament type of incentive scheme, the department would have to be able to sustain growth independently of the needs of its corporation. One possibility would be to sever the department from company needs by selling excess capacity to other companies or to employees or small businesses or even to outside law firms.[35] That is, one could imagine a firm that was a "law subsidiary" of a corporation, rather than a law department. The development of such firms would of course confront the long-standing ban on the practice of law by corporations.[36] It would be a firm with outside ownership, in this case a single owner. (Whether such firms would be permitted to practice is similar to the question of whether firms should be publicly held.)[37]

All of the formats discussed here leave undisturbed the basic architectural features of the system of legal services.[38] One of these is the division of the profession into what Heinz and Laumann call the individual and corporate hemispheres.[39] Specialization, they point out, is as much by client as body of

35. Cf. a description of one corporate law department that had developed expertise in the unitary tax area being retained by other corporate law departments (Liggio 1984, p. 107).

36. See Andrews (1989).

37. Could the in-house law department compete for a bigger share of corporate law business (without the connection to other clients)? One observer of law-firm history concluded that corporate legal business was originally located in big firms rather than law departments because "[t]he additional experience and connections that were developed by serving a variety of clients made the value of law firms so high that it was economically infeasible . . . [in the short-run] for corporations to 'buy out' corporate law firms, or to establish equivalent in-house legal departments" (Pinansky 1986–87, p. 634). If this observation is still relevant today, then the answer to our question is no. But if, as some believe, in-house law departments are populated with lawyers who have more experience, qualifications, business sense, and connections than ever before, perhaps the question remains open.

38. One of these architectural features is that all legal services to all kinds of clients are provided by members of a single, if highly differentiated and stratified, licensed profession. We suspect that in spite of intensified specialization and stratification, ideological and political considerations will keep law a single profession. In a 1921 Carnegie Foundation report that many hoped would be the Flexner report of legal education, Alfred Z. Reed (1921, pp. 237–38) proposed the formation of "[a]n Inner Bar distinguished from the General Body of Practitioners," to include "lawyers of superior attainments, of broader vision, of greater ability to identify themselves with a larger whole" and "less highly trained lawyers to administer, in behalf of the people, the law as it is." This aspect of the report received a frigid reception and was never acted upon. We see nothing in the present situation that suggests any new support for the notion of separate training and licensing of elite and/or business lawyers.

39. We have confined our attention to the corporate hemisphere. We would anticipate a similar

law.[40] Could the separation of hemispheres be overcome? Imagine for example a pool of personal-injury or labor lawyers serving comers on either side by the "cab rank" or common carrier principle. This in turn would involve a retreat from the strong identification with the client that has been such a distinctive characteristic of American lawyering. Further, we might imagine that legal services were provided as a public utility rather than in a competitive marketplace.[41] This would give an unaccustomed primacy to the theme of lawyers as public officers. We mention these more far-reaching proposals to put in perspective the new forms of practice that we discuss here, which leave in place the basic architecture of the system. (And we assume that the system will be peopled by lawyers much like those who people it today, not by alien creatures of strikingly different inclination.)

We can imagine an impulse to address the problems of big firms through public regulation. Various proposals can be conjectured: control of firm size, control of hierarchy within the firm, elimination of firms altogether. But we are skeptical of the need and efficacy of such reforms and believe that most such attempts misconstrue the nature of the big firm's problems.

Many of the problems the big firms face originate in the discomforts of the attorneys who must deal with the increasing pressures of growth. But that growth cannot be controlled in isolation. Much of it is a by-product of the very mechanism which allows lawyers to efficiently exchange their assets. So long as business attorneys have a need to share capital and labor, and so long as clients have a need for them to do so, there will be a demand for some mechanism to protect against the risks inherent in the exchange. The business-law firm and

---

proliferation of formats in the hemisphere that services individuals. Emergent formats of practice there might include:

—mass marketing: so-called "legal clinics" using salaried employees and/or franchises to provide relatively standardized services to consumers;

—specialty firms that do custom work on a selective basis, with business generated by referral rather than enduring relations with clients;

—generalists with back-up: small firms that can undertake a variety of things because of availability of backup from commercial services or collegial networks;

—legal services for the poor provided by innovative offices, for example, following strategies for group-oriented services (Bellow 1977);

—public-interest law firms, supported by external funding and recovery of attorneys' fees, addressing collective problems of diffuse constituencies.

40. Heinz and Laumann 1982, Chapter 10. LoPucki (1990) provides an elaborated account of patterns of lawyer specialization.

41. Thus, Marvin Frankel (1977, p. 92, 100) proposed a National Legal Service that would make "government law offices comprising salaried lawyers . . . available to serve all citizens, rich or poor, for every species of legal problems."

its promotion-to-partner tournament has played an integral part in safeguarding those interests. Growth, fortunately or unfortunately, has been a by-product of that structure. Attempts to limit by fiat the size, organization, or growth of firms, without also addressing the risks inherent in the underlying transaction, endanger the exchanges which allow skilled lawyers to address more issues and service more clients. Regulating growth might also jeopardize the very exchanges which permit young lawyers to develop the skills, experience, and reputation to assist business clients with increasingly large and complex problems.

We suspect that reforms that focus only on the structure of firms without also addressing how to safeguard the underlying exchanges would do little to alleviate the problems that trouble big-firm lawyers and would raise the transaction costs of utilizing their legal talent. For instance, suppose it was decreed that all attorneys had to work on their own (presumably they could hire such non-lawyers as secretaries) and were prohibited from employing other lawyers. What would happen? Unless somehow all lawyers' skills, training, contacts, and intelligence were equalized it is likely that some attorneys would still have more human capital than they could profitably use. Consequently, there would still be a desire to sell surplus human capital, which could be accomplished in several ways. First, a market for "almost lawyers" would develop. Lawyers would hire more paralegals and other nonlawyers with lawyer skills.

Second, there would be a great deal more contracting out. Lawyers with surplus capital would still contract with attorneys who had extra labor. But rather than govern the transaction inside firms, the transactions would take place across markets. The problems inherent in attempting to use markets to regulate transactions of this nature would not be abated, but the prevailing solution—firms—would be eliminated.

Third, perhaps a system like the securities market, with brokers and published prices, could be used to facilitate trades, but it is certainly not clear that this would be a superior or less costly structure. And it is not even very clear that the brokerage system would look greatly different than the present one. For example, like an assignment partner, the brokers would have to know quite a bit about the attorneys they used and would therefore be limited in the number of attorneys in their pool. To assure a broker that some attorneys would be available on a moment's notice retainer arrangements would need to be made. There would be no "partners," but there would be "higher-paid" lawyers because the system would be likely to pay premiums to attorneys with highly valued capital.

Fourth, much work would move in-house, where larger teams of lawyers could be put together—unless the limitation were to apply there (in a strong version it would eliminate in-house lawyers entirely).

We are skeptical of this type of regulation or any of the variants which attempt to place restrictions on the size of law firms. It seems doubtful that any major intervention is needed or justified to protect the lawyers. Lawyers are no more communal animals than the rest of us. They do not congregate in packs because they have some deeply felt need to be with large numbers of similarly trained professionals. To limit the size of firms does not eliminate the desire to share human capital or the problems of doing so. We believe that the firm has provided useful means of dealing with the monitoring and incentive compatibility problems associated with sharing human capital. Will it always? The answer is, not necessarily. But lawyers are neither unintelligent nor selfless. If it is possible to organize the exchange of human capital more efficiently without firms, enterprising lawyers are likely to do so and to gain a competitive edge over those who are slow to respond. But until that time, efforts to "break up" law firms will not eliminate the need to share human capital but will impose greater transaction costs on doing so.

If intervention in firm organization is justified it is not to make lawyers comfortable, but because firm organization affects the kind, quantity, quality, cost, or distribution of legal services. If, for example, we knew that the growth and transformation of business-law firms reduced the availability of legal services or made them more expensive or decreased their quality we would have cause for concern. In making such assessments, we should be interested not only in the way that firm organization affects the large firms' business clients. We should be equally concerned about the effect on wider publics. Does the growth of big firms increase the disparity in quality and quantity of legal services afforded to large corporations versus their smaller antagonists, or to representatives of diffuse and unorganized interests, or to public agencies? How do the changes in the market for legal talent brought about by growth in the number and size of large firms affect the supply of legal services for others? How do increases in the size, competitiveness, and hierarchy of large firms affect lawyers' independence in giving advice, their insistence on holding clients to legal or moral standards, their participation in legal reform, and so forth? There is little research that addresses these questions. What research there is suggests that lawyers have in the past displayed less of these noble attributes than we might have hoped.[42] It is far from clear that disparities in legal services between haves and have-nots have increased as law firms have grown. Nor is it evident that the recent growth in the scale of law firms has decreased the conferral of public benefits by lawyers. We think these are questions that deserve exploration. If the public intervenes in law firm organization it should be with an eye to protecting public interests, not lawyer comforts. And such intervention will have to keep in mind the way that the law firm is a solution to a tricky set of problems that flow from the very nature of the lawyers' craft.

42. Nelson 1988, Chapter 7.

As we survey the big firm of today, its variants, companions, and rivals, we may be seeing prefigurations of emergent forms of practice or we may be looking at sports and chimeras. What forms will prosper depends on unknown contingencies, among them the still-emergent preferences of lawyers. Notwithstanding, we want to close with a few speculations about the general contours of things to come.

The present era of transformation is reminiscent of the formative era of big firms. The big firm arose from lawyers' participation in the restructuring (by consolidations, mergers, reorganizations) and financing of business organizations and from handling the litigation that swirled around them in a legal setting of unprecedented complexity. Lawyers and clients were mobile; firm arrangements were fluid and volatile. The new kind of firm that crystallized provided services that ranged far beyond what had earlier been considered the boundaries of the practice of law.[43] Today, we are in another era of restructuring of business, the complexity of which is compounded by transnational flows of capital and new information technologies. As the demand for legal services changes, with more complex deals and more use of litigation as a business strategy, there is an expansion of services provided by lawyers. We can observe a volatility and organizational innovation that have been absent from the legal scene for generations.

As we talk about changes, we should recall the considerable stability of the world of big firms. Big law firms are still relatively small units, they have relatively small shares of their market, they are relatively unbureaucratic, they are dependent on particular kinds of clients, and they are constrained somewhat by an ideology of professionalism. These continuities coexist with powerful and enduring currents of change. We would not anticipate a reversal of the trend to rationalization: we expect that by cost accounting, specialized managers, and other means, firms will be more self-consciously strategic in their management and planning. We also anticipate that law firms will be increasingly entrepreneurial, oriented to finding new markets for their services, developing new services (including new combinations of "legal" and "nonlegal" services), and new forms of firm organization. Up to now there has been, with minor variations, basically one model of the big firm.[44] Lately, big firms are coming to look less alike as they try different strategies for coping. We anticipate pluralization—both that big firms will be less similar and that some of the work they presently do will be done by firms (or nonfirms) that are not big firms at all.

43. Pinansky 1986–87, p. 623.

44. On the tendency of organizations in a field to resemble each other, and the forces that support such isomorphism, see DiMaggio and Powell (1983).

But there is little to suggest that the great promotion-to-partner tournament is on the wane. Nothing has reduced both the partner's and associate's need for protection from opportunistic conduct. Partners still require a method of motivating and monitoring associates. Associates continue to need assurances that hard work will be honestly evaluated and rewarded. The promotion tournament solves both problems. We can envision firms having more and more elaborated tournaments, and we see evidence of that in the tiering of partnerships and the firing of some associates earlier. We can see the reduction of the promotion-to-partnership core relative to the entire mass of the firm, but we find no evidence that the core is not going to continue to grow. This does not mean that every firm will keep growing inexorably. Firms may break apart—but we would expect that the successor pieces would then recommence the pattern of exponential growth. We can also imagine a downward kink in which rates of growth (the portion of growth due to demand, etc.) would decrease so that overall growth would be slower, possibly even resulting in reduced promotion rates. We believe, though, that the basic transformation will continue to be *evolutionary*. There may be major discontinuities, but because of the inherent difficulties of monitoring the sharing of lawyers' human capital the changes will be in degree, not in kind. The changes which have occurred and, we believe, will continue to occur, are designed to extend and supplement the tournament, not to replace it.

Until recently, the big law firm was not only accounted a success in terms of institutional survival and technical performance, it was accepted as the paradigm of legal professionalism. A generation ago, Jerome Carlin studied the New York bar and found that large-firm lawyers not only had the largest incomes, served the most affluent clients, were best trained, and most technically skilled, but experienced "maximum pressure to conform to distinctively professional standards, as well as the more ordinary ethical norms; at the same time they are insulated from pressures to violate [those professional standards]."[45] In technical skill, collegiality, and probity, the large firm seemed to provide a venue for the most exemplary professionalism. Ironically, Geoffrey Hazard noted in his foreword to Carlin's book, the traditional badges of the profession—an independent general practice rendering personal service to all sorts of people—were no longer the marks by which the truly "professional" lawyer was identified. Instead it was large-firm lawyers who embodied the professional ideal.[46]

Since then, the big firms have continued to flourish. They have become larger, more numerous, more prosperous. There has been no diminution of specialization or technical skill. But the sense that such firms are the chosen

45. Carlin 1966, pp. 168–69.
46. Carlin 1966, p. xxiii.

vehicles of the professional ideal has waned. They have been assailed for abandoning their responsibilities as officers of public justice in favor of a narrow devotion to client interests. As they have grown and been transformed, they have been attacked as having sacrificed client interests to market considerations as well as having abandoned the collegiality and self-governance that made them good work-places. The relationship of the large firm to professionalism now seems quite problematic.

What kind of setting will these modified and new forms of practice provide for the admired qualities associated with professionalism (self-governance, independence of judgment, individualized treatment, and so forth)? There seems no reason to think that the big firm is the only possible container for these qualities—or even a uniquely good one. The transformation and displacement of the big law firm is not necessarily a danger to professionalism; indeed it may present an opportunity for new forms of pursuing professionalism.

Looking back on our story, we see the link of the big firm with aspirations to professionalism as ambivalent. Law practice, or at least that part of it that serviced large organizations, departed a century ago from the individual-practice format for doing legal work. But it never arrived at the great bureaucratic corporation as a format for practice.[47] Perhaps the promotion-to-partnership firm should be credited with averting such developments by permitting the development of sufficient size to undertake the largest and most complex work.[48] The big-firm form carried an inadvertent commitment to exponential growth, but that growth was sufficiently slow to be compatible for a long period with "professional" forms of governance. So law practice never suffered the separation of ownership from control; control of work by others was, in aspiration at least, only temporary. Compared to other business services, law remained relatively unconcentrated, decentralized, unbureaucratic, and worker-managed. As the big firm becomes a less congenial vehicle, lawyers enjoy new opportunities to use their institution-shaping skills to reorganize the formats of professional work to make it produce the services and protections desired by society while making it fulfilling for those who do the work.

47. On the specter of practice by corporations, see Bristol (1913); Dawson (1930, p. 274).

48. Apparently the big firm enjoyed some comparative advantage over internal law departments within corporations. See Pinansky (1986–87, pp. 632–35).

Appendix A: Data on the Size of
Law Firms

Alternative Measures of the "Size" of Law Firms. Our theory of law-firm growth is about the changing size of law firms. But what is the "size" of a law firm? On reflection this apparantly straightforward concept is not as clear as it first appears. For example, the size of firms might be measured by the total number of persons engaged in their efforts. This would count mailroom employees the same as senior partners. It would count employees who work thirty hours a week the same as employees who work sixty hours a week. But this would lead to the conclusion that a firm grew when a senior partner left and two mailroom employees were added—and that it shrunk when a partner was added and the two mailroom employees were replaced by a mailing machine or an outside service. Such a measure of size might be a useful one for the fire inspector who is responsible for seeing that everyone can be evacuated from the office in case of fire or the building engineer concerned with the capacity of the air-conditioning system. But it is not very helpful for our purposes, since it defines size in a way that is unrelated to the capacity to supply legal services.

We might improve this "total persons" model by adjusting for hours worked and skill levels to get a measure of the total amount of effort expended by the employees. But such a total-effort measure would not reflect changes in the productivity of that effort as the technology changes—for example, the replacement of typewriters by word processors, of library research by LEXIS. But if we were to move further, to a measure of total productivity, we might end up far from our intuitive notion of size. Measured by the value of services produced, a specialized boutique with ten lawyers might be "larger" than another firm with fifteen lawyers. Such a measure might be useful for measuring economic impact but not so useful if we want to know about the numbers and careers of lawyers.

Measuring the Number of Lawyers. Our thesis is about the core of each firm that consists of lawyers. It is an assertion about the inherent tendency of that number to grow once certain contractual relations are established. So, even though a measure of total personnel or effort or productivity might be more useful for other purposes, for our purposes we are interested in the number of lawyers employed by the firm. It is easier to measure the number of lawyers in a firm than to measure the firm's "size" in effort or productivity terms, but it is still far from simple.

Counting lawyers in a firm requires agreement on who is a lawyer, who is part of the firm, and who counts as "one."

Who is a "lawyer"?

• Is a newly hired but unadmitted associate a lawyer?
• Is a "paralegal" in one firm a lawyer if he does work identical to that done by trained and admitted lawyers in another firm?
• Is a summer intern or a part-time law student a lawyer?

Who is part of the firm?

• Is a lawyer affiliated with the firm as "of counsel" part of the firm?
• Is a "permanent associate" passed over for promotion part of the firm? Suppose he is designated "of counsel"?
• Are "temporary" lawyers hired for a specific task part of the firm?

Who counts as "one"?

• Does a retired partner who retains an office and does a fraction of the work she formerly did count as one?
• Does an associate or partner who is working part-time in order to fulfill child-care responsibilities count as one?
• Does a partner who is on leave for a sabbatical or for government service count as one?

It is easy to see that a census-taker who answered these questions one way would come up with a different count than other census-takers who answered them other ways. There is no one true way to count lawyers. It is no less "accurate" to count those "of counsel" than it is to exclude them. What is a good way to count lawyers depends on the purpose for which one is counting. If you are interested in what recent law graduates are doing you will want to include unadmitted lawyers. If you are interested in the total productive capacity of firms, you will want to discount retirees and part-timers.

We are concerned with tracing the growth of the core of partners and associates in each firm over a period of time—the longer the better. We do not have the luxury (and drudgery) of generating new data from scratch. There is no way that anyone could give us a fresh and accurate response to the question of how many lawyers were in X firm in 1926 or 1946. We have to rely on data that have been recorded over the years.

Sources of Time Series Data. There are two major sources of such data, each with its own problems. The first is the surveys of large firms that have been compiled since 1978 by the *National Law Journal (NLJ)*.[1] The other is the annual listing of attorneys in firms in the Martindale-Hubbell directories (for which we have access to the majority of volumes, beginning with 1922),[2] from which we were able to construct our own data set. Each of these data sets gives us an annual reading of the number of lawyers in each firm. Each uses a consistent but different method of measuring that number.

The *National Law Journal* collects figures annually on the 250 largest firms.[3] A questionnaire is mailed each year to firms on the previous year's list plus some 50 to 100 additional firms that are considered to be possible candidates for the list. The *NLJ* questionnaire is meant to be completed by a single respondent within each firm. Obviously, the respondent's knowledge may be imperfect, his perspective may be different from that of the predecessor who answered the previous year or from that of his counterparts in other firms.

The *National Law Journal* questionnaire asks for the number of partners and associates. It does not provide any instruction about who is to be counted as a partner or an associate, except that "of counsel" are to be excluded from these categories. "Of counsel" are counted separately, but the totals printed in the annual published surveys do not include them. We do not know how much respondents in different firms (or in the same firm from year to year) differ in the way they deal with the other "who is a lawyer" and "who counts as one" questions that we noted above. We suspect that there is some variation, but we have no reason to think that it introduces any systematic bias into the figures about firm growth.[4]

Martindale-Hubbell publishes an annual directory of lawyers that reports the names, but not the number, of lawyers at each firm. To estimate the number we have had our research assistants consult the directory listings (for each city) of

1. This is the longest-running and most continuous of the annual surveys of large firms conducted by several publications. *Legal Times* conducted surveys of 100 firms in 1979 and 1980, 200 firms in 1981–83, and 500 firms in 1984 and 1985. Starting in 1986, this national survey was dropped in favor of a listing of the 75 largest firms in Washington, D.C. Since 1987, *Of Counsel* has published a survey each April of the growth of the 500 largest law firms during the preceding year. Not only are more firms included than in the *National Law Journal* list, but there is information about "of counsel" lawyers and about hires and promotions, with laterals identified separately. Were it available for a long period of time, we would happily have used this source, but it is only available since 1987.

2. The *Martindale-Hubbell Law Directory*, published by Martindale-Hubbell, Inc., of New Providence, New Jersey, has appeared under that title since 1931. For some sixty years prior to that, the predecessor publications appeared as *Martindale's American Law Directory* and *Hubbell's Legal Directory*. Our information from before 1931 is taken from Martindale's directory.

3. From 1978 through 1982 the survey covered 200 law firms; since 1983, it has included 250.

4. If there are more nonequity partners or permanent associates or "provisional partners" or "provisional associates" that some firms are calling "of counsel," the exclusion of these from totals may lead to an understatement of firm growth.

the firms we are interested in and count the names. For each office of each firm, there are two lists, one in the firm "card" that appears in the "Geographical Bar Roster" section and the other a set of brief biographical sketches in the "Biographical" section. Our assistants counted the names of all lawyers that appeared in either section. This process was repeated for each year.

Martindale-Hubbell identifies lawyers as partners or associates or some other category (such as "of counsel"). In our data set, we have combined all the latter designations into a "miscellaneous" category. When we give firm totals, all lawyers are included: partners, associates, and miscellaneous. When we identify partners and associates, the miscellaneous are excluded.

Martindale-Hubbell sends a "Firm Report Form" annually to each firm that subscribes to its service and a "Personal Report Form" to every attorney admitted to the bar in every state and the District of Columbia. They enlarge their mailing list yearly by adding the names of newly admitted members of the bar as supplied by the state bar examiners. A lawyer is listed as part of a firm when the firm reports him as a member, indicating that he is admitted as an attorney, and this is verified by the lawyer mailing back the completed Personal Report Form.

Comparing our compilation from Martindale-Hubbell of the number of lawyers in firms with the number reported in the *National Law Journal* surveys, we see that the former systematically lists fewer lawyers than the number reported in the latter.[5] We can think of at least two reasons for this discrepancy. First, Martindale-Hubbell will often lag at least one year behind the *NLJ* survey. A new law-school graduate will generally be included by the firms' respondent to the *NLJ* survey as soon as that associate begins work (or even before—since the survey is filled out in the summer and many associates do not join their firms until the fall), regardless of his bar admission status. However, Martindale-Hubbell specifically declines to list that associate until assured that he has been admitted to the bar. Generally, notification of bar admissions occurs in the fall and spring. By the time that Martindale-Hubbell receives the lists from the states, mails the Personal Report Form, and receives the reply it is easy to imagine that someone who is counted on the *NLJ* survey in a given year will not be listed by Martindale-Hubbell until at least a year later.

If effective dates were the only difference between Martindale-Hubbell and the *NLJ,* we would expect to see a simple lag in the data: totals compiled from Martindale-Hubbell data would simply approximate the previous year's *NLJ* totals. But this does not appear to be the case. We believe that a second reason that Martindale-Hubbell numbers are lower than those in *NLJ* derives from differences in the methods by which the two publications collect their data. The *National Law Journal* is essentially asking one person at each law firm to fill

5. The magnitude of the discrepancy is discussed below at n. 6 and p. 144.

out a questionnaire. With persistent letter and phone follow-ups they can expect a reasonably high response rate, especially since firms are concerned that they be listed. Martindale-Hubbell on the other hand, requires every individual lawyer to provide information. If an attorney does not respond to requests for information, he will not be included in the directory.

Surveys like that of the *National Law Journal* are well suited to our research, but unfortunately they only report data back to 1978. Our study requires detailed growth histories over a period substantially longer than ten years. One solution would be to combine the *National Law Journal* data since 1978 with Martindale-Hubbell numbers for the period before 1978. But Martindale-Hubbell "undercounted" in the same way before 1978 that it does currently. So, combining its numbers with *National Law Journal* data would overstate the "jump" in the size of firms after 1978.

A second solution is to assume that Martindale-Hubbell understates the number of attorneys in any given firm in a fairly consistent manner over time. If that is the case, while the absolute numbers will be inaccurate, the observed changes over time will accurately reflect relative changes in the size of that firm. We do not make the further assumption that the "error" is uniform for all firms. Thus, we accept the possibility that our data is inaccurate as to the relative size of firm A and firm B in a given year.[6] We only claim that it is a useful indicator of the relative size of firm A in year 1 and year 5 and year 10. Even if the absolute numbers do not accurately represent the size of the firm at a given time, the rates of growth will accurately reflect those of the firm. Because we are concerned with rates of growth, not absolute size, we followed this second path.

Our Major Data Set. We have derived from Martindale-Hubbell histories of the size of one hundred large firms. Group I consists of fifty of the largest firms. We used the largest firms in the *National Law Journal* listings for 1986,[7] omitting on various grounds six firms listed among the fifty largest.[8] We present a

6. The ratios of Martindale-Hubbell to *National Law Journal* figures for firms in our Group I ranges from 64.1 percent to 101.1 percent for associates and from 86.1 percent to 108.1 percent for partners.

7. We used the *National Law Journal*'s rankings because Martindale-Hubbell prints names only and no summary statistics. Hence, to determine the largest firms solely from the directory would require us to have counted the number of lawyers in every major law firm in the country and then rank the results. We also make no claim that our sample represents the growth history of every law firm.

8. We omitted Hyatt Legal Services and Jacoby & Myers on grounds that they were not firms whose reward structure was built around the "promotion to partnership." Finley Kumble was omitted because its growth history was too short for our purposes. Akin, Gump, Strauss, Hauer & Field, Baker & McKenzie, and Wilson, Elser, Moskowitz, Edelman & Dicker were omitted because the way the raw data were reported made it very difficult to get accurate counts.

count of the partners and associates and total number of lawyers for each of these firms for each year. For two firms, Simpson Thacher and Bartlett and Sullivan and Cromwell, it was possible to construct alternate growth histories from published firm histories.[9] These data, which are included in the data set but not in the computations, confirm the general accuracy of the picture of growth derived from the Martindale-Hubbell data and the presence of the undercount.

Group II consists of fifty smaller but still large firms that that were roughly the two-hundreth to two-hundred-fiftieth in the *National Law Journal* list in 1988.[10] The two data sets are available in their entirety in hard copy and on disk from the Disputes Processing Research Program, Institute for Legal Studies, University of Wisconsin Law School, Madison, Wisconsin 53706. Graphs of the selected growth histories are found in figures 1 to 10 at the end of this Appendix.

We were able to derive a rough estimate of the extent of the Martindale-Hubbell undercount by comparing our Group I data with *National Law Journal* data on these same firms for the period from 1978 to 1986. Our Group I data accounted for 88 percent of the total lawyers in the *National Law Journal* counts of these fifty firms: 96 percent of the partners and 79.6 percent of the associates.[11]

The unchanging method and continuous collection of the underlying information persuades us that this data set is the most reliable for depicting long-term trends in law firms. We stress that we take these figures not as direct measurements of the absolute size of firms, but as reliable indicators of firm growth.

Other Data Sets. For specific purposes we have also compiled another data set that we refer to as the *"National Law Journal* Two Twenties" data set. This consists of data on twenty of the largest firms in New York (NY) and twenty of

9. Simpson, Thacher & Bartlett 1984; Sullivan & Cromwell 1981.

10. Once again the rankings, but not the counts, came from the *National Law Journal* annual survey of the 250 largest firms.

11. We suggested earlier that a significant portion of the undercount is attributable to Martindale-Hubbell's practice of counting only those attorneys admitted to the bar and the resulting lag between the time an attorney joins the firm and the time Martindale-Hubbell includes him in their directory. We can partially adjust for the lag by assuming that the actual number of lawyers with a firm in year t equals the sum of the Martindale-Hubbell listing of partners in year t and the associates listed in year t + 1. Combining the data in this way for Group I firms we derived estimates for associates that were 87 percent of those listed by the *National Law Journal.* While the resulting totals are generally still below the *National Law Journal* numbers, the lagged figures more closely approximate those numbers. We should not exclude the possibility that the *National Law Journal* count of associates is too high, based in many cases on optimistic midsummer estimation of the number of associates who will join the firm by late September.

the largest firms outside New York (ONY),[12] compiled from the *National Law Journal* surveys for 1980 and 1987. We have used this "Two Twenties" data set to document patterns of branching and use of paralegals, and to supplement our findings on leverage.

From time to time we have relied upon quantitative data compiled by various investigators who recorded the size and composition of a set of law firms at a single point in time. Reports by Klaw,[13] *Business Week*,[14] and *Juris Doctor*,[15] appear to be based on information supplied by the firms and we think they are highly reliable as cross-sectional portraits. But we have no assurance that the various counting questions were dealt with in the same way. Thus any comparisons of the findings of one of these with another is extremely suspect even if occasionally useful.

Although these different data sets should not be combined to support assertions about change, the presence of these multiple readings reinforces our confidence in the findings presented here. All of these data, collected for other purposes by various observers, are for our purpose indirect and "unobtrusive measures" of the underlying reality that we seek to address but cannot observe directly. Our confidence in our assertions about that underlying reality is reinforced by the "compensating error and converging corroboration from individually contaminated outcroppings."[16]

12. We omitted Hyatt Legal Services and Jacoby & Myers on grounds they were not "promotion-to-partnership" firms; Baker & McKenzie because we thought the relation of its offices might be distinctive; and Finley Kumble because it dissolved in 1987.

13. Klaw 1958.

14. *Business Week* 1968.

15. de Tocqueville (pseud.) 1972.

16. Webb, et al. 1966.

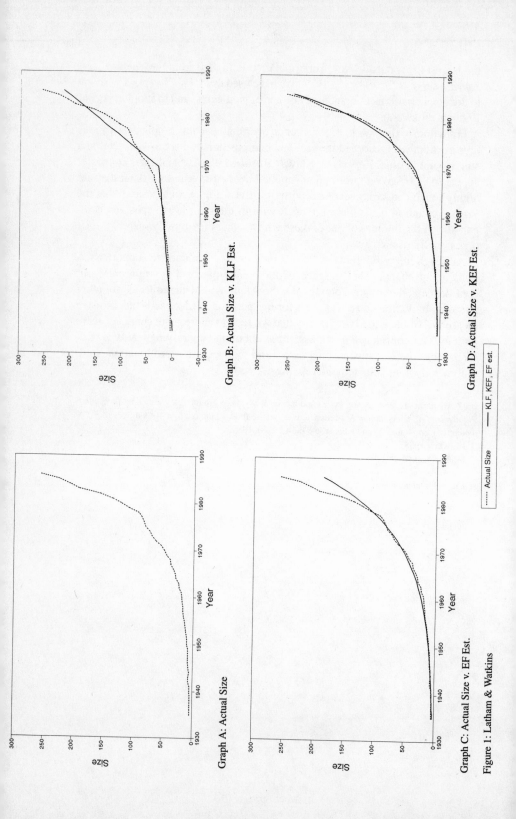

Graph A: Actual Size

Graph B: Actual Size v. KLF Est.

Graph C: Actual Size v. EF Est.

Graph D: Actual Size v. KEF Est.

Figure 1: Latham & Watkins

.... Actual Size   ——— KLF, KEF, EF est.

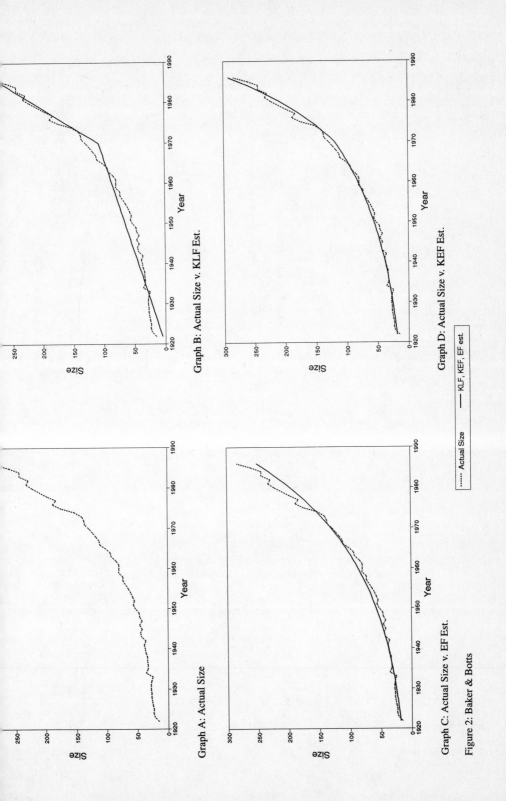

Graph A: Actual Size

Graph B: Actual Size v. KLF Est.

Graph C: Actual Size v. EF Est.

Graph D: Actual Size v. KEF Est.

Figure 2: Baker & Botts

······ Actual Size   —— KLF, KEF, EF est.

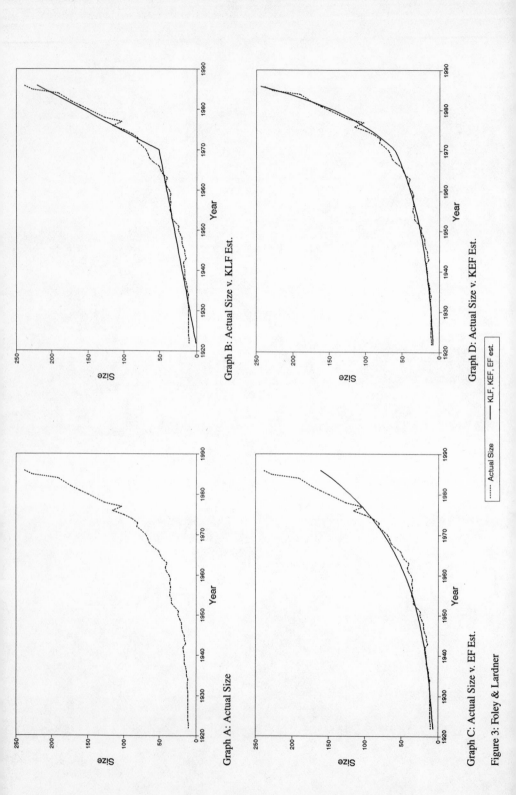

Graph A: Actual Size

Graph B: Actual Size v. KLF Est.

Graph C: Actual Size v. EF Est.

Graph D: Actual Size v. KEF Est.

Actual Size ·········   KLF, KEF, EF est. ———

Figure 3: Foley & Lardner

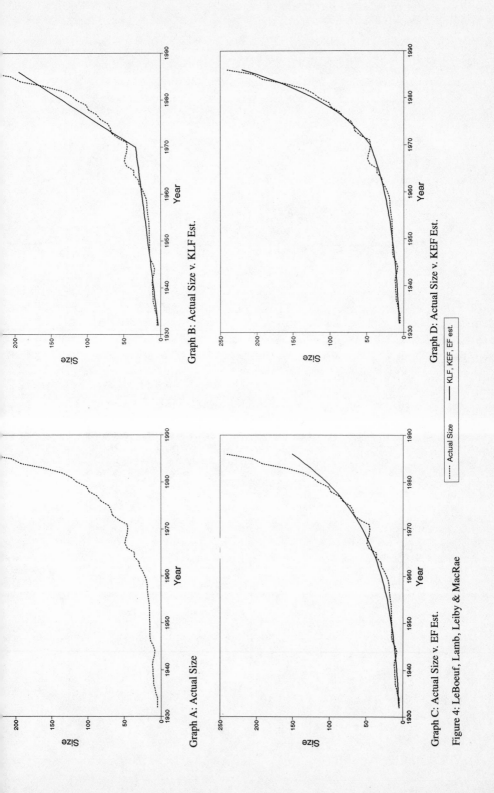

Graph A: Actual Size

Graph B: Actual Size v. KLF Est.

Graph C: Actual Size v. EF Est.

Graph D: Actual Size v. KEF Est.

Figure 4: LeBoeuf, Lamb, Leiby & MacRae

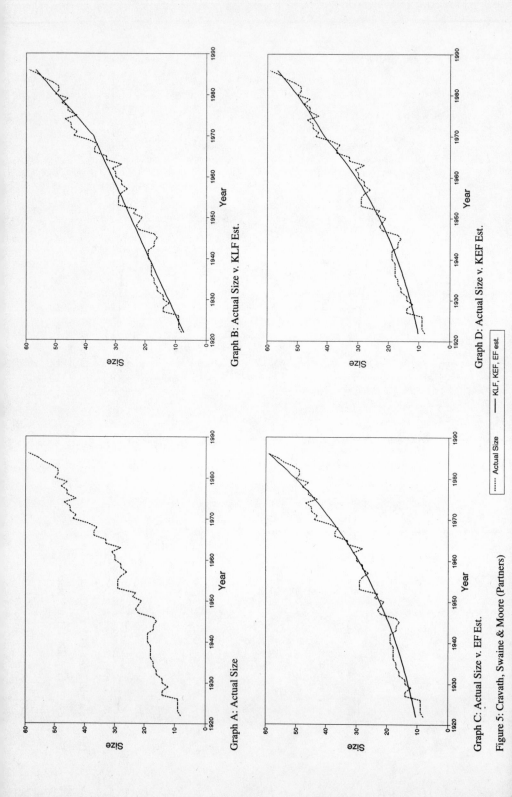

Graph A: Actual Size

Graph B: Actual Size v. KLF Est.

Graph C: Actual Size v. EF Est.

Graph D: Actual Size v. KEF Est.

········ Actual Size   ——— KLF, KEF, EF est.

Figure 5: Cravath, Swaine & Moore (Partners)

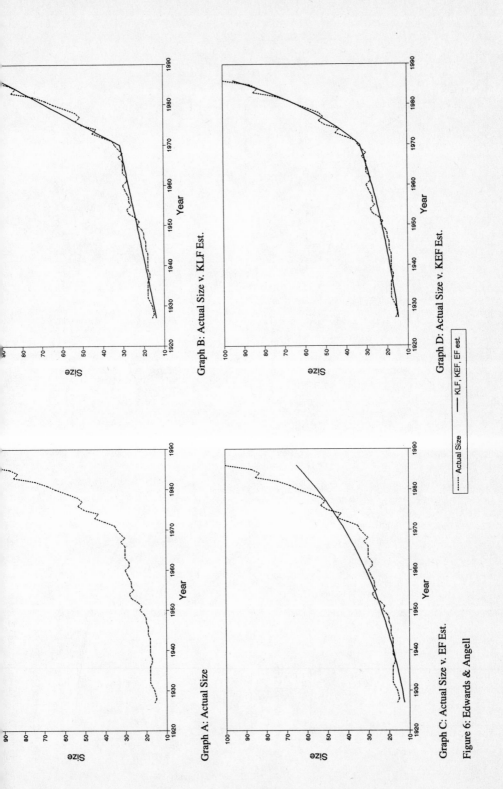

Graph A: Actual Size

Graph B: Actual Size v. KLF Est.

Graph C: Actual Size v. EF Est.

Graph D: Actual Size v. KEF Est.

Figure 6: Edwards & Angell

······ Actual Size ——— KLF, KEF, EF est.

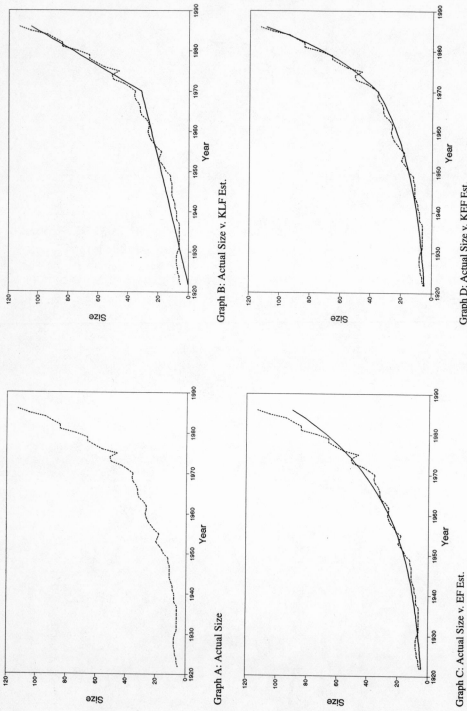

Graph A: Actual Size

Graph B: Actual Size v. KLF Est.

Graph C: Actual Size v. EF Est.

Graph D: Actual Size v. KEF Est.

······ Actual Size   ——— KLF, KEF, EF est.

Figure 7: Ice, Miller, Donadio & Ryan

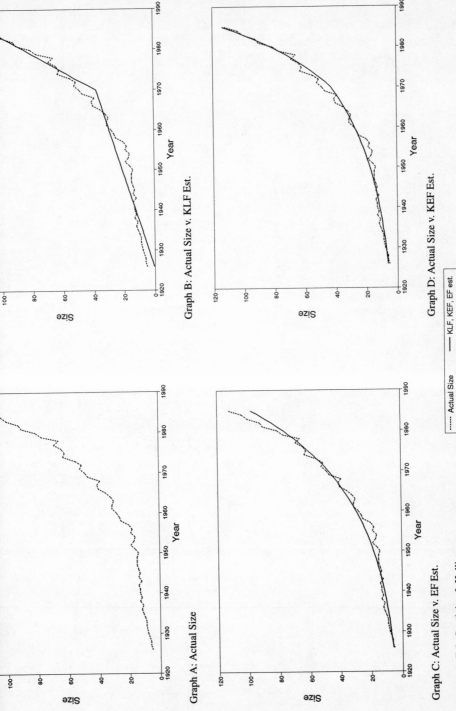

Graph A: Actual Size

Graph B: Actual Size v. KLF Est.

Graph C: Actual Size v. EF Est.

Graph D: Actual Size v. KEF Est.

Actual Size ......   KLF, KEF, EF est. ——

Figure 8: Taft, Stettinius & Hollister

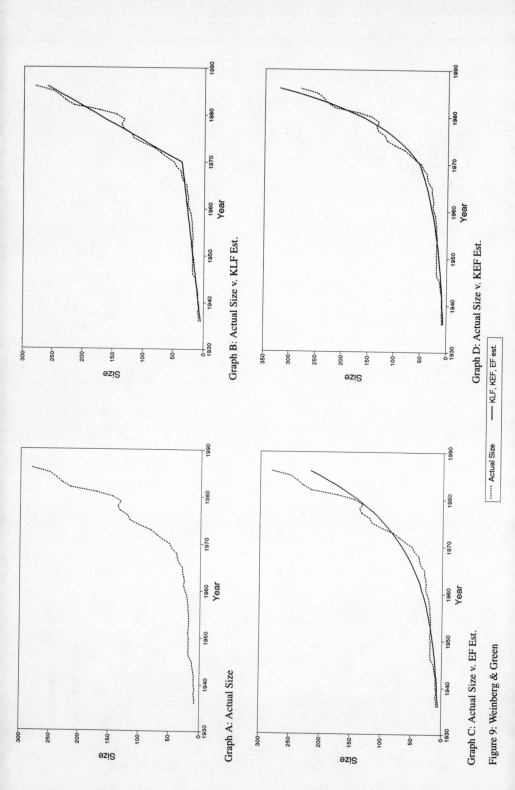

Graph A: Actual Size

Graph B: Actual Size v. KLF Est.

Graph C: Actual Size v. EF Est.

Graph D: Actual Size v. KEF Est.

Actual Size .... KLF, KEF, EF est. ———

Figure 9: Weinberg & Green

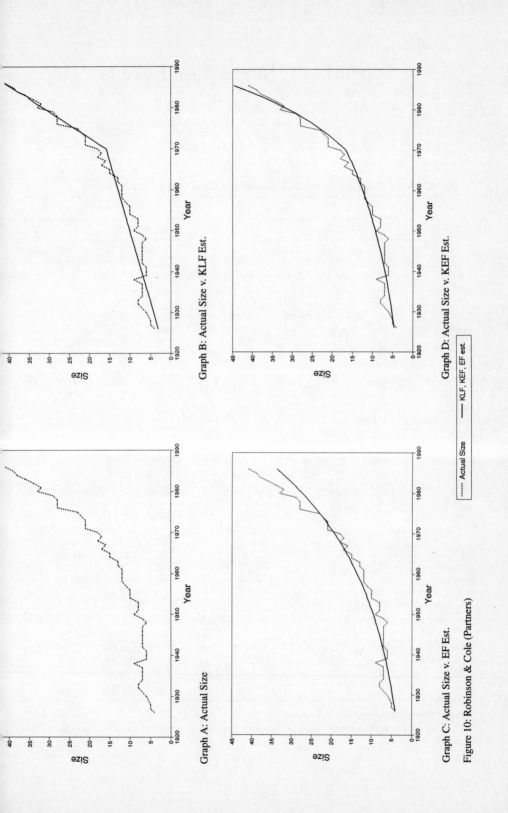

Graph A: Actual Size

Graph B: Actual Size v. KLF Est.

Graph C: Actual Size v. EF Est.

Graph D: Actual Size v. KEF Est.

Actual Size ·········   KLF, KEF, EF est. ——

Figure 10: Robinson & Cole (Partners)

Appendix B: Regression Results

Table B1 Group I Firms: Estimated Parameters and R^2 for KLF, EF, and KEF Models

		Totals				Partners			
		Constant	T_1	T_2	R^2	Constant	T_1	T_2	R^2
Arnold & Porter	KLF	−7.687	2.175	5.911	0.99	−3.564	1.111	2.573	0.97
			(15.781)	(17.241)			(11.745)	(10.938)	
	EF	1.094	0.109		0.90	0.649	0.1		0.93
			(18.076)				(21.618)		
	KEF	0.76	0.136	−0.083	0.92	0.362	0.124	−0.071	0.95
			(14.985)	(3.66)			(18.569)	(4.302)	
Baker & Botts	KLF	2.681	2.13	8.604	0.98	8.274	1.099	3.972	0.98
			(22.392)	(20.651)			(13.346)	(17.675)	
	EF	2.859	0.041		0.96	2.391	0.051		0.95
			(60.777)				(27.86)		
	KEF	2.916	0.038	0.018	0.98	2.499	0.043	0.028	0.96
			(49.682)	(5.478)			(16.688)	(3.996)	
Baker & Hostetler	KLF	17.311	0.856	11.933	0.95	5.405	0.596	0.6032	0.97
			(4.571)	(17.566)			(5.973)	(19.344)	
	EF	2.689	0.043		0.91	1.773	0.051		0.94
			(23.051)				(27.49)		
	KEF	2.915	0.03	0.065	0.98	2.029	0.039	0.052	0.98
			(22.021)	(13.138)			(22.288)	(9.541)	
Brobeck, Phleger & Harrison	KLF					−2.248	0.668	2.687	0.97
							(15.33)	(15.713)	
	EF					0.927	0.06		0.98
							(51.043)		
	KEF					0.904	0.061	−0.007*	0.98
							(36.627)	(1.07)	
Cadwalader, Wickersham & Taft	KLF					9.511	0.267	2.171	0.96
							(10.33)	(19.335)	
	EF					2.184	0.024		0.86
							(19.749)		
	KEF					2.336	0.017	0.047	0.95
							(15.876)	(10.22)	
Cahill, Gordon & Reindel	KLF	8.217	1.672	4.278	0.98	2.396	0.691	0.587	0.98
			(25.962)	(15.234)			(29.758)	(5.811)	
	EF	2.887	0.036		0.97	1.971	0.034		0.97
			(42.256)				(40.958)		

Note: Absolute t-statistics are in parentheses.

*Not significant at the 5 percent level. All other estimates of T_1 and T_2 significant at the 5 percent (or better) level.

Table B1 (*Continued*)

		Totals				Partners			
		Constant	T_1	T_2	R^2	Constant	T_1	T_2	R^2
	KEF	2.897	0.035	0.003*	0.97	1.911	0.037	−0.019	0.97
			(29.133)	(0.611)			(35.917)	(4.195)	
Cleary, Gottlieb,	KLF					3.177	1.001	2.295	0.96
Steen							(8.911)	(8.72)	
& Hamilton	EF					1.835	0.064		0.98
							(40.146)		
	KEF					1.803	0.067	−0.008*	0.98
							(23.246)	(1.14)	
Coudert Brothers	KLF	22.299	1.47	8.533	0.97	5.553	0.376	3.013	0.96
			(1.98)	(7.776)			(9.283)	(18.941)	
	EF	2.838	0.082		0.98	1.841	0.033		0.82
			(33.503)				(16.2)		
	KEF	2.972	0.068	0.022	0.98	2.095	0.022	0.061	0.91
			(10.605)	(2.257)			(10.543)	(7.403)	
Cravath, Swaine	KLF					6.714	0.628	0.577	0.97
& Moore							(26.575)	(5.62)	
	EF					2.324	0.027		0.96
							(37.76)		
	KEF					2.294	0.029	−0.009	0.96
							(29.357)	(2.169)	
Davis, Polk	KLF					9.464	0.589	1.302	0.96
& Wardwell							(20.388)	(9.72)	
	EF					2.494	0.025		0.97
							(45.136)		
	KEF					2.524	0.024	0.01	0.97
							(32.936)	(2.998)	
Dechert, Price	KLF	−8.891	2.234	6.621	0.98	−1.884	1.056	2.441	0.98
& Rhoads			(22.098)	(18.942)			(23.282)	(15.576)	
	EF	1.676	0.073		0.92	1.433	0.06		0.94
			(25.11)				(28.037)		
	KEF	1.521	0.082	−0.043	0.94	1.318	0.067	−0.032	0.95
			(20.342)	(3.104)			(22.442)	(3.104)	
Dewey,	KLF	84.473	3.292	0.364	0.90	23.133	1.296	0.761	0.95
Ballantine,			(5.294)	(0.38)			(6.135)	(2.344)	
Bushley,	EF	4.483	0.027		0.90	3.189	0.039		0.96
Palmer			(15.479)				(23.958)		
& Wood	KEF	4.464	0.029	−0.004*	0.90	3.184	0.04	−0.001*	0.96
			(6.277)	(0.598)			(8.952)	(0.162)	
Dorsey	KLF	3.837	1.19	9.513	0.98	1.91	0.769	4.61	0.97
& Whitney			(11.559)	(23.458)			(12.462)	(18.726)	
	EF	2.212	0.049		0.95	1.771	0.047		0.92
			(29.151)				(25.907)		
	KEF	2.357	0.041	0.045	0.98	1.885	0.041	0.034	0.94
			(24.588)	(6.895)			(17.684)	(3.703)	
Dykema,	KLF	2.645	0.747	8.435	0.98	0.905	0.385	4.393	0.98

(*continued*)

Table B1 (*Continued*)

		Totals				Partners		
		Constant	T_1	T_2	R^2	Constant	T_1	T_2	R^2
Gossett,			(8.137)	(25.329)			(8.186)	(25.713)	
Spencer,	EF	1.628	0.06		0.95	0.784	0.064		0.97
Goodnow			(30.213)				(41.439)		
& Trigg	KEF	1.828	0.047	0.061	0.98	0.942	0.054	0.048	0.99
			(25.798)	(9.183)			(38.475)	(9.41)	
Foley & Lardner	KLF	−0.301	1.049	9.555	0.98	−0.653	0.532	5.409	0.98
			(14.187)	(28.453)			(13.076)	(29.308)	
	EF	1.896	0.049		0.96	1.143	0.05		0.93
			(38.88)				(28.169)		
	KEF	2.032	0.042	0.046	0.98	1.315	0.042	0.059	0.96
			(38.382)	(9.277)			(23.606)	(7.364)	
Fried, Frank,	KLF	33.374	1.962	8.723	0.97	−0.634	0.663	2.809	0.97
Harris, Shriver			(13.427)	(16.451)			(13.057)	(15.245)	
& Jacobson	EF	3.048	0.078		0.94	1.316	0.052		0.93
			(29.53)				(26.644)		
	KEF	3.039	0.077	0.006*	0.94	1.418	0.046	0.029	0.94
			(19.552)	(0.398)			(17.101)	(2.979)	
Fulbright	KLF	17.997	2.6	12.527	0.99	11.692	1.396	5.598	0.99
& Jaworski			(24.447)	(26.209)			(17.177)	(28.904)	
	EF	1.818	0.064		0.99	2.549	0.062		0.98
			(64.787)				(42.125)		
	KEF	1.774	0.066	−0.015	0.99	2.624	0.055	0.02	0.99
			(51.383)	(2.578)			(25.422)	(3.97)	
Gibson, Dunn	KLF	13.65	1.404	14.734	0.96	3.879	0.808	5.951	0.99
& Crutcher			(6.773)	(19.475)			(13.447)	(27.127)	
	EF	2.754	0.048		0.93	1.881	0.052		0.98
			(26.897)				(46.284)		
	KEF	2.953	0.036	0.059	0.98	2.004	0.044	0.037	0.99
			(26.676)	(11.974)			(51.18)	(11.637)	
Hinshaw,	KLF	3.205	0.64	6.191	0.95	−1.988	0.477	1.582	0.95
Culbertson,			(4.563)	(14.518)			(9.266)	(10.107)	
Moelmann,	EF	1.476	0.065		0.97	0.19	0.076		0.97
Hoban			(40.725)				(37.219)		
& Fuller	KEF	1.618	0.055	0.038	0.99	0.137	0.08	−0.014*	0.97
			(30.878)	(6.928)			(24.922)	(1.44)	
Hunton	KLF	1.51	0.726	12.66	0.97	2.59	0.379	4.193	0.99
& Williams			(6.573)	(25.267)			(14.209)	(34.621)	
	EF	1.583	0.053		0.94	1.26	0.045		0.93
			(30.781)				(28.918)		
	KEF	1.797	0.042	0.073	0.99	1.393	0.039	0.045	0.96
			(39.445)	(15.058)			(22.67)	(5.85)	
Jones, Day,	KLF	30.782	1.593	16.679	0.92	25.949	1.597	3.981	0.92
Reavis			(3.074)	(11.178)			(5.177)	(5.87)	
& Pogue	EF	3.255	0.05		0.92	3.274	0.044		0.96
			(22.347)				(31.152)		
	KEF	3.469	0.035	0.056	0.97	3.331	0.038	0.014	0.97

Table B1 (*Continued*)

		Totals				Partners			
		Constant	T_1	T_2	R^2	Constant	T_1	T_2	R^2
			(15.42)	(8.592)			(15.553)	(2.509)	
Kaye, Scholer,	KLF	19.219	2.645	5.811	0.98	−5.126	1.002	1.804	0.96
Fierman, Hays			(16.527)	(10.765)			(15.115)	(8.066)	
& Handler	EF	1.193	0.085		0.97	1.059	0.065		0.98
			(40.521)				(55.807)		
	KEF	0.972	0.099	−0.061	0.99	0.975	0.07	−0.023	0.99
			(50.279)	(9.255)			(46.929)	(4.633)	
Kelley, Drye	KLF					10.062	0.313	1.212	0.87
& Warren							(8.483)	(7.563)	
	EF					2.326	0.022		0.92
							(26.531)		
	KEF					2.378	0.019	0.016	0.93
							(18.23)	(3.606)	
Kirkland & Ellis	KLF	36.912	2.099	8.212	0.99	2.717	1.313	2.773	0.93
			(15.982)	(20.464)			(27.026)	(13.726)	
	EF	3.645	0.037		0.97	2.381	0.04		0.97
			(38.811)				(50.442)		
	KEF	3.743	0.03	0.026	0.99	2.342	0.043	−0.012	0.97
			(34.813)	(10.056)			(38.4)	(2.569)	
Latham	KLF	−1.111	0.844	10.742	0.96	−0.503	0.441	4.265	0.97
& Watkins			(4.659)	(18.504)			(6.512)	(19.639)	
	EF	1.012	0.081		0.99	0.407	0.077		0.96
			(63.989)				(36.167)		
	KEF	1.143	0.073	0.035	1.00	0.497	0.072	0.024	0.97
			(60.567)	(9.186)			(22.644)	(2.412)	
LeBoeuf, Lamb,	KLF	2.28	0.809	9.223	0.95	0.777	0.459	3.353	0.96
Leiby,			(5.195)	(17.09)			(7.751)	(16.389)	
& MacRae	EF	1.551	0.063		0.96	1.035	0.057		0.92
			(35.407)				(23.966)		
	KEF	1.706	0.054	0.045	0.98	1.183	0.048	0.041	0.93
			(27.65)	(6.639)			(15.005)	(3.724)	
Mayer, Brown	KLF	23.288	1.986	8.365	0.96	6.177	1.213	4.327	0.97
& Platt			(9.147)	(13.026)			(12.819)	(13.825)	
	EF	3.253	0.045		0.95	2.409	0.047		0.96
			(29.627)				(32.543)		
	KEF	3.36	0.038	0.03	0.97	2.504	0.041	0.028	0.97
			(19.32)	(5.218)			(21.818)	(4.503)	
McDermott, Will	KLF	−0.241	2.073	9.159	0.99	−2.067	1.068	6.024	0.97
& Emery			(13.145)	(22.428)			(7.19)	(15.655)	
	EF	2.159	0.072		0.98	0.93	0.09		0.94
			(43.527)				(26.207)		
	KEF	2.166	0.072	0.001*	0.98	0.776	0.1	−0.032	0.95
			(25.532)	(0.187)			(18.212)	(2.251)	
Milbank, Tweed,	KLF					7.285	0.728	1.644	0.96
Hadley							(19.546)	(10.16)	
& McCloy	EF					2.316	0.032		0.91

(*continued*)

Table B1   (*Continued*)

		Totals				Partners			
		Constant	T_1	T_2	R^2	Constant	T_1	T_2	R^2
							(24.882)		
	KEF					2.312	0.032	−0.001*	0.91
							(17.806)	(0.162)	
Morgan, Lewis	KLF	1.216	2.355	14.768	0.98	0.925	1.269	5.607	0.97
& Bockius			(13.406)	(23.766)			(13.973)	(17.457)	
	EF	2.584	0.058		0.98	2.09	0.052		0.97
			(49.815)				(38.71)		
	KEF	2.688	0.051	0.031	0.99	2.174	0.047	0.025	0.98
			(43.401)	(7.285)			(27.406)	(4.03)	
Morrison	KLF	24.082	0.073*	11.892	0.98	4.35	0.203	4.7	0.95
& Foerster			(0.222)	(18.431)			(3.465)	(19.507)	
	EF	2.479	0.072		0.88	1.15	0.044		0.89
			(14.934)				(21.358)		
	KEF	2.948	0.031	0.095	0.98	1.427	0.031	0.074	0.97
			(7.718)	(12.096)			(20.236)	(11.601)	
O'Melveny	KLF	0.498	1.8	12.178	0.98	1.642	0.612	4.376	0.98
& Myers			(15.845)	(23.85)			(15.433)	(24.556)	
	EF	2.445	0.048		0.96	1.61	0.044		0.96
			(37.726)				(39.479)		
	KEF	2.52	0.044	0.025	0.97	1.711	0.039	0.033	0.98
			(27.459)	(3.397)			(32.017)	(6.052)	
Paul, Weiss,	KLF					10.139	1.125	1.405	0.99
Rifkind,							(18.872)	(10.721)	
Wharton	EF					2.539	0.047		0.99
& Garrison							(50.601)		
	KEF					2.527	0.048	−0.003*	0.99
							(27.306)	(0.728)	
Pepper, Hamilton	KLF	0.18	1.134	8.483	0.96	−0.068	0.707	2.936	0.97
& Scheetz			(11.644)	(20.042)			(16.641)	(15.908)	
	EF	2.038	0.047		0.96	1.585	0.044		0.98
			(38.312)				(56.294)		
	KEF	2.159	0.041	0.038	0.98	1.616	0.043	0.01	0.98
			(30.825)	(6.527)			(39.951)	(2.094)	
Pillsbury,	KLF					−1.166	1.133	4.92	0.97
Madison							(13.871)	(16.605)	
& Sutro	EF					1.693	0.059		0.98
							(47.298)		
	KEF					1.712	0.057	0.006*	0.98
							(32.07)	(0.911)	
Proskauer, Rose,	KLF					1.256	0.492	2.985	0.98
Goetz							(19.55)	(27.33)	
& Mendelson	EF					1.382	0.044		0.96
							(39.327)		
	KEF					1.468	0.039	0.027	0.97
							(29.215)	(4.641)	

Table B1 (*Continued*)

		Totals				Partners			
		Constant	T_1	T_2	R^2	Constant	T_1	T_2	R^2
Rogers & Wells	KLF					2.478	0.585 (15.226)	2.457 (14.715)	0.96
	EF					1.819	0.037 (31.629)		0.94
	KEF					1.907	0.032 (22.753)	0.028 (4.49)	0.96
Shea & Gould	KLF	5.558	1.097 (2.472)	8.533 (9.679)	0.95	4.65	0.567 (3.534)	3.299 (10.358)	0.96
	EF	1.784	0.092 (46.361)		0.98	1.483	0.076 (30.726)		0.97
	KEF	1.838	0.087 (22.503)	0.01* (1.354)	0.98	1.571	0.069 (14.457)	0.017 (1.808)	0.97
Shearman & Sterling	KLF					6.287	0.821 (22.081)	3.123 (18.103)	0.98
	EF					2.331	0.035 (51.88)		0.98
	KEF					2.377	0.032 (39.738)	0.016 (4.189)	0.98
Sidley & Austin	KLF	24.076	1.158 (3.773)	20.65 (22.728)	0.97	1.174	0.825 (12.022)	8.568 (32.439)	0.99
	EF	2.856	0.058 (21.905)		0.91	1.661	0.054 (30.94)		0.94
	KEF	3.148	0.037 (19.924)	0.077 (13.778)	0.98	1.866	0.043 (28.125)	0.059 (9.908)	0.98
Simpson, Thacher & Bartlett	KLF					4.703	0.636 (17.174)	2.076 (12.892)	0.96
	EF					2.093	0.033 (37.733)		0.96
	KEF					2.143	0.031 (26.689)	0.016 (3.14)	0.96
Simpson, Thacher & Bartlett (BOOK)	KLF	5.961	2.454 (24.434)	8.927 (17.848)	0.98	4.431	0.713 (17.221)	2.176 (10.55)	0.95
	EF	3.039	0.041 (47.5)		0.97	2.157	0.034 (40.186)		0.96
	KEF	3.059	0.039 (34.624)	0.008* (1.357)	0.97	2.198	0.032 (29.708)	0.016 (2.947)	0.97
Skadden, Arps, Slate, Meagher & Flom	KLF	14.242	−0.711* (0.0841)	21.344 (12.278)	0.94	6.413	−0.231* (0.802)	6.126 (10.337)	0.92
	EF	1.083	0.125 (29.959)		0.96	0.64	0.1 (23.425)		0.94
	KEF	1.441	0.09 (19.281)	0.084 (8.659)	0.99	1.032	0.062 (15.565)	0.091 (11.12)	0.99
Squire, Sanders & Dempsey	KLF	26.575	1.81 (11.566)	10.945 (20.744)	0.98	16.698	0.699 (10.14)	4.354 (17.311)	0.96

(*continued*)

Table B1 (*Continued*)

		Totals				Partners			
		Constant	T_1	T_2	R^2	Constant	T_1	T_2	R^2
	EF	3.36	0.039 (21.871)		0.90	2.789	0.031 (18.137)		0.86
	KEF	3.543	0.027 (16.07)	0.051 (8.819)	0.96	2.964	0.021 (11.977)	0.048 (7.557)	0.93
Stroock & Stroock & Lavan	KLF	8.567	1.66 (4.58)	7.745 (10.385)	0.96				
	EF	2.373	0.079 (54.876)		0.99				
	KEF	2.411	0.076 (26.969)	0.009* (1.512)	0.99				
Sullivan & Cromwell	KLF					15.386	0.488 (10.55)	2.364 (11.765)	0.93
	EF					2.735	0.023 (16.294)		0.81
	KEF					2.846	0.017 (10.218)	0.035 (4.784)	0.86
Sullivan & Cromwell (BOOK)	KLF	36.957	1.825 (15.583)	10.25 (10.857)	0.94				
	EF	3.731	0.026 (20.522)		0.88				
	KEF	3.79	0.022 (16.573)	0.044 (3.999)	0.91				
Vinson & Elkins	KLF	41.259	3.197 (18.735)	10.302 (24.222)	0.99	15.099	0.972 (7.58)	6.606 (20.671)	0.98
	EF	3.779	0.046 (42.047)		0.98	2.623	0.053 (19.208)		0.90
	KEF	3.873	0.039 (33.35)	0.023 (8.037)	0.99	2.85	0.035 (11.31)	0.056 (7.391)	0.96
Weil, Gotschell & Manges	KLF	3.95	0.955 (8.553)	12.949 (33.544)	0.99	1.733	0.34 (15.314)	2.991 (38.957)	0.99
	EF	1.609	0.074 (31.224)		0.95	0.901	0.057 (31.806)		0.95
	KEF	1.739	0.064 (20.97)	0.048 (4.58)	0.96	1.047	0.048 (22.252)	0.041 (5.484)	0.97

Table B2 Group II Firms: Estimated Parameters and R^2 for KLF, EF, and KEF Models

		Totals				Partners			
		Constant	T_1	T_2	R^2	Constant	T_1	T_2	R^2
Adams, Duque & Hazeltine	KLF					1.089	0.613 (8.624)	0.877 (5.609)	0.95
	EF					1.165	0.067 (31.281)		0.97
	KEF					1.048	0.077 (22.808)	−0.026 (3.531)	0.98
Bond, Schoeneck & King	KLF	−0.311	0.811 (34.21)	2.567 (27.31)	0.99	−4.349	0.53 (15.11)	1.577 (11.322)	0.96
	EF	1.705	0.044 (28.643)		0.93	0.572	0.053 (33.417)		0.95
	KEF	1.678	0.045 (20.33)	−0.004* (0.511)	0.93	0.578	0.053 (23.139)	0.001* (0.147)	0.95
Breed, Abbot & Morgan	KLF					11.65	0.363 (9.717)	0.261* (1.816)	0.82
	EF					2.499	0.019 (15.938)		0.82
	KEF					2.465	0.021 (12.13)	−0.009* (1.38)	0.82
Briggs & Morgan	KLF	−1.412	0.898 (15.001)	3.252 (19.958)	0.99				
	EF	1.168	0.074 (46.36)		0.98				
	KEF	1.188	0.073 (27.149)	0.005* (0.69)	0.98				
Calfee, Halter & Griswold	KLF	−3.043	0.574 (13.65)	3.945 (23.65)	0.98	−2.689	0.383 (12.122)	2.112 (16.847)	0.96
	EF	0.897	0.054 (37.577)		0.96	0.249	0.057 (24.947)		0.92
	KEF	1.049	0.047 (28.684)	0.037 (5.702)	0.98	0.347	0.052 (16.533)	0.024 (1.921)	0.92
Choate, Hall & Stewart	KLF	29.177	0.611 (5.765)	3.171 (11.308)	0.95	8.095	0.441 (35.654)	0.278 (5.662)	0.98
	EF	3.239	0.028 (21.059)		0.91	2.344	0.022 (39.542)		0.96
	KEF	3.36	0.019 (13.118)	0.03 (7.965)	0.97	2.311	0.023 (31.212)	−0.008 (2.743)	0.97
Curtis, Mallet-Prevost, Colt & Mosie	KLF	13.449	0.673 (13.974)	2.517 (13.163)	0.96	8.417	0.337 (18.316)	0.519 (7.094)	0.95
	EF	2.728	0.026 (25.41)		0.92	2.266	0.021 (30.803)		0.94
	KEF	2.836	0.021 (18.06)	0.026 (5.673)	0.95	2.286	0.02 (20.799)	0.005* (1.349)	0.94

Note: Absolute t-statistics are in parentheses.

*Not significant at the 5 percent level. All other estimates of T_1 and T_2 significant at the 5 percent (or better) level.

Table B2 (*Continued*)

		Totals				Partners			
		Constant	T_1	T_2	R^2	Constant	T_1	T_2	R^2
Dilworth, Paxson, Kalish & Kaufman	KLF	10.08	0.97 (4.665)	4.363 (9.863)	0.96	6.167	0.661 (8.484)	1.467 (8.843)	0.97
	EF	2.308	0.063 (36.052)		0.97	1.968	0.054 (41.429)		0.98
	KEF	2.393	0.055 (18.14)	0.02 (3.053)	0.98	2.009	0.05 (20.631)	0.01* (1.899)	0.98
Edwards & Angell	KLF	13.496	0.404 (12.71)	3.264 (27.38)	0.98	9.11	0.299 (12.779)	1.757 (20.032)	0.97
	EF	2.491	0.028 (22.874)		0.90	2.142	0.027 (26.604)		0.93
	KEF	2.66	0.019 (27.719)	0.047 (17.954)	0.99	2.265	0.021 (22.435)	0.033 (9.434)	0.97
Fennemore Craig	KLF	2.481	0.263 (5.865)	3.299 (18.52)	0.95	3.359	0.114 (4.881)	1.734 (18.699)	0.95
	EF	1.145	0.041 (19.197)		0.86	0.981	0.034 (17.3)		0.84
	KEF	1.43	0.029 (14.151)	0.07 (8.671)	0.94	1.254	0.022 (12.751)	0.067 (9.838)	0.94
Foley, Hoag & Eliot	KLF	0.161	0.896 (16.492)	3.863 (26.182)	0.99	−0.094	0.459 (16.743)	2.163 (29.054)	0.99
	EF	1.146	0.079 (23.073)		0.93	0.403	0.081 (31.55)		0.96
	KEF	1.112	0.081 (14.359)	−0.009* (0.57)	0.93	0.363	0.084 (19.858)	0.01* (0.905)	0.96
Foster, Pepper & Riviera	KLF								
	EF								
	KEF								
Fox, Rothschild, O'Brien & Frankel	KLF	0.031	0.495 (12.848)	2.891 (17.867)	0.96	−1.553	0.377 (15.759)	0.991 (9.759)	0.95
	EF	1.146	0.047 (27.92)		0.93	0.668	0.046 (40.266)		0.96
	KEF	1.213	0.044 (19.061)	0.02 (2.012)	0.93	0.677	0.046 (28.327)	0.003* (0.399)	0.96
Frost & Jacobs	KLF					−0.708	0.263 (8.407)	2.734 (21.992)	0.97
	EF					0.208	0.056 (31.348)		0.94
	KEF					0.385	0.048 (22.74)	0.044 (5.209)	0.96
Haight, Brown & Bonesteel	KLF	0.22	0.263 (3.403)	3.955 (15.464)	0.94	0.498	0.119 (3.794)	1.199 (11.512)	0.80
	EF	−0.49	0.093		0.92	−0.431	0.068		0.91
	KEF	−0.481	0.093 (15.205)	0.003* (0.133)	0.92	−0.35	0.063 (14.923)	0.024* (1.695)	0.91

Table B2   (*Continued*)

		Totals				Partners			
		Constant	T_1	T_2	R^2	Constant	T_1	T_2	R^2
Hazel, Thomas,	KLF								
Fiske,	EF								
Beckhorn	KEF								
& Hanes									
Hinckley, Allen,	KLF	12.373	0.256	2.135	0.94	6.373	0.245	0.753	0.88
Snyder			(7.285)	(15.311)			(8.523)	(6.612)	
& Comen	EF	2.36	0.023		0.86	1.936	0.022		0.90
			(19.208)				(22.202)		
	KEF	2.519	0.016	0.039	0.94	1.999	0.02	0.015	0.91
			(14.346)	(8.96)			(14.473)	(2.881)	
Ice, Miller,	KLF	−0.646	0.648	3.956	0.98	2.305	0.286	1.752	0.95
Donadio			(18.704)	(26.256)			(10.606)	(14.962)	
& Ryan	EF	1.378	0.048		0.96	1.311	0.035		0.86
			(41.058)				(19.505)		
	KEF	1.465	0.043	0.027	0.97	1.475	0.027	0.051	0.91
			(30.358)	(4.391)			(13.175)	(5.795)	
Jackson & Kelly	KLF	8.614	0.165	3.445	0.94	7.543	0.064	1.266	0.88
			(3.453)	(18.202)			(2.526)	(12.537)	
	EF	1.823	0.03		0.81	1.751	0.019		0.61
			(15.903)				(9.566)		
	KEF	2.125	0.017	0.074	0.97	2.015	0.008	0.065	0.83
			(14.588)	(16.121)			(3.962)	(8.465)	
Jackson, Lewis,	KLF								
Schnitzler	EF								
& Krumpman	KEF								
Kramer, Levin,	KLF								
Nessen,	EF								
Kamin &	KEF								
Frankel									
Lane, Powell,	KLF	0.442	0.339	4.486	0.97	1.146	0.175	2.087	0.97
Moss & Miller			(7.453)	(24.841)			(8.083)	(24.303)	
	EF	0.824	0.051		0.87	0.598	0.043		0.85
			(19.445)				(17.942)		
	KEF	1.11	0.038	0.07	0.92	0.907	0.029	0.076	0.93
			(12.996)	(5.996)			(12.616)	(8.277)	
Lewis & Roca	KLF	1.945	1.673	1.163	0.96	2.372	0.906	1.294	0.99
			(9.037)	(3.352)			(17.114)	(13.032)	
	EF	2.065	0.071		0.91	1.65	0.07		0.98
			(17.426)				(34.073)		
	KEF	1.733	0.101	−0.064	0.96	1.542	0.08	−0.021	0.98
			(17.497)	(5.896)			(23.659)	(3.301)	
Luce, Forward,	KLF	−0.228	0.619	3.316	0.98	1.125	0.305	1.604	0.97
Hamilton			(14.896)	(22.349)			(12.05)	(17.736)	
& Scripps	EF	1.263	0.054		0.97	0.96	0.046		0.89

(*continued*)

Table B2   (*Continued*)

		Totals				Partners			
		Constant	T_1	T_2	R^2	Constant	T_1	T_2	R^2
			(41.991)				(20.66)		
	KEF	1.381	0.047	0.033	0.98	1.117	0.037	0.044	0.92
			(32.861)	(6.326)			(12.929)	(4.295)	
Manat, Phelps, Rothenberg & Phillips	KLF EF KEF								
Miller, Nash, Wiener, Hagar & Carlsen	KLF	−3.35	0.723	2.741	0.98	−1.286	0.399	1.359	0.97
			(16.332)	(17.445)			(15.005)	(14.394)	
	EF	0.709	0.067		0.96	0.539	0.057		0.93
			(35.682)				(25.992)		
	KEF	0.642	0.071	−0.018*	0.96	0.573	0.055	0.009*	0.93
			(25.882)	(1.841)			(16.831)	(0.794)	
Mintz, Levin, Cohn, Ferris, Glovsky & Popeo	KLF	6.558	0.232*	3.979	0.90				
			(1.265)	(9.178)					
	EF	1.458	0.064		0.94				
			(24.778)						
	KEF	1.674	0.047	0.051	0.98				
			(15.866)	(7.214)					
Mitchell, Silberberg & Krupp	KLF	2.282	0.643	3.797	0.98	0.855	0.325	1.812	0.97
			(15.428)	(23.688)			(13.179)	(19.063)	
	EF	1.62	0.047		0.93	0.923	0.046		0.94
			(26.502)				(30.801)		
	KEF	1.719	0.042	0.027	0.94	1.03	0.041	0.029	0.96
			(17.441)	(2.936)			(21.028)	(3.863)	
Palmer & Dodge	KLF	15.317	0.307	3.949	0.96	11.197	0.126	1.993	0.96
			(5.094)	(18.866)			(4.506)	(20.476)	
	EF	2.519	0.03		0.81	2.191	0.024		0.73
			(14.632)				(11.601)		
	KEF	2.742	0.016	0.065	0.95	2.42	0.01	0.066	0.93
			(10.053)	(11.608)			(6.255)	(12.003)	
Parker, Chapin & Flattau	KLF	6.898	1.282	2.406	0.96	5.971	0.403	1.194	0.96
			(7.467)	(7.048)			(5.893)	(8.771)	
	EF	2.296	0.063		0.97	1.764	0.052		0.95
			(31.614)				(25.133)		
			(14.966)	(0.499)			(11.13)	(2.773)	
Patterson, Belknap, Webb & Tyler	KLF	11.164	0.663	3.987	0.97	4.624	0.458	1.013	0.95
			(5.027)	(13.743)			(7.416)	(7.466)	
	EF	2.274	0.057		0.96	1.662	0.051		0.93
			(29.757)				(22.894)		
	KEF	2.426	0.043	0.036	0.98	1.729	0.045	0.016*	0.94
			(17.59)	(6.619)			(10.998)	(1.77)	
Patton, Boggs & Blow	KLF	7.126	0.453*	4.052	0.98	3.386	0.212*	2.063	0.97
			(0.787)	(5.819)			(0.613)	(4.925)	
	EF	1.814	0.123		0.96	1.087	0.125		0.96

Table B2 (*Continued*)

		Totals				Partners			
		Constant	T_1	T_2	R^2	Constant	T_1	T_2	R^2
			(23.649)				(22.077)		
	KEF	1.73	0.141	−0.022*	0.96	0.919	0.161	−0.045*	0.96
			(5.939)	(0.775)			(6.464)	(1.479)	
Phelps, Dunbar,	KLF	−0.189	0.472	3.874	0.977	−0.419	0.297	1.403	0.951
Marks,			(11.912)	(24.614)			(11.489)	(13.675)	
Claverie	EF	1.166	0.047		0.921	0.775	0.042		0.889
& Sims			(26.075)				(21.596)		
	KEF	1.369	0.038	0.05	0.953	0.928	0.035	0.038	0.911
			(19.089)	(6.253)			(14.1)	(3.767)	
Phillips, Lytle,	KLF					8.429	0.319	1.112	0.941
Hitchcock,							(13.517)	(10.828)	
Blaine	EF					2.172	0.024		0.922
& Huber							(27.337)		
	KEF					2.224	0.021	0.016	0.934
							(18.767)	(3.287)	
Pitney, Hardin,	KLF	14.49	0.228	3.101	0.97	10.544	0.055	0.704	0.76
Kipp & Szuch			(7.693)	(26.315)			(2.351)	(7.65)	
	EF	2.414	0.024		0.79	2.199	0.011		0.55
			(14.597)				(8.33)		
	KEF	2.653	0.013	0.059	0.93	2.342	0.005	0.035	0.71
			(10.188)	(11.218)			(3.229)	(5.572)	
Plunkett	KLF					−2.854	0.706	4.306	0.96
& Cooney							(4.38)	(12.157)	
	EF					−0.037	0.118		0.93
							(21.507)		
	KEF					0.16	0.102	0.043	0.94
							(10.545)	(2.042)	
Preston,	KLF	5.205	0.063*	4.979	0.96	3.343	0.056*	2.134	0.94
Thorgimson,			(1.432)	(26.893)			(2.121)	(19.181)	
Ellis	EF	1.026	0.041		0.77	0.76	0.035		0.79
& Holman			(13.845)				(14.853)		
	KEF	1.446	0.021	0.123	0.97	1.079	0.02	0.093	0.95
			(13.734)	(19.261)			(12.753)	(14.21)	
Robinson & Cole	KLF	4.774	0.392	3.266	0.96	2.809	0.289	1.289	0.97
	EF	1.683	0.04		0.95	1.383	0.035		0.92
			(31.39)				(26.244)		
	KEF	1.84	0.032	0.043	0.98	1.502	0.029	0.033	0.95
			(29.265)	(10.301)			(18.323)	(5.375)	
Ross & Hardies	KLF	5.074	0.744	1.211	0.88	1.5	0.382	0.716	0.90
			(11.869)	(4.443)			(8.831)	(5.298)	
	EF	2.291	0.03		0.93	1.623	0.03		0.88
			(27.963)				(18.817)		
	KEF	2.296	0.03	0.001*	0.93	1.716	0.027	0.013*	0.89
			(19.742)	(0.206)			(10.956)	(1.714)	

(*continued*)

Table B2 *(Continued)*

		Totals				Partners			
		Constant	T_1	T_2	R^2	Constant	T_1	T_2	R^2
Schulte, Roth	KLF								
& Zabel	EF								
	KEF								
Schwabe,	KLF	3.709	0.756	4.205	0.979	2.793	0.335	2.103	0.968
Williamson			(8.038)	(17.539)			(5.907)	(14.514)	
& Wyatt	EF	1.539	0.069		0.985	1.092	0.062		0.924
			(51.84)				(22.083)		
	KEF	1.639	0.066	0.011	0.987	1.243	0.05	0.037	0.941
			(29.102)	(1.974)			(11.405)	(3.285)	
Shook, Hardy	KLF	0.755	0.55	2.663	0.98	1.037	0.281	1.745	0.97
& Bacon			(12.725)	(19.237)			(9.996)	(19.34)	
	EF	1.156	0.059		0.97	0.699	0.056		0.95
			(41.113)				(29.28)		
	KEF	1.215	0.055	0.016	0.97	0.824	0.048	0.034	0.96
			(25.955)	(2.325)			(18.573)	(4.07)	
Steel, Hector	KLF	4.42	0.249	3.871	0.95	0.284	0.285	1.364	0.94
& Davis			(4.728)	(17.538)			(10.625)	(12.153)	
	EF	1.328	0.043		0.92	0.699	0.046		0.92
			(24.256)				(30.227)		
	KEF	1.513	0.033	0.06	0.97	0.765	0.043	0.022	0.93
			(21.056)	(9.172)			(20.574)	(2.466)	
Sullivan	KLF	−6.378	0.617	4.678	0.97	−2.905	0.408	2.078	0.97
& Worcester			(10.222)	(19.415)			(13.062)	(16.682)	
	EF	0.189	0.067		0.96	0.392	0.054		0.96
			(34.126)				(35.523)		
	KEF	0.344	0.06	0.039	0.97	0.5	0.049	0.027	0.97
			(24.027)	(3.947)			(24.711)	(3.418)	
Taft, Stettinius	KLF	−0.461	0.852	3.837	0.98	0.725	0.34	2.022	0.96
& Hollister			(16.99)	(19.884)			(9.77)	(15.11)	
	EF	1.702	0.048		0.98	0.903	0.048		0.96
			(47.819)				(35.908)		
	KEF	1.777	0.044	0.021	0.98	0.976	0.044	0.02	0.96
Webster	KLF	1.637	0.924	2.805	0.98	1.212	0.451	1.135	0.98
& Sheffield			(13.478)	(15.387)			(14.432)	(12.975)	
	EF	1.725	0.059		0.97	1.067	0.057		0.96
			(37.051)				(30.832)		
	KEF	1.764	0.057	0.009*	0.97	1.052	0.058	−0.004*	0.96
			(21.511)	(1.242)			(18.978)	(0.447)	
Weinberg	KLF	−9.689	0.861	3.502	0.97	−5.144	0.0433	1.545	0.95
& Green			(16.428)	(16.842)			(12.484)	(11.223)	
	EF	0.075	0.074		0.97	−0.404	0.067		0.93
			(43.813)				(27.828)		
	KEF	−0.054	0.079	−0.032	0.98	−0.4	0.067	0.001*	0.93
			(36.442)	(3.649)			(19.298)	(0.077)	

Table B2 (*Continued*)

		Totals				Partners			
		Constant	T_1	T_2	R^2	Constant	T_1	T_2	R^2
White	KLF	16.24	0.497	3.18	0.98	7.136	0.36	0.765	0.98
& Williams			(5.258)	(15.802)			(11.424)	(11.415)	
	EF	2.591	0.045		0.94	1.955	0.04		0.98
			(23.277)				(37.274)		
	KEF	2.776	0.028	0.043	0.99	2.022	0.033	0.016	0.98
			(17.165)	(12.522)			(20.023)	(4.424)	
Whiteford,	KLF	3.189	0.194	2.934	0.95	1.784	0.189	1.308	0.95
Taylor			(3.132)	(15.535)			(5.772)	(13.106)	
& Preston	EF	0.842	0.06		0.91	0.648	0.053		0.95
			(21.241)				(29.451)		
	KEF	1.045	0.046	0.055	0.94	0.782	0.044	0.036	0.97
			(12.972)	(5.147)			(19.754)	(5.389)	
Wyman,	KLF	6.578	2.791*	1.563*	0.86	1.496	1.488	0.097*	0.87
Bautzer,			(2.034)	(0.895)			(2.779)	(0.143)	
Christensen,	EF	2.564	0.092		0.89	1.664	0.093		0.87
Kuchek			(12.415)				(11.373)		
& Silbert	KEF	2.17	0.171	−0.103	0.93	1.185	0.188	−0.125	0.93
			(7.715)	(3.668)			(8.408)	(4.403)	

Appendix C: Graphs of 1988 Actual versus Estimated Size

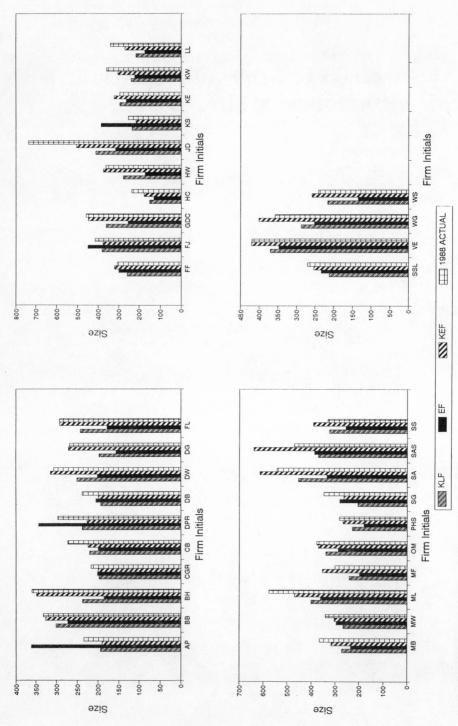

Figure 11: 1988 Actual v. Estimated Size (Group I)

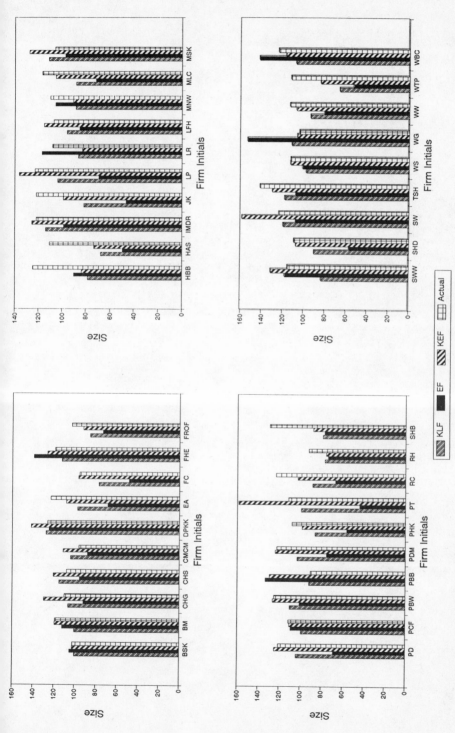

Figure 12: 1988 Actual v. Estimated Size (Group II)

Bibliography

Abel, Richard. 1989. *American Lawyers.* New York: Oxford University Press.

Adams, Edward. 1989. "Longer Partnerships Odds at N.Y. Firms." *New York Law Journal,* July 17:1, 6.

Alperson, Myra. 1983. "Asbestos Defendants Begin to Cooperate in Litigation." *Legal Times,* September 19:3, 10.

Altman, Mary Ann. 1988. "Two-Tiered Ownership Approaches." *Law Firm Agreements and Disagreements,* pp. 59–66. New York: Practicing Law Institute.

Altman & Weil, Inc. 1985. "Special Report on Law Department Functions and Expenditures—1982." In *Management for In-House Counsel: Techniques, Tools, Approaches,* ed. M. Goldblatt, pp. 75–100. Chicago: Corporate Law Department Management Committee, Section of Economics of Law Practice, American Bar Association.

American Bar Association. 1959. *Lawyers' Economic Problems and Some Bar Association Solutions.* Chicago: Special Committee on the Economics of Law Practice, American Bar Association.

———. 1973. *Law Schools and Bar Admission Requirements—A Review of Legal Education.* Chicago: Section of Legal Education and Admissions to the Bar, American Bar Association.

———. 1985. *A Review of Legal Education in the United States; Law School and Bar Admission Requirements.* Chicago: Section of Legal Education and Admission to the Bar, American Bar Association.

———. 1986a. *Dispute Resolution Handbook of State and Local Bar Associations.* Monograph Series No. 3. Chicago: Standing Committee on Dispute Resolution, American Bar Association.

———. 1986b. *In the Spirit of Public Service: A Blueprint for the Rekindling of Lawyer Professionalism.* Chicago: Committee on Professionalism, American Bar Association.

———. 1989. *A Review of Legal Education in the United States; Law School and Bar Admission Requirements.* Chicago: Section of Legal Education and Admission to the Bar, American Bar Association.

———. 1990. Recommendation and Report on Law Firms' Ancillary Business Activities. Discussion draft, 8 February, 1990. Chicago: Section of Litigation, American Bar Association.

American Bar Foundation. 1979. *1979 Annotated Code of Professional Responsibility.* Chicago: American Bar Foundation.

American Corporate Counsel Institute. 1987. *Corporate Law Department Trends and the Effect of the Current Bar Admission System: A Survey of Corporate Counsel.* Washington, D.C.: American Corporate Counsel Institute.

American Lawyer. 1895. "The Commercialization of the Profession." *American Lawyer*, March: 84–85.

American Lawyer. 1989. "The Am Law 100." *American Lawyer*, July–August: Pull-Out Supplement 4-58.

Andrews, Champ. 1907. "The Law—A Business or a Profession?" *Yale Law Journal* 17:602–10.

Andrews, Thomas. 1989. "Nonlawyers in the Business of Law: Does the One Who Has the Gold Really Make the Rules?" *Hastings Law Journal* 40:577–656.

Annual Reports of the Administrative Offices of the United States Courts. Williamsburg, Va.: National Center for State Courts' Court Statistics.

Annual Report of the Director of the Administrative Office of the United States Courts. Washington, D.C.: U.S. Government Printing Office.

Appleson, Gail. 1983. "Boutique Firms Hold Their Own." *National Law Journal*, March 1:1, 22.

Arrow, Kenneth. 1969. "The Organization of Economic Activity: Issues Pertinent to the Choice of Market Versus Nonmarket Allocation." In *The Analysis and Evaluation of Public Expenditure: The PPB System*, vol. 1. pp. 47–64. U.S. Joint Economic Committee, 91st Congress, 1st Session. Washington, D.C.: Government Printing Office.

Arthur Andersen & Co. 1985. "The Corporate Market for Legal Services." Marketing study. Chicago: Arthur Andersen & Co.

———. 1990. "Personnel by Divisions." Intrafirm publication. Chicago: Arthur Andersen & Co.

Arthurs, Harry; Weisman, Richard; and Zemans, Frederick. 1988. "Canadian Lawyers: A Peculiar Professionalism." In *Lawyers in Society*, vol. 1, *The Common Law World*, ed. R. Abel and P. Lewis, pp. 123–85. Berkeley: University of California Press.

Auerbach, Jerold. 1976. *Unequal Justice: Lawyers and Social Change in Modern America*. New York: Oxford University Press.

———. 1983. *Justice without Law?* New York: Oxford University Press.

Austin, Edwin. 1957. "Some Comments on Large Firms." *Law Practice Forum* 3(4):8–16.

Ayre, Randolph. 1982. "In House—Better Than Ever: Corporate Legal Departments—More Visible, More Attractive." *National Law Journal*, February 15:11.

Banks, Robert. 1983. "Companies Struggle to Control Legal Costs." *Harvard Business Review* 61(2):168–70.

Barnett, Chris. 1981. "Image-Building Professional Style." *Republic Scene*, April: 42–43.

Bellon, Lee Ann. 1988. "Southeast Boasts an Expanding Legal Community." *National Law Journal*, January 18:19, 20.

Bellow, Gary. 1977. "Turning Solutions into Problems: The Legal Aid Experience." *NLADA Briefcase* 34:106–25.

Berkman, Barbara. 1988. "Temporarily Yours: Associates for Hire." *American Lawyer*, March 24:24, 26–27.

Berkow, Robert, and Spiciarich, Lisa. 1985. "Inside Counsel Gets More Competitive." *National Law Journal*, November 4:13.

Berle, Adolph A. 1933. "Modern Legal Profession." *Encyclopedia of the Social Sciences* 5:340–45.

Bernstein, Howard. 1987–88. "Does a Hiring Crisis Threaten the Profession?" *National Law Journal,* December 28–January 4:20, 22.

Bernstein, Peter. 1978. "The Wall Street Lawyers Are Thriving on Change." *Fortune* 97(5):104–12.

———. 1982. "Profit Pressures on the Big Law Firm." *Fortune* 105(8):84–100.

Berman, Jerry, and Cahn, Edgar. 1970. "Bargaining for Justice: The Law Student's Challenge to Law Firms." *Harvard Civil Rights—Civil Liberties Law Review* 5:16–31.

Blum, Bill, and Lobaco, Gina. 1988. "When Associates Don't Make Partner." *California Lawyer* 8(1):51–54.

Bodine, Larry. 1979. "Law Firm Ladder Gets a New Rung." *National Law Journal* March 12:1, 17.

Bowers, Lloyd. 1904. "The Lawyer To-Day." *American Law Review* 38:823–35.

Brill, Steven. 1989a. "The End of Partnership?" *American Lawyer,* December:3, 35.

———. 1989b. "The Law Business in the Year 2000." *American Lawyer,* June: Management Report.

Bristol, George. 1913. "The Passing of the Legal Profession." *Yale Law Review* 22:590–613.

Brooks, John. 1983. "Advocate?" *The New Yorker* 59(14):46–81.

Business Disputing Group. 1989. "Corporation in Court: Trends in American Business Litigation." Report prepared for Arthur Anderson & Co. by M. Galanter, S. Macaulay, T. Palay and J. Rogers, University of Wisconsin Law School, Madison, Wisconsin.

Business Week. 1968. "Why Law Is a Growth Industry." *Business Week,* January 13:78–79.

———. 1984. "A New Corporate Powerhouse: The Legal Department." *Business Week,* April 9:66–71.

Cardozo Law Review. 1985. Symposium on Critical Legal Studies. *Cardozo Law Review* 6(4).

Carlin, Jerome. 1962. *Lawyers on Their Own: A Study of Individual Practitioners in Chicago.* New Brunswick, N.J.: Rutgers University Press.

———. 1966. *Lawyers' Ethics: A Survey of the New York City Bar.* New York: Russell Sage Foundation.

Carter, Terry. 1989a. "Now, a Novel Twist on Flex-Time: NALP Chief Moves to California." *National Law Journal,* July 3:4.

———. 1989b. "Students Grill Potential Bosses: What is Life Really Like There?" *National Law Journal,* June 19:4.

Center for Public Resources. 1983–. *Alternatives to the High Cost of Litigation.* New York.

———. 1982. *Corporate Dispute Management 1982: A Manual of Innovative Corporate Strategies for the Avoidance and Resolution of Legal Disputes.* New York: Matthew Bender.

Chamberlayne, Charles. 1906. "The Soul of the Profession." *Green Bag* 18:396–401.

Chambers, David. 1989. "Accommodation and Satisfaction: Women and Men Lawyers and the Balance of Work and Family." *Law & Social Inquiry* 14:251–87.

Chase, Anthony. 1986. "Lawyers and Popular Culture: A Review of Mass Media Portrayals of American Attorneys." *American Bar Foundation Research Journal* 1986:281–300.

Chayes, Abram, and Chayes, Antonia. 1985. "Corporate Counsel and the Elite Law Firm." *Stanford Law Review* 37:277–300.

Clark, David. 1981. "Adjudication to Administration: A Statistical Analysis of Federal District Courts in the Twentieth Century." *Southern California Law Review* 55:65–152.

Coffee, John. 1986. "Understanding the Plaintiff's Attorney: The Implications of Economic Theory for Private Enforcement of Law Through Class and Derivative Actions." *Columbia Law Review* 86:669–727.

Couric, Emily. 1985. "Firms Adapt to New Era." *National Law Journal,* July 8:1.

———. 1988. "New Relationships, New Rules." *National Law Journal,* August 1: Pull-Out Supplement 2.

Coyle, Marcia. 1987. "Boutique Shakeout: Merger Can Be an Attractive Option." *National Law Journal,* March 2:1, 16–18.

Cox, Gail. 1987. "Fees Keep Coming for Seattle Bar." *National Law Journal,* April 13:1, 32–34.

Crossen, Cynthia. 1981. "13 Great Small Firms." *American Lawyer,* April:27.

Curran, Barbara. 1985. *The Lawyer Statistical Report: A Statistical Profile of the U.S. Legal Profession in the 1980's.* Chicago: American Bar Foundation.

———. 1986. *Supplement to the Lawyer Statistical Report: The U.S. Legal Profession in 1985.* Chicago: American Bar Foundation.

Damaska, Mirjan. 1975. "Structures of Authority and Comparative Criminal Procedure." *Yale Law Journal* 84:480–544.

d'Amato, Anthony. 1983. "Legal Uncertainty." *California Law Review* 71:1–55.

Darby, D. Weston. 1985. "Are You Keeping Up Financially?" *American Bar Association Journal* 71:66–68.

Dawson, Mitchell. 1930. "Frankenstein, Inc." *American Mercury* 19:274–80.

Delaney, William, and Feingold, Alan. 1970. "Wall Street Lawyer in the Provinces." *Administrative Science Quarterly* 15:191–201.

de Tocqueville, Alexis [pseud.]. 1972. "Money Talks: Why It Shouts to Some Lawyers and Whispers to Others." *Juris Doctor* 2(4):55–57.

Dill, James. 1903. "The Business Lawyer of Today." *Albany Law Journal* 65:111–13.

Di Maggio, Paul, and Powell, Walter. 1983. "The Iron Cage Revisited: Institutional Isomorphism and Collective Rationality in Organizational Fields." *American Journal of Sociology* 48(2):147–60.

Dockser, Amy. 1988. "Midsize Law Firms Struggle to Survive." *Wall Street Journal,* October 19:B1.

Dos Passos, John. 1907. *The American Lawyer: As He Was—As He Is—As He Can Be.* New York: The Banks Law Publishing Co.

Dungworth, Terence. 1988. *Product Liability and the Business Sector: Litigation Trends in Federal Courts.* Santa Monica, Calif.: RAND Corporation: Institute for Civil Justice.

Dunne, Finley. 1963. *Mr. Dooley on the Choice of Law,* ed. E. J. Bander. Charlottesville: Michie Co.

Dye, Ronald A. 1984. "The Trouble with Tournaments." *Economic Inquiry* 22:147–49.

Earle, Walter. 1963. *Mr. Shearman and Mr. Sterling and How They Grew: Being Annals of Their Law Firms.* New Haven: Yale University Press.

Earle, Walter, and Perlin, Charles. 1973. *Shearman & Sterling 1873–1973.* 2d. ed. New York.

Epstein, Cynthia Fuchs. 1981. *Women in Law.* New York: Basic Books.

Falk, Carol. 1970. "Many Lawyers Take Up Political, Social Causes on Their Firms' Time." *Wall Street Journal,* May 20:1, 15.

Feeley, Malcolm. 1976. "The Concept of Laws in Social Science: A Critique and Notes on an Expanded View." *Law & Society Review* 10:497–523.

Fisk, Margaret. 1988. "What Does the Future Have in Store?" *National Law Journal,* September 26:49–50.

Fitzpatrick, James. 1989. "Legal Future Shock: The Role of Large Law Firms by the End of the Century." *Indiana Law Journal* 64:461–71.

Flaharty, Francis. 1983a. "Comparison Shopping Hits the Law: Companies Cut Costs." *National Law Journal,* October 31:1, 9–11.

———. 1983b. "Right-Wing Firms Pick Up Steam." *National Law Journal,* May 23:1.

Flood, John. 1989. "Megalaw in the U.K.: Professionalism or Corporatism? A Preliminary Report." *Indiana Law Journal* 64:569–92.

Forbes. 1971. "The Gilt-Edged Profession." *Forbes* 108(6):30–38.

Fortune. 1960a. "The Fortune Directory Part II." *Fortune* 62(8):135–44.

———. 1960b. "The Fortune Directory: The 500 Largest U.S. Industrial Corporations." *Fortune* 62(7):131–50.

———. 1988a. "The Fortune 500 Largest U.S. Industrial Corporations. *Fortune* 117(9):D11–60.

———. 1988b. "The 500 Largest Service Corporations." *Fortune* 117(12):D7–38.

Fowler, Elizabeth, M. 1990. "Ever-Rising Demand for Paralegals." *New York Times,* January 9:37.

Frankel, Marvin. 1977. "An Immodest Proposal." *New York Times Magazine,* December 4:92–104.

Freeman, Martha. 1987. "Alternatives to the Old Up or Out." *California Lawyer* 7(12):44–45, 104–5.

Friedman, Lawrence. 1985. *Total Justice.* New York: Russell Sage Foundation.

Galante, Mary Ann. 1983a. "Firms Look Closer at How to Create Lawyer Categories." *Los Angeles Daily Journal,* August 22:1, 14.

———. 1983b. "Meet the Permanent Associate." *National Law Journal,* October 24:1, 28, 30.

———. 1985. "Firms Finding More Value in Marketing." *National Law Journal,* November 18:1, 28–29.

Galanter, Marc. 1983. "Mega-Law and Mega-Lawyering in the Contemporary United States." In *The Sociology of the Professions: Lawyers, Doctors and Others,* ed. R. Dingwall and P. Lewis, pp. 152–76. London: Macmillan.

———. 1985. "Presidential Address: The Legal Malaise; Or, Justice Observed." *Law & Society Review* 19:537–56.

———. 1988. "The Life and Times of the Big Six; or, The Federal Courts Since the Good Old Days." *Wisconsin Law Review* 1988:921–54.

Galanter, Marc, and Palay, Thomas. 1990a. The Size of Large Law Firms: Data on One Hundred Firms. Unpublished Paper, University of Wisconsin Law School.

———. 1990b. Data on Associate Promotion Rates. Unpublished Paper, University of Wisconsin Law School.

———. 1990c. "Why the Big Get Bigger: The Promotion-to-Partner Tournament and the Growth of Large Law Firms." *Virginia Law Review* 76(4):747–811.

Galanter, Marc, and Rogers, Joel. 1988. "The Transformation of American Business Disputing? Some Preliminary Observations." Paper delivered at the annual meeting of the Law and Society Association, 9–12 June 1988, at Vail, Colorado.

Gartner, Michael. 1973. "Guest Opinion: Are Outside Directors Taking Outside Chances?" *Juris Doctor* 3(3):4–5, 37.

Gawalt, Gerard. 1984. *The New High Priests: Lawyers in the Post Civil War America.* Westport, Conn.: Greenwood Press.

Gibbons, Thomas F. 1989. "Branching Out." *American Bar Association Journal* 75:70–76.

Gilson, Ronald, and Mnookin, Robert. 1985. "Sharing Among the Human Capitalists: An Economic Inquiry into the Corporate Law Firm and How Partners Split Profits." *Stanford Law Review* 37:313–92.

———. 1989. "Coming of Age in the Corporate Law Firm: The Economics of Associate Career Patterns." *Stanford Law Review* 41:567–95.

Glick, Henry, and Pruet, George. 1986. "Dissent in State Supreme Courts: Patterns and Correlates of Conflict." In *Judicial Conflict and Consensus: Behavioral Studies of American Appellate Courts,* ed. S. Goldman and C. Lamb, pp. 199–214. Lexington, KY: University Press of Kentucky.

Goffman, Erving. 1969. *Strategic Interaction.* Philadelphia: University of Philadelphia Press.

Goldberg, Victor. 1985. "Price Adjustment in Long-Term Contracts." *Wisconsin Law Review* 1985:527–43.

Goldstein, Tom. 1979. "Demystifying the Profession." *New York Times,* June 1:D3.

———. 1983. "Review: *The American Lawyer.*" *Columbia Lawyer Review* 83:1351–63.

Gordon, Robert. 1988. "The Independence of Lawyers." *Boston University Law Review* 68:1–83.

Graham, Deborah. 1983. "New 'Senior Attorney' Program Draws Attention at Davis Polk." *Legal Times* 5(38):3, 7.

Granelli, James. 1978. "Hiring Out: Boon for Small Firm." *National Law Journal,* November 6:1, 21.

———. 1980. "The Battle of Law Firm Consultants." *National Law Journal,* June 16:1, 27.

Green, Mark. 1970. "Law Graduates: The New Breed." *The Nation* 210:658–60.

Griggs, Peter, and McNeill, Daviryne. 1987–88. "Upper Ranks Add Heft at Most Big D.C. Firms." *Legal Times* 10(30):4.

Hallam, Kirk. 1983. "Big Firms Search for Alternatives to Traditional Form." *Los Angeles Daily Journal,* March 18:1, 14.

Handler, Joel. 1978. *Social Movements and the Legal System: A Theory of Law Reform and Social Change.* New York: Academic Press.

Handler, Joel; Hollingsworth, Ellen; and Erlanger, Howard. 1978. *Lawyers and the Pursuit of Legal Rights*. New York: Academic Press.

Hankin, Faye A., and Krohnke, Duane W. 1965. *The Lawyer Statistical Report*. Chicago: American Bar Foundation.

Harrington, John. 1927. "The Big Shops of the Law." *American Mercury* 11(42):143–49.

Harrington, William. 1984. "A Brief History of Computer-Assisted Legal Research." *Law Library Journal* 77:543–56.

Haserot, Phyllis. 1986. "How to Get Associates into the Act." *National Law Journal*, August 25:15, 21.

———. 1987. "Multiprofessional Mixes Are Proliferating." *National Law Journal*, October 19:16, 18.

Hayes, Arthur S. 1989a. "How Does Brad Hildebrandt Manage?" *American Lawyer*, May:90–94, 96–98.

———. 1989b. "Lawyers Hire Ghostwriters, Raising Spectre of Liability." *Wall Street Journal*, December 5:B1.

Heintz, Bruce. 1982. "New Trends in Partner Profit Distribution." *Wisconsin Bar Bulletin* 55(10):24–26, 45.

———. 1983. "Elements of Law Firm Competition." *National Law Journal*, December 26:15, 19–42.

Heinz, John, and Laumann, Edward. 1982. *Chicago Lawyers: The Social Structure of the Bar*. New York: Russell Sage Foundation; Chicago: American Bar Foundation.

Hildebrandt, Bradford W., and Kaufman, Jack. 1990. "Two-Tier Partnerships: A New Look." *National Law Journal*, January 8:15, 19.

Hirsch, Ronald L. 1985. "Are You on Target?" *The Barrister Magazine* 12(1):17–20, 49–50.

Hobson, Wayne. 1986. *The American Legal Profession and the Organizational Society 1890–1930*. New York: Garland Publishing.

Hoffman, Paul. 1973. *Lions in the Street: The Inside Story of the Great Wall Street Firms*. New York: Saturday Review Press.

———. 1982. *Lions of the Eighties: The Inside Story of the Powerhouse Law Firms*. Garden City, N.Y.: Doubleday.

Holley, Dannye, and Kleven, Thomas. 1987. "Minorities and the Legal Profession: Current Platitudes, Current Barriers." *Thurgood Marshall Law Review*, 12:299–345.

Holmes, Deborah. 1988. "Structural Causes of Dissatisfaction Among Large-Firm Attorneys: A Feminist Perspective." Working Paper 3:3. Institute for Legal Studies, University of Wisconsin-Madison.

Holmstrom, Bengt R., and Tirole, Jean. 1989. "The Theory of the Firm." In *Handbook of Industrial Organization*, ed. R. Schmalensee and R. D. Willig, pp. 61–133. New York: North-Holland.

Houck, Oliver. 1984. "With Charity for All." *Yale Law Journal* 93:1415–1563.

Hurst, James Willard. 1950. *The Growth of American Law: The Law Makers*. Boston: Little, Brown.

Jensen, Rita. 1987a. "Partners Work Harder to Stay Even." *National Law Journal*, August 10:12.

———. 1987b. "The Rainmakers." *National Law Journal*, October 5:1, 28, 30.

————. 1988a. "Banking Clients More Willing to Shop for Firms." *National Law Journal,* January 18:1, 18.

————. 1988b. "Networking: The Future of Law Firms." *National Law Journal,* March 7:1, 10.

————. 1988c. "Seeking a Balance." *National Law Journal,* July 18:1, 22–23.

————. 1989. "Past Woes Don't Deter Hyatt Plans." *National Law Journal,* July 3:1.

————. 1990. "Minorities Didn't Share in Firm Growth." *National Law Journal,* February 19:1, 28–31, 35.

Johnson, Earl. 1974. *Justice and Reform: The Formative Years of the OEO Legal Services Program.* New York: Russell Sage Foundation.

Johnston, Richard. 1957. "Stevenson Joins a Law Firm Here." *New York Times,* April 20:1, 7.

Katsh, M. Ethan. 1989. *The Electronic Media and the Transformation of Law.* New York: Oxford University Press.

Kiechel, Walter. 1978. "Growing Up at Kutak, Rock & Huie." *Fortune* 98(8):112–20.

Kiernan, Laura. 1979. "Legal Publications Invading Law Firms' Inner Sanctums." *Washington Post,* November 26:C1, C3.

Kingson, Jennifer. 1988. "Women in the Law Say Path is Limited by 'Mommy Track'." *New York Times,* August 8:1, 15.

Klaw, Spencer. 1958. "The Wall Street Lawyers." *Fortune* 57(2):140–44, 192–98, 202.

Klemesrud, Judy. 1985. "Women in the Law: Many Are Getting Out." *New York Times,* August 9:14.

Kogel, Otto. 1953. *Walter S. Carter: Collector of Young Masters or the Progenitor of Many Law Firms.* New York: Roundtable Press.

Labaton, Stephen. 1988. "Lawyers Debate Temporary Work." *New York Times,* April 18:D2.

Ladinsky, Jack. 1963a. "Career Lawyers, Law Practice and Legal Institutions." *American Sociological Review* 28:47–54.

————. 1963b. "The Impact of Social Backgrounds of Lawyers on Law Practice and the Law." *Journal of Legal Education* 16:127–44.

Lauter, David. 1984. " 'Outsiders' Who Work for Firms." *National Law Journal,* February 6:1.

Lavine, Douglass. 1981. "Outside Counsel Are Feeling the Corporate Whip: Economy Tightens Reins." *National Law Journal,* January 26:1.

Lazear, Edward, and Rosen, Sherwin. 1981. "Rank Order Tournaments as Optimum Labor Contracts." *Journal of Political Economy* 89:841–64.

Lee, Edward. 1923. "Large Law Offices." *American Law Review* 57:788–92.

Levy, Beryl. 1961. *Corporation Lawyer: Saint or Sinner.* Philadelphia: Chilton Co.

Lewin, Tamar. 1984. "The New National Law Firms." *New York Times,* October 4:D1, D6.

————. 1986. "At Cravath, $65,000 to Start." *New York Times,* April 18:D1, D18.

————. 1987. "Outside Ventures Transform Law Firms." *New York Times,* February 11:D1, D7.

Lewis, Neil A. 1990. "Non-Lawyers to Be Partners in Nation's Capital." *New York Times,* March 2:B8.

Lieberman, Jethro. 1978. *Crisis at the Bar: Lawyers' Unethical Ethics and What to Do About It*. New York: Norton.

Liggio, Carl. 1984. Remarks in Federal Bar Council, Conference Proceedings of 1984 Bench and Bar Conference, 29 January–5 February, 1984, at Dorado, Puerto Rico.

Lipset, Seymour, and Schneider, William. 1987. *The Confidence Gap: Business, Labor and Government in the Public Mind*. Rev. ed. Baltimore: Johns Hopkins University Press.

Lisagor, Nancy, and Lipsius, Frank. 1988. *A Law Unto Itself: The Untold Story of the Law Firm Sullivan & Cromwell*. New York: Morrow.

Llewellyn, Karl. 1931. "Book Reviews." *Columbia Law Review* 31:1215–20.

———. 1933. "The Bar Specializes—With What Results?" *Annals* 167:177–92.

LoPucki, Lynn. 1990. "The DeFacto Pattern of Lawyer Specialization." Disputes Processing Research Program Working Paper Series 9, Institute for Legal Studies, Madison, Wisconsin.

Lortie, Dan. 1959. "Laymen to Laymen: Law Schools, Careers and Professional Socialization." *Harvard Education Review* 29:352–69.

Lundberg, Ferdinand. 1939. "The Law Factories: Brains of the Status Quo." *Harper's Magazine* 179:180–92.

Lyons, James. 1985. "Baker and McKenzie: The Belittled Giant." *American Lawyer*, October: 115–22.

Macaulay, Stewart. 1963. "Non-Contractual Relations in Business." *American Sociological Review* 28:55–67.

Mackaye, Milton. 1932. "Profiles: Public Man." *New Yorker* 7(46):21–24.

Mairs, Patricia. 1988. "Bringing Up Baby." *National Law Journal*, March 14:1, 7–8.

Malcomson, James. 1984. "Work Incentives, Hierarchy, and Internal Labor Markets." *Journal of Political Economy* 92(3):486–507.

Mansnerus, Laura. 1988. "Law Firms, Too, Hire Lawyers." *New York Times*, March 4:B10.

———. 1989. "Rule on Temporary Lawyers Changes Again." *New York Times*, June 2:B6.

Marcus, Ruth. 1986. "Lawyers Branch Out from the Law." *Washington Post*, March 13:A1, A17.

Mason, Alpheus. 1946. *Brandeis: A Free Man's Life*. New York: Viking Press.

Mastrangelo, Paul. 1986. "Lawyers and the Law: A Filmography II." *Legal Reference Services* 5(4):5–42.

Mayer, Martin. 1956a. "The Wall Street Lawyers, Part II: Keepers of the Business Conscience." *Harper's Magazine* 212(1269):50–56.

———. 1956b. "The Wall Street Lawyers, Part I: The Elite Corps of American Business." *Harper's Magazine* 212(1268):31–37.

———. 1966. *The Lawyers*. New York: Harper & Row.

———. 1968. *Emory Buckner*. New York: Harper & Row.

McConnell, Michael. 1987. "The Counter-Revolution in Legal Thought." *Policy Review* 41:18–25.

McGrath, Phyllis. 1979. *Redefining Corporate-Federal Relations: A Research Report from the Conference Board's Division of Management Research*. New York: The Board.

Meier, Kenneth J. 1985. *Regulation: Politics, Bureaucracy and Economics.* New York: St. Martin's Press.

Mendelsohn, Oliver, and Lippman, Matthew. 1979. "The Emergence of the Corporate Law Firm in Australia." *University of New South Wales Law Journal* 3:78–98.

Middleton, Martha. 1984. "Getting Support." *National Law Journal,* June 4:1, 26, 28.

Nalebuff, Barry J., and Stiglitz, Joseph E. 1984. "Prizes and Incentives: Towards a General Theory of Compensation and Competition." *Bell Journal of Economics* 14:21–43.

National Industrial Conference Board. 1959. "Organization of Legal Work." *The Conference Board Business Record* 16:463–68.

National Law Journal. 1980. "Ma Bell: Top Lawyer Employer." *National Law Journal,* February 4:1, 24–25.

———. 1981. "Largest 100: 4th Annual NLJ Survey." *National Law Journal,* September 21:1, 27–31.

———. 1986. "The NLJ 250." *National Law Journal,* September 22:S1–23.

———. 1988. "The NLJ 250." *National Law Journal,* September 26:S1–28.

———. 1989a. "Legal Search Profession Annual Survey." *National Law Journal,* June 12:S1–52.

———. 1989b. "Mass Firing in Seattle." *National Law Journal,* July 24:2.

———. 1990. "Non-Lawyer Partner Rule Released." *National Law Journal,* March 12:7.

Nelson, Robert. 1988. *Partners with Power: The Social Transformation of the Large Law Firm.* Berkeley: University of California Press.

———. 1990. "Analysis of Hirsch Data by Robert L. Nelson." In *The Law and Ethics of Lawyering,* ed. Geoffrey C. Hazard, Jr., and Susan P. Koniak, p. 1033. Westbury, N.Y.: Foundation Press.

Nelson, Steve. 1989. "Law Firms Adopt Staff Attorney Option at 'Revolutionary' Pace." *Of Counsel* 7(8):14–15.

Nelson, William E. 1990. "Contract Litigation and the Elite Bar in New York City, 1960–1980." *Emory Law Journal* 39(2):413–62.

New York Times. 1957. "Bar Groups Back Bid by Stevenson." *New York Times,* May 7:38.

———. 1989. "New Partner in the Firm: The Marketing Director." *New York Times,* June 2:B6.

Nevins, Francis. 1984. "Law, Lawyers and Justice in Popular Fiction and Film." *Humanities Education* 1(2):3–12.

Noah, Timothy. 1990. "Washington's Plan to Let Lobbyists Be Partners in Law Firms Strikes Some Lawyers as Appalling." *Wall Street Journal,* April 27:A14.

Of Counsel. 1989. "Of Counsel 500." *Of Counsel* 8(8):18–20.

O'Keefe, Mary; Viscusi, W. Kip; and Zeckhauser, Richard J. 1984. "Economic Contests: Comparative Reward Schemes." *Journal of Labor Economics* 2:27–56.

Oliver, Myrna. 1987. "1-Man Jolt for Legal Journalism." *Los Angeles Times,* June 20:1, 28–30.

O'Neill, Suzanne. 1989. "Associates Can Attract Clients, Too." *National Law Journal,* January 16:17, 20.

Orey, Michael. 1987. "Staff Attorneys: Basic Work at Bargain Prices." *American Lawyer,* September:20.

Palay, Thomas. 1986. "Relational Contracting, Transaction Cost Economics and the Governance of HMO's." *Temple Law Quarterly* 59:927–50.

Parsons, Talcott. 1951. *The Social System.* Glencoe: The Free Press.

Penoyer, Ronald. 1981. *Directory of Federal Regulatory Agencies.* 3d ed. St. Louis: Center for the Study of American Business, Washington University.

Perez Perdomo, Rogelio. 1988. "The Venezuelan Legal Profession: Lawyers in an Inegalitarian Society." In *Lawyers in Society,* vol. II, *The Common Law World,* ed. R. Abel and P. Lewis, pp. 380–99. Berkeley: University of California Press.

Peterson, Mark. 1987. *Civil Juries in the 1980s: Trends in Jury Trials and California and Cook County, Illinois.* Santa Monica, Calif. RAND Corporation: Institute for Civil Justice.

Pinansky, Thomas. 1986–87. "The Emergence of Law Firms in the American Legal Profession." *University of Arkansas at Little Rock Law Review* 9:593–640.

Pindyck, Robert, and Rubenfeld, Daniel. 1981. *Econometric Models and Economic Forecasts.* 2d ed. New York: McGraw-Hill.

Posner, Richard. 1985. *The Federal Courts: Crisis and Reform.* Cambridge, Mass: Harvard University Press.

————. 1987. "The Decline of Law as an Autonomous Discipline: 1962–1987." *Harvard Law Review* 100:761–80.

Pound, Roscoe. 1909. "The Etiquette of Justice." *Proceedings of the Nebraska State Bar Association* 3:231–51.

Powell, Michael. 1985. "The New Legal Press: Reflecting and Facilitating Changes in the Legal Profession." Paper presented at the Annual Meeting of the Law and Society Association, June 1985, at San Diego, California.

Practicing Law Institute. 1965. "Managing Law Offices." Edited transcript prepared from forum, 20–21 May 1965, at Statler Hilton Hotel, New York.

Ranii, David. 1981. "Specialized Bars Strive to Survive." *National Law Journal,* September 14:1, 18.

Reed, Alfred. 1921. *Training for the Public Profession of the Law.* The Carnegie Foundation for the Advancement of Teaching. Boston: Merrymount Press, D. B. Updike.

Repa, Barbara Kate. 1988. "Is There Life after Partnership?" *American Bar Association Journal* 74:70–75.

Rosen, Robert Eli. 1989. "Ethical Soap: *L.A. Law* and the Privileging of Character." *University of Miami Law Review* 43(5):1229–61.

Rosen, Sherwin. 1986. "Prizes and Incentives in Elimination Tournaments." *American Economic Review* 76(4):701–15.

Rottenberg, Dan. 1979. "The Pinstripe Revolution." *Chicago Magazine* 28(7):98–124.

Saks, Michael. 1989. "Law Journals: Their Shapes and Contents, 1960 and 1985." Preliminary Draft Report presented to Executive Committee's Symposium on Legal Scholarship at Annual Meeting of the Association of American Law Schools, 6 January, 1989, at New Orleans.

Salibra, Lawrence. 1986. "Controlling the Cost of Litigation." *International Financial Law Review,* February:27–29.

Saltonstall, Susan, and Lane, Page. 1988. "Consultancies Develop with Specialties, Client Needs." *National Law Journal,* June 6:25, 28–29.

Samborn, Randall. 1989. "Rudnick and Wolfe Partners 'De-Equitized.' " *National Law Journal,* November 20:2.

———. 1990. "Non-Lawyers as Firm Partners." *National Law Journal,* March 5:B1, B46–47.

Sander, Richard, and Williams, Douglas. 1989. "Why Are There So Many Lawyers? Perspectives on a Turbulent Market." *Law & Social Inquiry* 14:431–79.

Schaeffer, Jan. 1981. "Cost-Cutting Legal Boutiques Tailor Services to Clients." *Philadelphia Inquirer,* November 16:6B.

Schenkman, Martin, and Ross, Kurt. 1989. "Firms Light Own Media Spotlight." *National Law Journal,* December 18:15.

Schept, Kenneth. 1980. "Small Firms Are Getting Big Clients." *National Law Journal,* October 27:1, 7.

Schmidt, Sally. 1986. "Firm Development Mobilized by a 'New Breed' of Resource." *National Law Journal,* August 25:15, 17, 19.

Schneyer, Ted. 1989. "Professionalism as Bar Politics: The Making of the Model Rules of Professional Conduct." *Law and Social Inquiry* 14(4):677–737.

Schuman, Jerome. 1971. A Black Lawyer Study. *Howard Law Journal* 16:225–313.

Schuyt, Kees. 1988. "The Rise of Lawyers in the Dutch Welfare State." In *Lawyers in Society,* vol. II, *The Common Law World,* ed. R. Abel and P. Lewis, pp. 200–224. Berkeley: University of California Press.

Seron, Carroll. Forthcoming. "Managing Legal Services: The Transformation of Small-Firm Practice." In *Lawyers' Ideals and Lawyers' Practices: Professionalism and the Transformation of the American Legal Profession,* ed. R. Nelson, D. Trubek, and R. Solomon.

Sherman, Rorie. 1988. "The Media and the Law." *National Law Journal,* June 6:32–34.

Siconolfi, Michael. 1985. "Law Firms Aren't Simply for Law as Attempts to Diversify Begin." *Wall Street Journal,* November 18:33.

Siddall, Roger. 1956. *A Survey of Large Law Firms in the United States.* New York: Vantage Press.

Siegel, Sidney. 1956. *Non-Parametric Statistics for the Behavioral Sciences.* New York: McGraw-Hill.

Sikes, Bette H.; Carson, Clara N.; and Gorai, Patricia. 1972. *The 1971 Lawyer Statistical Report.* Chicago: American Bar Foundation.

Silas, Faye. 1986. Diversification. *American Bar Association Journal* 72:17–18.

Simon, Herbert. 1957. *Models of Man: Social and Rational; Mathematical Essays on Rational Human Behavior in a Social Setting.* New York: John Wiley & Sons.

———. 1961. *Administrative Behavior: A Study of Decision-Making Processes in Administrative Organization.* 2d ed. New York: The Free Press.

———. 1976. *Administrative Behavior: A Study of Decision-Making Processes in Administrative Organization.* 3d ed. New York: The Free Press.

Simon, Ruth. 1988. "Paralegals: The Hottest Job Market." *National Law Journal,* July 4:1.

Simpson, Thatcher & Bartlett. 1984. *The First One Hundred Years, 1884–1984.* Vermont: Stinehour Press.

Singer, Amy. 1987. "Senior Attorney Programs: Half a Loaf." *American Lawyer*, January–February: 12.

Smigel, Erwin. 1960. "The Impact of Recruitment on the Organization of the Large Law Firm." *American Sociological Review* 25:56–66.

———. 1969. *The Wall Street Lawyer: Professional Organization Man?* Bloomington: Indiana University Press.

Smith, Beverly. 1925. "The Business-Getter." *American Mercury* 5(18):199–201.

Smith, Larry. 1989a. "National Study: Lateral Hiring Continues Unabated." *Lawyer Hiring and Training Report* 9(13):6–8.

———. 1989b. "Notable Gains and Losses Punctuate Another Stable Growth Year." *Of Counsel* 8(8):1.

———. 1989c. "Renaissance in Style: Firms Adopt New Lawyer Categories." *Of Counsel* 8(8):15–17.

Smith, Reginald. 1940a. "Law Office Organization I." *American Bar Association Journal* 26:393–96.

———. 1940b. "Law Office Organization II." *American Bar Association Journal* 26:494–96, 502.

———. 1940c. "Law Office Organization III." *American Bar Association Journal* 26:610–12.

———. 1940d. "Law Office Organization IV." *American Bar Association Journal* 26:648–51.

Snider, Robert. 1987. McLaw: Lawyering for the Masses. *California Lawyer* 8(12):29–33.

Spangler, Eve. 1986. *Lawyers for Hire: Professionals as Salaried Employees*. New Haven: Yale University Press.

Stanford Law Review. 1984. Critical Legal Studies Symposium. *Stanford Law Review*. 36(1–2).

Star, Jack. 1981. "Legal Eagle." *Chicago Magazine*, July:16.

Stark, Steven. 1987. "Perry Mason Meets Sonny Crockett: The History of Lawyers and the Police as Television Heroes." *University of Miami Law Review* 42:229–83.

State Court Caseload Statistics: Annual Report. 1984–. Williamsburg, Va.: National Center for State Courts.

Stevens, Mark. 1987. *Power of Attorney: The Rise of the Giant Law Firms*. New York: McGraw-Hill.

Stevenson, Tom. 1973. "The Talent Peddlers." *Juris Doctor* 3(7):12, 13.

Stille, Alexander. 1985. "When Law Firms Start Their Own Businesses." *National Law Journal*, October 21:1, 20–22.

Stone, Harlan. 1934. "The Public Influence of the Bar." *Harvard Law Review* 48:1–14.

Strasser, Fred. 1985. "In-House Lure Gets Stronger: Corporations Compete for Best and Brightest." *National Law Journal*, July 22:1.

Strong, Theron. 1914. *Landmarks of a Lawyer's Lifetime*. New York: Dodd, Mead.

Stuart, Mary. 1986. "Anderson Russel's Classless Society." *American Lawyer*, December:10.

Sullivan & Cromwell. 1981. *Lamplighters: The Sullivan & Cromwell Lawyers April 2, 1879 to April 2, 1979*.

Susman, Steven. 1987. "Eighties Shakeout." Transcript from presentation at *American Lawyer* symposium, 1–2 June 1987, at New York City.

Swaine, Robert. 1946a. *The Cravath Firm and Its Predecessors, 1819–1947*. Vol. 1. New York: Ad Press.

———. 1946b. *The Cravath Firm and Its Predecessors, 1819–1947*. Vol. 2. New York: Ad Press.

Taylor, Stuart. 1988. "Lifting of Secrecy Reveals Earthy Side of Justices." *New York Times,* February 22:16.

Tomasic, Roman, and Pentony, Brendon. 1989. "The Expanding Role of the Large Corporate Law Firm in Australia: The Case of Takeover Litigation." Paper prepared for the Annual Meeting of the Law and Society Association, 8–11 June 1989, at Madison, Wisconsin.

Tucker, Marilyn; Albright, Laurie A.; and Busk, Patricia. 1989. "What Ever Happened to the Class of 1983?" *Georgetown Law Journal* 78:153–95.

Tullock, Gordon. 1975. "On the Efficient Organization of Trials." *Kyklos* 28:745–62.

———. 1980. *Trials on Trial: The Pure Theory of Legal Procedure*. New York: Columbia University Press.

Tybor, Joseph. 1981. "Bad Day at Kutak Rock." *National Law Journal,* November 2:1, 8–9.

Untermeyer, Samuel. 1933. "What Every Present-Day Lawyer Should Know." *Annals* 167:173–76.

U.S. Bureau of the Census. 1976. *Historical Statistics of the United States: Colonial Times to 1970*. Washington, D.C.: Government Printing Office.

———. 1987. *Statistical Abstract of the United States*. Washington, D.C.: Government Printing Office.

———. 1989. *Statistical Abstract of the United States*. Washington, D.C.: Government Printing Office.

U.S. Bureau of Labor Statistics. 1988. *Labor Force Statistics Derived from the Current Population Survey, 1948–87*. Bulletin 2307. Washington, D.C.: U.S. Department of Labor, Bureau of Labor Statistics.

U.S. Department of Commerce. 1986. *The National Income and Product Accounts of the United States, 1929–1982*. Washington, D.C.: Government Printing Office.

U.S. Department of Commerce, Bureau of the Census. 1976. *1972 Census of Selected Service Industries*. Summary and subject statistics, p. 4–36. Washington, D.C.: Government Printing Office.

———, 1981. *1977 Census of Service Industries*. Subject statistics p. 5–52, Washington, D.C.: Government Printing Office.

———, 1985. *1982 Census of Service Industries*. Miscellaneous Subjects p. 5–109. Washington, D.C.: Government Printing Office.

———. 1988. *Survey of Current Business*. Washington, D.C.: Government Printing Office.

U.S. President. 1987. *Economic Report of the President*. Washington, D.C.: Government Printing Office.

———. 1988. *Economic Report of the President*. Washington, D.C.: Government Printing Office.

————. 1989. *Economic Report of the President.* Washington, D.C.: Government Printing Office.

Vilkin, Richard. 1982. "Firms Court Clients with Seminars." *National Law Journal,* November 8:1, 34–35.

Vogel, David. 1981. "The New Social Regulation in Historical and Comparative Perspective." In *Regulation in Perspective: Historical Essays,* ed. T. McCraw, pp. 155–85. Cambridge, Mass.: Harvard University Press.

Wall Street Journal. 1988. "The Strange Case of the Vanishing Firms." *Wall Street Journal,* July 29:17.

Warner, Henry E. 1950. Excerpt from his Reminiscences. From the files of Warner and Stackpole, Boston, Massachusetts.

Warren, Charles. 1911. *A History of the American Bar.* Boston: Little, Brown.

Warshauer, Irene. 1984. "Litigation Management Techniques." *Alternatives to the High Cost of Litigation* 2(11):7–11.

Watson, Richard, and Downing, Rondal. 1969. *The Politics of the Bench and Bar.* New York: Wiley.

Webb, Eugene; Campbell, Donald; Schwartz, Richard; and Sechrest, Lee. 1966. *Unobtrusive Measures: Nonreactive Research in the Social Sciences.* Chicago: Rand McNally.

Weber, Max. 1978. *Economy and Society: An Outline of Interpretive Sociology,* ed. G. Roth and C. Wittich. Berkeley: University of California Press.

Weidenbaum, Murray, and Penoyer, Ronald. 1983. *The Next Step in Regulatory Reform: Updating the Statutes.* St. Louis: Center for the Study of American Business, Washington University.

Weil, Fred B. 1968. *The 1967 Lawyer Statistical Report.* Chicago: American Bar Foundation.

Weinstein, Henry. 1975. "Defending What? The Corporation's Public Interest." *Juris Doctor* 5(6):39–43.

Weisbrod, Burton; Handler, Joel; and Komesar, Neil. 1978. *Public Interest Law: An Economic and Institutional Analysis.* Berkeley: University of California Press.

Weisenhaus, Doreen. 1988. "Still a Long Way to Go for Women, Minorities." *National Law Journal,* February 8:1, 48, 50, 53.

Weiss, Kenneth. 1989. "If There's a Law, There's a Newsletter." *New York Times,* June 2:A11.

Weklar, Diane. 1988. "Strategies for Legal Marketing." *National Law Journal,* August 1:22, 26.

Wermiel, Stephen. 1986. "Shroud of Secrecy That Veils the Supreme Court Lifts as Justices Assume Higher Public Profiles." *Wall Street Journal,* July 1:54.

Williamson, Oliver. 1975. *Markets and Hierarchies: Analysis and Antitrust Implications: A Study in the Economics of Internal Organization.* New York: The Free Press.

————. 1979. "Transaction Cost Economics: The Governance of Contractual Relations." *Journal of Law and Economics* 22:233–61.

————. 1985. *The Economic Institutions of Capitalism: Firms, Markets, and Relational Contracting.* New York: The Free Press; London: Collier Macmillan.

Wise, Daniel. 1987. "Psst! Wanna Make Partner?" *National Law Journal,* October 26:1, 32–33.

Woodward, Robert, and Armstrong, Scott. 1979. *The Brethren: Inside the Supreme Court.* New York: Simon and Schuster.

Wright, Edward. 1970. "The Code of Professional Responsibility: Its History and Objectives." *Arkansas Law Review* 24:1–18.

Yale Law Journal. 1964. "The Jewish Law Student and New York Jobs—Discriminatory Effects in Law Firm Hiring Practice." *Yale Law Journal* 73:625–60.

———. 1989. Symposium on Popular Culture. *Yale Law Journal* 98(8).

Zion, Sidney. 1968a. "Law Firms Across U.S. Raising Pay." *New York Times,* February 17:31.

———. 1968b. "New Lawyers to Find Salary Market Bullish." *New York Times,* February 15:45.

Zlokower, Harry. 1981. "Choosing a Public Relations Firm." *National Law Journal,* November 2:19, 23–25.

Zweigenhaft, Richard, and Domhoff, G. William. 1982. *Jews in the Protestant Establishment.* New York: Praeger.

Index